Contents

Abbreviations

The following abbreviations are used:

Alt. Dem.   Alternative Demonstration
App.   Appendix
Ax.   Axiom
Cor.   Corollary
DA#   Definitions of the Affects
Def.   Definition
Dem.   Demonstration
Exp.   Explanation
Lem.   Lemma
NS   From the Curley translation of Spinoza, referring to a posthumous edition of 1677, *De Nagelate Schriften van B.D.S.*
Post.   Postulate
Praef.   Preface
Schol.   Scholium

AT   Adam and Tannery's *Œuvres de Descartes* (1909)
CWS   *The Collected Works of Spinoza*, trans. Edwin Curley, cited by volume and page number
KV   *Short Treatise on God, Man, and His Well-Being* (*Korte Verhandeling*; e.g. KV II, 2, 2 refers to Part II, Chapter 2, Section 2
TdIE   *Treatise on the Emendation of the Intellect* (*Tractatus de Intellectus Emendatione*)
TP   *Political Treatise* (*Tractatus politicus*; e.g. TP I, 5 refers to Chapter 1, paragraph 5)

The Spinoza–Machiavelli Encounter

Spinoza Studies
Series editor: Filippo Del Lucchese, Brunel University London

Seminal works devoted to Spinoza that challenge mainstream scholarship

This series aims to broaden the understanding of Spinoza in the Anglophone world by making some of the most important work by continental scholars available in English translation for the first time. Some of Spinoza's most important themes - that right is coextensive with power, that every political order is based on the power of the multitude, the critique of superstition and the rejection of the idea of providence - are explored by these philosophers in detail and in ways that will open up new possibilities for reading and interpreting Spinoza.

Editorial Advisory board

Books available

Affects, Actions and Passions in Spinoza: The Unity of Body and Mind by Chantal Jaquet, translated by Tatiana Reznichenko

The Spinoza-Machiavelli Encounter: Time and Occasion by Vittorio Morfino, translated by Dave Mesing

Forthcoming

Affirmation and Resistance in Spinoza: Strategy of the Conatus by Laurent Bove, translated and edited by Émilie Filion-Donato and Hasana Sharp

Politics, Ontology and Knowledge in Spinoza by Alexandre Matheron, translated and edited by Filippo Del Lucchese, David Maruzzella and Gil Morejón

Experience and Eternity in Spinoza by Pierre-François Moreau, translated by Robert Boncardo

https://edinburghuniversitypress.com/series-spinoza-studies.html

The Spinoza–Machiavelli Encounter
Time and Occasion

Vittorio Morfino

Translated by Dave Mesing

EDINBURGH
University Press

Edinburgh University Press is one of the leading university presses in the UK. We publish academic books and journals in our selected subject areas across the humanities and social sciences, combining cutting-edge scholarship with high editorial and production values to produce academic works of lasting importance. For more information visit our website: edinburghuniversitypress.com

Il tempo e l'occasione: l'incontro Spinoza Machiavelli © Vittorio Morfino, 2002
Published by LED – Edizioni Universitarie du Lettere Economia Diritto, Milan
English translation © Dave Mesing, 2019, 2020

Edinburgh University Press Ltd
The Tun – Holyrood Road
12(2f) Jackson's Entry
Edinburgh EH8 8PJ

First published in hardback by Edinburgh University Press 2019

Typeset in 10/12 Goudy Old Style by
Servis Filmsetting Ltd, Stockport, Cheshire, and
printed and bound by CPI Group (UK) Ltd,
Croydon, CR0 4YY

A CIP record for this book is available from the British Library

ISBN 978 1 4744 2124 9 (hardback)
ISBN 978 1 4744 7452 8 (paperback)
ISBN 978 1 4744 2125 6 (webready PDF)
ISBN 978 1 4744 2126 3 (epub)

The right of Vittorio Morfino to be identified as the author of this work has been asserted in accordance with the Copyright, Designs and Patents Act 1988, and the Copyright and Related Rights Regulations 2003 (SI No. 2498).

Published with the support of the University of Edinburgh Scholarly Publishing Initiatives Fund.

TTP   *Theological-Political Treatise* (*Tractatus theologico-politicus*; e.g.
               TTP XVII, 7 refers to Chapter 17, paragraph 7, where the par-
               agraph number corresponds to the Bruder edition, reproduced
               in Curley's *Collected Works, Volume II*)

Translator's Introduction:
Unscripted Space, Devoured Time

Vittorio Morfino's *Il tempo e l'occasione: l'incontro Spinoza-Machiavelli* constitutes a decisive intervention for contemporary studies of Spinoza. Owing in part to Spinoza's apparent paucity of references to Machiavelli, Spinoza's relation to him has often implicitly been treated as occasional: perhaps the two share some affinities for realist or anti-utopian political positions, with Spinoza taking up certain Machiavellian or Machiavellian-like insights, but the relation does not go beyond this point. This book challenges such assumptions by demonstrating a connection between Spinoza and Machiavelli as specific as it is pervasive, arguing that Spinoza's understanding of causality in the *Ethics* owes much to his study of Machiavelli's writings on history and politics, a claim with multiple implications for Spinoza's own views on history and politics as well as temporality. Morfino succinctly treats different approaches to the Spinoza–Machiavelli question in the introduction, and I will not rehearse them here.[1] Instead, I will briefly recapitulate the main steps in his overall analysis in order to frame it in terms of the object alluded to in the title of the book – Spinoza's encounter with Machiavelli.

After synthetically summarising different approaches to the Spinoza–Machiavelli question throughout the twentieth century in the introduction, Morfino proceeds to carry out four steps in the remainder of the text. First, in chapter 1, through close examination of Spinoza's own library, Morfino delivers a clear and thorough framework of the possible means through which Spinoza read Machiavelli. His analysis shows that Spinoza had multiple access points to the Florentine's work: Machiavelli's complete works in Italian (which Spinoza seemed capable of understanding, given the presence of an Italian–Spanish dictionary in his library, as well as an Italian-

---

[1] One notable exception to this implicit consensus is Del Lucchese 2009, which had not been published when Morfino wrote this book.

language monograph), a Latin translation of *The Prince*, and discussions of Machiavelli in texts of Bacon, Descartes and others. Morfino is careful to note that these basic facts, of course, do not necessarily mean that Spinoza studied Machiavelli in these ways, or only in these ways, since such information cannot speak to the practical aspects of reading or other kinds of study. As such, in addition to his detailed account of these possible means, Morfino outlines Spinoza's general approach to citation, where proper names are rare, and together with impersonal figures (such as the 'theologians and metaphysicians' in the appendix to *Ethics* I), negative, except for a remark about ancient atomists in a letter to Hugo Boxel.[2] Morfino then considers Spinoza's direct citations of the 'ever shrewd'[3] Machiavelli.

Both of the latter two elements also contribute to Morfino's extensive analysis of the *Theological-Political Treatise* and *Political Treatise* in chapter 2. He does this through the rubric of 'Machiavelli's implicit presence', by which he does not intend an esoteric reading of Spinoza's work, showing some kind of secret fidelity to an atemporal Machiavellianism. Instead, again undertaking a precise and painstaking labour, Morfino demonstrates substantive links between arguments within Spinoza's political works and Machiavelli's texts, above all *Discourses on Livy* and *The Prince*. Some key aspects that Morfino outlines in this chapter, which simultaneously constitutes a kind of mini-treatise on Spinoza's political works, include the decisiveness of Machiavelli's conceptual pair 'virtue' and 'fortune' for Spinoza's discussion of election in the *Theological-Political Treatise*, and the deployment of Machiavelli's remarks on keeping pacts in the framework of natural law theory, especially in contrast to Hobbes. In the unfinished *Political Treatise*, Morfino outlines Machiavelli's presence in what he terms the 'skeletal structure' of the text, emphasising the idea that *imperium* represents a momentary equilibrium of forces, rather than a model of politics where civil society names a stabilised transcendence of the state of nature.

Third, Morfino draws out the consequences of his reconstruction of Spinoza's use of Machiavellian arguments even more fully, in what are undoubtedly some of the most exciting pages in the book. A full reckoning with these details is best left to the text itself, but we can note here that the consequences Morfino uncovers are especially relevant for Spinoza's concepts of causality and eternity, and by extension, for how to think Spinoza's political works in tandem with the *Ethics*. The idea at the heart of the chapter is that Spinoza's encounter with Machiavelli's approach to history and

---

[2] *Ep.* LVI [to Hugo Boxel]; CWS II, 423–4
[3] *TP* V, 7; CWS II, 531.

politics bears its most dazzling traces in the structure of Spinoza's account of common notions and the third kind of knowledge.[4] In a famous passage on teleological prejudice in the appendix to *Ethics* I, Spinoza lists mathematics as what provides a standard of truth that breaks the circle between human experience and the inscrutability of levels of divine providence and will.[5] Morfino both cautions against reading the passage from superstition to science, or imagination to reason, as a necessary law, and suggests that mathematics be understood a singular event among others.

In the same passage, Spinoza also remarks that other causes break with teleological prejudice and lead to true knowledge of things, but does not list them. Morfino suggests that these causes are physics and political theory. Based on Spinoza's remark that the causes are unnecessary to enumerate 'here', Morfino further suggests that Spinoza has written or will write about these causes elsewhere. If Spinoza discusses physics in the short treatise of *Ethics* II, it is less clear that he discusses political theory in the same way, even though many readers have productively utilised material from the *Ethics* in this sense, especially parts three and four. However, Morfino argues that 'there are two specific passages where, more strictly than elsewhere, Spinoza traces a line of demarcation between the teleological knowledge of history and politics and the knowledge of the essence and characteristics of the political body – that is, between the imaginary sanctification of history and power, and the knowledge of their dynamics'.[6] These passages are *TTP* III, where Spinoza uses the Machiavellian concepts of virtue and fortune in his conceptual critique of the election of the Hebrew people, and the opening of *TP* I, where Spinoza differentiates himself from theorists of reason of state, emphasising a need for what we could call, with some simplification, political realism.

Machiavelli stands out as the point of departure for both of these political critiques of teleological prejudice. On the basis of the hypothesis that physics and political theory also constitute ways of breaking with imagination and superstition, Morfino proceeds to further argue that these ways of knowing are also helpful for thinking about one of the most difficult problems in Spinoza's work, the third kind of knowledge or intuitive science. Following

---

[4] I have referred generically to Machiavelli's 'approach' to history and politics, partly in keeping with the broad engagement to Machiavelli's work that Morfino exhibits. For a useful recent collection of texts on Machiavelli, see Del Lucchese, Frosini and Morfino (eds) 2015.

[5] *Ethics* I, App.; CWS I, 441–2.

[6] Page 122 below.

Machiavelli and a number of others including Aristotle, Morfino emphasises a parallelism between medicine and politics. Intuitive science thus concerns adequate knowledge of a singular physical body or adequate knowledge of a singular social body.

These arguments are best considered in their full detail in chapter 3, but two further insights which undergird this section of Morfino's analysis concern causality and eternity. Morfino claims that one of the most fundamental effects of Spinoza's encounter with Machiavelli is a shift in his conception of causality, from a serial and linear understanding in his early *Treatise on the Emendation of the Intellect* to an immanent and structural understanding in the *Ethics*, as well as implicitly in several passages of the *TTP* and *TP*. An important corollary to these arguments is a claim concerning Spinoza's 'anti-humanist' conception of eternity, which treats eternity not as a totalising concept, but rather as a principle of intelligibility for the connection of durations that make up the temporal fabric of being.[7] 'As such', Morfino concludes, 'eternity forbids the conception of history as both a straight line and a cycle, in order to open on to an anti-humanistic conception of eternity as the aleatory interweaving of necessity, an eternity that does not impose any binary as obligatory for history.'[8]

In this way, the fourth and final step of the overall argument takes on the idea of philosophy of history, in order to examine a possible general way of reading Spinoza and Machiavelli. Morfino thus begins the final chapter by sketching a basic orientation that extends beyond Spinoza's encounter with Machiavelli, or arguments in the texts of either. Morfino analyses two thinkers who have proposed such readings: Lessing in the case of Spinoza's *TTP*, and Vico in the case of a combination of Machiavellian and Spinozist insights. The chapter is organised around a refusal to conceive history as a univocal stream of time, flowing towards the progressive realisation of necessary, universal knowledge. The examinations of both Lessing and Vico thus serve as models that further specify the stakes of a general approach to Spinoza and Machiavelli, and Morfino reconstructs their readings in order to highlight the implications of extracting a philosophy of history from them. He concludes that instead of such a picture of history, what the Spinoza–Machiavelli encounter urges is knowledge of the singular connection particular to an object. In the case of a historical object, it is this model that Spinoza's *TTP* and Machiavelli's *Discourses on Livy* exemplify.

---

[7] The material throughout this chapter constitutes some elements of what Morfino will later develop as the theory of plural temporality. See Morfino 2014, especially 132–73.

[8] Page 158 below.

If such a refusal of a general philosophy of history constitutes one of the key implications at the intersection of Spinoza's and Machiavelli's philosophy, one thing that remains somewhat opaque is the question of exactly in what their encounter consists. While it should not prevent us from wagering yet more hypotheses on the basis of careful examination of their work, specificity in this regard is fraught with difficulties. Morfino suggests thinking their encounter as necessarily plural, involving some of the materials he excavates at the outset of the argument, and perhaps more encounters devoured by time.[9] The Spinoza–Machiavelli encounter is also plural if we judge it by the results of the book in your hands: in addition to the historical material that Morfino excavates, he offers an extensive discussion of key arguments across Spinoza's work, new insights regarding the content of Spinoza's understanding of causality, and an appreciation for how it is interwoven in key moments of Spinoza's mature work. As such, a productive response to the material in *The Spinoza–Machiavelli Encounter* lies not in searching for the origin of the unscripted space opened up by this book, but rather in the challenges and uses it presents for Spinoza scholarship and contemporary philosophy. One aspect of such a programme might be the displacement of the ideological couple 'origin' and 'end' for the pair 'encounter' and 'relation'. Spinoza's relation to Machiavelli is thus indeed an occasional one, provided we understand an occasion in the same sense as the Florentine secretary. In a history abounding with occasions, the existence of such unscripted space is necessary. What continues to be left to chance is the efficacy of relations between encounters that have taken hold, as so many footholds for finding balance in a history without guarantees.

---

[9] Although it is not explicitly conceptualised in this book, one understanding of the encounter that bears a strong affinity to the suggestions raised by its arguments is Althusser's unfinished manuscript (2006). See Morfino 2014: 89–112.

Translator's Note and Acknowledgments

References to Spinoza's works cite the paragraph or section numbers from Curley's translations, which have been used systematically throughout this book to ensure consistency. I have signalled in the footnotes when Curley's translation has been altered. While Spinoza's Latin terms *potestas* and *potentia* have distinct correlates in Italian (*potere* and *potenza*), English provides only a single term, *power*. I have left this translation issue unresolved in the book, translating both terms with power and indicating the corresponding Latin or Italian term in brackets for clarity.

References to Machiavelli's works cite the part and chapter numbers, and include a corresponding reference to the English translation and page number. When possible I have used Mansfield's translation, and any alterations are signalled in the footnotes. For reasons of readability, I have chosen to translate Machiavelli's concepts of *virtù* and *fortuna*, even though they do not neatly correspond with the common English senses of virtue and fortune. The best introduction to the difficulty of these terms is through a careful study of Machiavelli's works, as Morfino practises throughout the book.

* * *

I want to thank the following people, who read parts of the translation at various stages of the drafting process and provided me with invaluable feedback: Andrew Anastasi, Erik Beranek, Aaron Berman, Chris Drain, Asad Haider, Ryan J. Johnson, David Maruzzella, Christopher P. Noble, Charles Prusik, Joseph Serrano and Charlie Strong. As series editor, Filippo Del Lucchese provided boundless enthusiasm and a decisively sharp eye. Jason E. Smith's encouragement predates the genesis of this project, which would never have taken hold without his steadfast counsel. Vittorio Morfino's passion for materialism and exemplary modelling of philosophy as *presa di posizione* were wellsprings of motivation throughout the entire process. I thank him for his patience and tirelessness in responding to my many questions. I also want to thank Carol Macdonald, Kirsty Woods and James Dale at Edinburgh University Press for their support and hard work throughout the process of editing, formatting and revising the translation. Any faults in this book remain my own.

For Ricky, Arianna, Carlos, Attilio and Nestor

Introduction

For almost two centuries, the question of the relationship between Machiavelli and Spinoza was only addressed in negative terms, mostly in Catholic and Reformed apologetics. Then for the entire twentieth century it remained at the margins of the imposing philological and critical labour dedicated to Spinoza's work: here we find far more hints of a path to follow than genuine efforts to follow it. Adolph Menzel was the first to take up the question at the beginning of the twentieth century. While he stressed Machiavelli's importance for the political theory of Spinoza's *Political Treatise* (but not, however, the *Theological-Political Treatise*),[1] Menzel did not go beyond an analysis of the two direct citations,[2] emphasising a common anti-utopian method of presentation. The latter would become commonplace in the Italian and German studies between the two world wars, and its fascination would not escape Maggiore,[3] Solari,[4] Ravà,[5] Strauss and Gebhardt. Spinoza's polemic in

---

[1] 'No politician has influenced Spinoza's political doctrine more powerfully than Machiavelli' (Menzel 1902: 567). 'In [the *TTP*], there is no trace of Machiavelli's influence' (Menzel 1902: 571).

[2] Emilio Villa dedicated an article exclusively to analysing of the first of these citations in 1919. His interpretation primarily lies in demarcating Spinoza's reading of *The Prince* from the Republican tradition (Rousseau, Alfieri, Foscolo). Villa claims that *The Prince* is not a work which feigns teaching to kings in order actually to instruct the people, but rather the theory of the factual conditions of tyranny as well as freedom: 'Just as determinate causes create tyranny', Villa writes, 'so also do others necessarily bring about freedom. Freedom is demonstrated to be possible: here is the highest apology and glorification that can be made of it, which Machiavelli made with admirable profundity. In this consists the value of Machiavelli and, I dare say, also the true end of his entire work' (Villa 1919: 195).

[3] Maggiore 1927: 207–9.

[4] Solari 1927: 317–53; Solari 1974: 195–250.

[5] Ravà 1958: 91–113. Ravà offers a fascinating suggestion in this early article, which he

TP I, 1 was thus held to be directly inspired by the well-known passages from *The Prince* on effectual truth. The only noteworthy result of the analysis of this theme was Strauss's observation in *Spinoza's Critique of Religion* that the tones of the two authors' anti-utopian polemics are different: Machiavelli's text is lucid and cold, combating utopia exclusively in its practical effects, while Spinoza's is harsh and sarcastic, combating utopia in the name of philosophy with an attitude that is fundamentally non-political.[6]

This point, however, exhausted the anti-utopian discussion. Other themes examined by these authors were first of all that of virtue: both Maggiore and Ravà[7] highlight the influence of Machiavelli's concept of virtue for Spinoza's theory of *virtus sive potentia*.[8] Second, these authors also give a date for the Spinoza–Machiavelli encounter. Building on the work of Guzzo, Ravà opposes Menzel's restriction of Machiavelli's influence to the *TP* by locating it instead already in the chapters on Hebrew history in the *TTP*.[9] In his work, Gebhardt takes stock of the results achieved by these studies. In the inventory of the sources of the two works, he proposes the first sparse and largely incomplete list of Spinozian passages inspired by

does not, however, pursue in later analyses: 'Machiavelli', he writes, 'is one of the main sources of Spinoza's political thought, and *not only of his political thought*' (Ravà 1958: 91, my emphasis).

[6] Strauss 1965.

[7] Ravà proposes a parallelism between Machiavellian virtue and Spinozian *potentia* by understanding them 'as a summing up of a person who has succeeded in social conflicts' (Ravà 1930: 105).

[8] It should be noted that Maggiore's work has a clearly fascist inspiration: 'Is there another here that is not implicated in Machiavelli's concept of virtue? And yet far from Greek virtue, which, when it is not confused with cold wisdom, with sexual pleasure [*voluttà*] and lethargy, meant the just and temperate equilibrium between the two. For to be virtuous, it is not enough to be wise, resting on good intentions, sitting in the balance between good and evil on the brink of a thinking almost fearful of brimming over into action; one needs to fight against luck [*fortuna*], and to dare, grasping at any means in order to reach the end and look evil in the face, instead of hiding one's face, in order to win and to transform it into good' (Maggiore 1927: 208).

[9] 'Menzel, who studied the relation between Machiavelli and Spinoza *ex professo*, claims that Machiavelli's influence makes itself felt only in the final writings of Spinoza, particularly the *TP*, while the *TTP* would not have any trace. And yet to those who seriously know the *Discourses on Livy*, the entire *TTP* appears as an attempt to explain the victories of the Hebrew people, and to draw political conclusions from them, with the same spirit of objective inquiry that Machiavelli uses to study the history of the Roman people' (Ravà 1930: 103). With regard to the history of the Hebrew people in the *TTP*, Guzzo writes in a 1924 work: 'Here Spinoza makes a series of extremely sharp and well-chosen observations, which convey an accurate reading of the Latin historians, especially Tacitus, and our own Machiavelli' (Guzzo 1924: 403).

Machiavelli, without, however, devoting any critical reflection to the problem.[10]

After a long period punctuated by Carla Gallicet Calvetti's book, which I will consider below, there was a rebirth of interest in Spinoza's Machiavellianism within French and Italian Marxism in the second half of the twentieth century. Alexandre Matheron, author of two important studies on Spinoza at the turn of the 1970s, showed how *TP* I, 2 refers to 'popular Machiavellianism'[11] rather than the true teaching of Machiavelli, which is much more comprehensive.[12] He claims that by means of a radical subversion of the position of both philosophy and politics (displayed in the first two paragraphs of *TP* I), Spinoza moves beyond the political-philosophical dilemma, genuinely changing the terrain. Spinoza rejects philosophy, inasmuch as it produces a utopia, and as for politics, 'conforming without doubt to the teaching of the authentic Machiavelli, he reveals the arcane "Machiavellianisms" as derisive pragmatic formulas'.[13] Regarding the continuity between Machiavelli and Spinoza, Laurent Bove, who was a student of Matheron, takes into consideration the concepts of prudence, virtue and necessity in the Dutch philosopher. In keeping with the thesis of his book on the theory of *conatus* in Spinoza, Bove maintains that 'for Spinoza, reading Machiavelli [confirmed] the identification of actual essence (the *conatus*) and a logic of being [*une logique de l'existant*] striving to endure, consisting of a strategic dynamic determined by affirmation and resistance'.[14]

Pervaded by a sensibility that is more theoretical than historical-philosophical, Negri's and Althusser's Marxist readings of the Spinoza–Machiavelli relation attempt to identify a materialist and revolutionary tradition of thought, and end up in a perfectly oppositional symmetry. First in *The Savage Anomaly* and then in *Insurgencies*, Negri identifies the line of Machiavelli–Spinoza–Marx as a humanistic and revolutionary tradition opposed to the dominant bourgeois tradition of modernity.[15] In several

---

[10] Spinoza 1925: 242–3.

[11] Matheron 1978: 43.

[12] 'There is no question, of course, of reducing Machiavelli to this broad outline: if these different features are effectively claimed by him, he integrates them, once again, in a much vaster ensemble; Spinoza knows this, which leaves in suspense the question of the true meaning of Machiavelli's work, including *The Prince*' (Matheron 1978: 49).

[13] Matheron 1978: 59.

[14] Bove 1999: 49.

[15] 'The history of modern thought must be seen as a problematic of the new productive force. The ideologically hegemonic vein of thought is that which functions toward the development of the bourgeoisie. This vein yields to the ideology of the market, in

posthumously published writings, Althusser sketches instead an underground current of materialism, which he defines as a materialism of the
encounter or the aleatory. For Althusser, Machiavelli, Spinoza and Marx,
as well as other authors, represent an anti-humanist tradition in which
reality is thought beyond every teleological and theological order, and, what
amounts to the same thing, beyond every legitimisation of existing reality.[16]
We owe an analysis of one of the ways in which this underground current
has been transmitted to Gabriel Albiac, a Spanish student of Althusser and
the author of an essential study on the Marrano sources of Spinozism. Albiac
shows that in the texts of Abraham Pereira, who attempted to reconstruct
rabbinic orthodoxy after two centuries of Marranism, Machiavelli appears
as the sworn enemy who makes religion into a pure functional cover for
domination.[17] Precisely in becoming detached from the Jewish community
of Amsterdam, Spinoza could have appealed to this sworn enemy of all
religion by theoretically radicalising him. From this perspective, in fact, 'the
path for a rigorously materialist conception of virtue remains open. After
Machiavelli, Spinoza is on the lookout. It is with him that the final decom-

---

the determinate form imposed by the new mode of production. The problem, as we
have amply demonstrated, is the hypostasis of the dualism of the market within the
metaphysical system from Hobbes to Rousseau, from Kant to Hegel. This is, then, the
central vein of modern philosophy: The mystification of the market becomes a utopia
of development. In opposition, there is the Spinozian rupture – but, before it, there is
already the one worked by Machiavelli, and after it, the one sanctioned by Marx. The
dystopia of the market becomes, in this case, an affirmation of the productive force as
a terrain of liberation. We could never insist enough on this immanent and possible
alternative in the history of Western thought. It is a sign of dignity, to the same extent
that the other is an emblem of infamy' (Negri 1991: 219).

[16] Althusser 2006: 163–207; Althusser 1997.

[17] 'It is above all the will to set up politics as a theoretical discipline in the margins of
moralising pretensions or transcendent foundations which appears in Machiavelli as
the peril that must be discarded. The reduction of the study of politics to an analytic of
the mechanisms of power, according to their strict functionality, insofar as it excludes
any presupposition of teleological orientation from historical processes, leaves a difficult situation – we should say rather that it sweeps away, it removes forever from the
theoretical horizon the old problem of the ethical dimensions of the act of power:
good and evil definitively pack their bags and definitively cede their deteriorated foundation to the subtle dynamic of games of force and domination. Virtue here consists
in "knowing the times and orderings of things and accommodating oneself to them",
no longer having any connection to the Christian tradition; and, certainly, no longer
with any other soteriological tradition. No other option remains, on the terrain of
power [potestas], than to annihilate or be annihilated. Virtue means nothing but power
[potentia]. All else is only servitude' (Albiac 1988: 39).

position of the Christian prince occurs – and also the subject, which is its shadow.'[18]

The research of Carla Gallicet Calvetti, a Catholic scholar of Spinoza and author of the only monograph on the Spinoza–Machiavelli relation in the twentieth century, is situated between these two periods. Her study, which has the undisputed merit of widening the points of agreement between the two thinkers in comparison to Gebhardt, starts from a double interpretative presupposition which constitutes perhaps its strongest limitation. First, Gallicet Calvetti argues that Machiavelli's influence is only detectable at a political level and that the method of effectual truth itself produces a fracture between politics and metaphysics.[19] Second, she maintains that the relation is legible only in the terms of fulfilment.[20]

This marginality of the Spinoza–Machiavelli question within the basic lines of Spinozist research must be explained. It is true that, with the exception of two long citations in the *TP*, nothing seems to link Machiavelli the politician with Spinoza the metaphysician. But the same proximity in political theory, explicitly signalled by the two long passages in the *TP*, has long remained incidental within Spinozist criticism when compared to, for example, the attention given to Spinoza's relationship to Hobbes, as well as to natural law theory more generally.[21] This situation mirrors the way that attention has not been given until recently to the only current of ancient thought in which Spinoza openly takes part: atomism.[22] Thus, the possibility of demonstrating the existence of a truly philosophical relationship between Machiavelli and Spinoza has only been intimated by some critics, and as such, what we find are

[18] Albiac 1988: 52.

[19] 'It seems [. . .] that, if in the *metaphysical domain*, the human creature, genetically joined to divine substance and therefore bearing the divine stigmata, denounces, however, a special degradation of the divine represented precisely by the "properties" of existing humans, in the *political domain* such degradation assumes a more precise shape and remains an ethical assessment, not free of Machiavellian "tricks"' (Gallicet Calvetti 1972: 54).

[20] 'Spinoza's Machiavellianism [. . .] assumes an original countenance that sometimes represents the singular re-elaboration of the thought of the Italian politician, sometimes the overcoming of his position, and sometimes a kind of overturning of the very convictions of Machiavelli according to his own assumptions' (Gallicet Calvetti 1972: 65).

[21] Bertman, De Dijn and Walther 1987; Bostrenghi 1992b; Giancotti 1995; Di Vona 1990; Lazzeri 1998.

[22] This lacuna has been in part bridged by the special issue of *Archives de Philosophie* 1994 and Barbaras 1996.

merely passing observations, more the fruit of intuition than rigorous research.

What explains this lack of interrogation of texts whose very materiality seems to demand it is, I think, the relations of force traversing their interpretation. A powerful general interpretation is in fact capable of eliminating the possibility of a particular question, reducing material traces on the basis of which it could have been posed to the artefact of a meticulous philology. It is not difficult to identify in the Romantic and in particular Hegelian image of Spinoza the cause of one such exclusion. It was indeed precisely Hegel who in the *Science of Logic* and the *Encyclopedia* established the interpretative lines of Spinozist thought for the future.[23] Hegel interprets Spinoza's thought as a philosophy of the infinite, in which the passage to the finite is nothing but *verschwinden*, vanishing, and not *aufheben*, dialectical overcoming. For Hegel, Spinozism is a philosophy of eternity without temporality, and therefore without history and without politics; it is a philosophy of which Spinoza's illness, tuberculosis (*Schwindsucht*, which etymologically means the tendency to disappear), is the symbol. For a long time this powerful shadow cast over Spinoza's philosophy by the all-encompassing [*alles zermalmende*] Hegelian system oriented the research of academic historiography, and it was not until the 1960s that a new perspective in Spinoza studies emerged. In particular, the work of Gueroult, Matheron and Deleuze changed the relations of force composing the field of Spinoza interpretations, at first only in France, and then in most of Europe. With regard to my own work, however, by far the most important page in this recent history is the dazzling and obscure one that Althusser devotes to Spinoza in the opening lines of *Reading Capital*:

> The first person ever to have posed the problem of reading, and in consequence, of writing, was Spinoza, and he was also the first in the world to have proposed both a theory of history and a philosophy of the opacity of the immediate. With him, for the first time ever, a man linked together in this way the essence of reading and the essence of history in a theory of the difference between the imaginary and the true. This explains to us

[23] Hegel 1976: 382–3. In the *Encyclopedia*, Hegel synthesises the core of his reading of Spinoza in a few lines: 'Apart from the fact that Spinoza does not define God as the unity of God and the world, but as the unity of *thinking* and extension (the material world), this unity does already imply – even when it is taken in that first very clumsy way – that, on the contrary, the world is determined in the Spinozist system as a mere phenomenon without genuine reality [*als ein Phänomen, dem nicht wirkliche Realität zukomme*], so that this system must rather be seen as *acosmism*' (Hegel 1991: 97).

why Marx could not have possibly become Marx except by founding a theory of history and a philosophy of the historical distinction between ideology and science, and why in the last analysis this foundation was consummated in the dissipation of the religious myth of reading.[24]

This Althusserian detour through Spinoza allows for an entirely new reading of the Spinozist theory of the finite, no longer reducible to the universalised manifestation of Schopenhauerian *noluntas*. Metaphysics and politics are thought against one another in a theory of history elaborated on the basis of the distinction between the true and the imaginary, itself made possible by an analysis of biblical discourse as meaning rather than truth. From this perspective, the question of the Spinoza–Machiavelli relation becomes central, if we only consider the fact that here Spinoza takes up the distinction between the imagination of the thing and effectual truth from *The Prince* XV.

Certainly Machiavelli is not a philosopher in the strict sense, but rather a political thinker. However, once again taking up some Althusserian hints in 'Is it Simple to Be a Marxist in Philosophy?', I have searched in Machiavelli's politics for his philosophy, finding in this way, in a virtuous or vicious circle, Spinoza's philosophy, or at least a new shade of Spinoza's philosophy, that is, a new way of confronting the materiality of his texts. Properly understood, such research does not pretend to be the objective confrontation of two thinkers given as a conclusive totality. It is by means of the continual passage from one to the other, each taken into consideration in the materiality of every fragment, that I have tried to answer the questions I have posed. These questions are not purely historiographical: in the space between [*Zwischen*], which at once separates and binds Machiavelli and Spinoza, I have sought the means to think history independently from every philosophy of history, but also from the tired song of its absence, intoned by nihilism.

---

24 Althusser et al. 2015: 14–15.

1

Machiavelli in Spinoza's Library and Texts

Interrogating the Spinoza–Machiavelli relation first requires an analysis of some empirical facts which make up the basis of this problem in the last century. On the one hand, we have those texts of Machiavelli that were present in Spinoza's library, and on the other, the passages of the *TP* in which Spinoza cites Machiavelli and comments on him. To this we must add an investigation of works in Spinoza's library that discuss or repeat Machiavellian thought in both open and disguised ways, as well as a study of the role of citation in Spinoza's work. The former will allow us to emphasise the material traces of interpretations of Machiavelli through which Spinoza presumably elaborated his own interpretation, while the latter will enable us to stress the strategic significance of the occurrence of Machiavelli's name in Spinoza's lexicon.

Machiavelli's Texts in Spinoza's Library

We will first focus on the texts by Machiavelli that were present in Spinoza's library. In this regard, I think it is important to remember, as a preliminary methodological observation, that the presence of a text in the inventory of Spinoza's library does not *ipso facto* mean that it was read or studied by him. This inventory thus cannot retrace Spinoza's cultural horizon. The latter clearly extends over a much wider range and includes, beyond books that did not end up in the inventory, also those that he read without owning, and the entire atmosphere of knowledge that derives from oral communication in different social practices.

With this clarification, we come to the analysis of what Kant would define as a historical fact, since it is ratified by a local authority. In the inventory of objects left by Spinoza and sold at the public auction after his death, which is conserved in the notary archives of The Hague, there are two by Machiavelli:[1]

Among the books *in quarto*, n. 14: *Opere di Machiavelli*. 1550.
Among the books *in octavo*, n. 16: *Machiavel*. Basel.

The first of these corresponds to the edition of Machiavelli's works without an indication of the place of publication and dated 1550, known as the 'Testina' edition because of the type used by the press ('testino' characters). Thanks to the work of Bartolomeo Gamba, we know that this edition was reprinted five different times.[2] Gerber has been able to establish that these five reprints are all from the seventeenth century, indicating their order of appearance with the letters A, B, C, D, E.[3] And finally, Georges Bonant has established the probable dates for the appearance of each reprint:

> A emerged out of Geneva, around 1615, B appeared around 1628 thanks to the press of Pierre Aubert, C was carried out jointly by Pierre Aubert and Pierre Chouet around 1635, D on the typography of Jacques Stoer on behalf of Pierre Chouet and eventually the heirs of Pierre Aubert around 1640, and finally, E was printed for Samuel Chouet around 1660.[4]

Bonnant also provides a completely convincing explanation of the earlier dating in the 'Testina':

> It was desirable to give to these texts the authority of an edition close to the first publications of the author. In addition, by taking the date 1550, nine years prior to the condemnation of Machiavelli's writings by the Holy Office, these works benefited from the approval that they had earlier received from the Papacy.[5]

[1] On Spinoza's library, cf. Servas van Rooijen 1888; Land 1889; Meinsma 1983; Nourisson 1892; Vulliaud 1934; Pozzi 1994.
[2] Gamba 1839.
[3] Gerber 1906: 171–4, 193–7. Here is Gerber's general description of the work: 'The edition, as would be expected at this time, is just as little a critical edition in the current sense of the term as the first Aldina edition, if we note that it does not attempt to reconstruct a possible original text [*ursprüngliche Text*] on the basis of either manuscripts or the oldest accessible printed texts. Instead, Comin da Trino's *Histories*, the 1535 *The Prince*, Zanetti's *Discourses on Livy*, and Wolf's final two volumes were used as a model [*Druckvorlagen*] in order to remedy as much as possible, with the help of other editions, omissions which hinder comprehension as well as printing errors, but equally set out to improve its readability as a rule, thanks in particular to more modern punctuation' (Gerber 1962: 93–4). For further details on the five variations of the *Testina* edition, cf. Gerber 1962: 94–104.
[4] Bonnant 1965: 88.
[5] Bonnant 1965: 88. Cf. de Bujanda et al. 1990.

The presence of this work in Spinoza's library supplies us with an unequivocal fact: at a minimum, Spinoza had the possibility of reading the complete works of Machiavelli in Italian, a language that he seemed to be capable of understanding, as demonstrated by the presence in his library of an Italian–Spanish dictionary (*in octavo* Lorenzo Franciosini, *Vocabolario Italiano e Spagnolo*, Geneva: S. Chovët, 1665, 2 tomes in 1 volume), and another Italian-language work (Gregorio Leti's *Le visioni politiche*).

The second item refers to a widely circulated Latin translation of *The Prince* that was the point of departure for Machiavelli's reception in northeast Europe. It was very likely[6] a translation out of Basel from 1560; the

---

[6] Gerber points out two editions of the Latin translation of *The Prince*, the first edited by Tegli in 1560 and the second corrected by Stupanus in 1580 (of which Gerber mentions three variations). The second edition appeared 'with two speeches extracted from Cassius Dio and two anonymous Huguenot writings. [. . .] The two speeches come from Gaius Maecenas and Agrippa and are for and against the acceptance of the empire by Augustus. The Huguenot writings are entitled *Vindicae contra tyrannos sive, de principis in populum, populique in principem, legitima potestate* and *De jure magistratuum in subditos, et officio subditorum erga magistratus*. The former was written by Philippe de Mornay and reworked and edited by Hubert Languet, and it opposes absolute monarchy and the religious oppressions it puts into practice, justifying armed resistance against it' (Gerber 1962: 60). For passages in the *Vindicae contra tyrannos* against Machiavelli and Machiavellians, cf. Gerber 1962: 61. The facsimile I consulted in the reconstructed Rijnsburg library does not contain the *Vindicae*. To have an idea of what Spinoza could have found on Machiavelli, it suffices to read a passage from the French translation: 'I was not unaware, princes, that when I published these investigations of Stephanus Junius Brutus into the true right and power of a prince over the people and of the people over a prince, there would be some who would rebuke me. For these inquiries diametrically conflict with the evil arts, vicious counsels, and false and pestiferous doctrines of Niccolò Machiavelli the Florentine, whom these men consider to be a guide in governing the commonwealth. [. . .] So about two years ago, when I had extensive discussions with that learned, prudent gentleman Brutus concerning the disasters in Gaul, and when each of us had fully traversed their origins and causes, their beginnings and their development, we eventually came to the conclusion that, among other things, it was chiefly through the books of Machiavelli that some were sharpening their minds so that they might embrace the artifices of disrupting the commonwealth on the basis of the authority of those who rule it. It was sufficiently apparent to both of us that he established the foundations of such artifices in these books, by enunciating shocking precepts on that topic here and there. It was also clear that there could be no more certain and prompt remedy than if the rule [*imperium*] of princes and the right of peoples [*ius popularum*] (who are under them) were referred to their legitimate and certain first principles. By this means the power of both would be kept within bounds [*fines*], beyond or short of which the right administration of the commonwealth clearly could not survive; nor, of course, could the teachings of Machiavelli, which are completely overturned by these principles, be accepted. [. . .] But when this

edition was produced by two Italians, the translator Silvestro Tegli and the printer Pietro Perna, who took refuge in Basel from religious persecution.[7] In the introduction to the translation, Tegli maintains the ritual distance from the presented text:

> Nevertheless, I am well aware of the accusations and the numerous clamourings against the author, as well as the motives advanced by those who decree that it would be necessary to distance the souls of men from his lesson: of course, it would have been necessary first of all to celebrate the glory of the sovereign prince, to care for him alone, and propose him as the ultimate goal of our studies. Men, in contemplating and admiring the work of God, are made to sing praises, honour, worship, and serve with a pure spirit the sovereign author of all things. Once such a foundation is laid, there is nothing that could not be helpful to us.[8]

Regarding the translation, we cannot completely adhere to Procacci's judgement that the translator has 'considered it prudent to censor some of the more indecent passages and made use of Latin to domesticate certain crude expressions'.[9] Instead, a closer look shows that Tegli gave shape to Machiavelli's Italian insofar as the language allowed him. Certainly, he does not maintain any consistency in the translation of terms, but rather than domesticating Machiavelli's style, this renders it, if anything, more confusing. For example, he translates both *popolo* and *sudditi* with the term *populus*, while using *multitudo* to translate *università*, *universale*, *popolo*, *sudditi* and *moltitudine*. In the same way, he translates *ordini* with *leges et instituta* as

firm bond of human society is constituted, and the limits [*metae*] and boundaries [*fines*] which these investigations demonstrate – determined and fixed according to true and just principles – are established, surely the doctrine of Machiavelli entirely collapses without further ado? Should it not be rooted out as worthless, impious, and highly dangerous to the human race?' (Languet 1994: 8–11).

[7] 'The fact that precisely Basel was selected to give a universal linguistic guise to Machiavelli does not only depend on the general importance it had as a printing centre for northern Europe, but also the particular environment out of which the Latin version of *The Prince* comes: the environment of Italian emigrants. Neither the translator nor the printer were from Basel. The translator, Silvestro Tegli, is known almost only for the preface of the book. [. . .] In Basel he met another person from Lucca: the printer Perna who probably commissioned the translation of Machiavelli' (Kaegi 1960: 158). On the reasons why Calvinist immigrants took interest in Machiavelli, cf. Kaegi 1960: 160–3; Perini 1967. Regarding Perna's catalogue, see Perini 1990.

[8] Machiavelli 1560: 4v–6r. Cf. also Stupanus's epistle dedicatory in the 1580 edition (Machiavelli 1580: 2–4).

[9] Procacci 1995: 130–1.

well as with *leges* (which obviously he also uses to translate *leggi*), or even with *instituta* or *ordines*.[10] In each case this discontinuity does not enable a clear interpretation.

The censorship Procacci refers to in Tegli's translation is limited to two cases. The first omission is in fact without meaning and is probably a simple oversight of translation. Tegli does not translate the passage in chapter six where Machiavelli claims that 'armed prophets have always conquered, while disarmed ones have been destroyed'. However, he does not hide anything in Machiavelli's argumentation in the chapter, of which this formula is nothing but a summary.

The second case concerns chapter eighteen, and Tegli's intervention is more complex. First, after translating the first two lines of the chapter (*Quam sit omni laude dignum in principe pactam fidem servare, atque vitae integritatem sine ullo dolo malo retinere, nemo est qui non intelligat*),[11] Tegli eliminates Machiavelli's reference to his own time, of which he notes that 'princes who have done great things are those who have taken little account of faith and have known how to get around men's brains with their astuteness; and in the end they have overcome those who have founded themselves on loyalty'.[12]

In the next paragraph, after accurately establishing the theory of the doubling of politics in man and beast, Tegli does not translate the conclusion that 'the one without the other is not lasting'.[13] In the third paragraph, he does translate the passages about the good use of the beast in the double-form of lion and fox, a metaphor for force and cunning, but he modifies the meaning of the central passage. Where Machiavelli writes that 'a prudent lord, therefore, cannot observe faith, nor should he, when such observance turns against him, and the causes that make him promise have been eliminated',[14] Tegli translates:

> Therefore, the prince who is gifted with wisdom must avoid the promises he considers will be contrary to his interest [*Princeps propterea qui sapientia sit praeditus, debet ea promissa vitare, quae suis commodis contraria fore fidet*].[15]

---

[10] Machiavelli makes a clear distinction between laws [*leggi*] and orders [*ordini*] in *Discourses on Livy* I, 18; Machiavelli 1996: 49–52.

[11] Machiavelli 1560: 110; Machiavelli 1580: 122.

[12] *The Prince* XVIII; Machiavelli 1985: 69. Gerber also emphasises the suppression [*Unterdrückung*] of this passage in Gerber 1962: 65–6.

[13] *The Prince* XVIII; Machiavelli 1985: 69.

[14] Ibid.

[15] Machiavelli 1560: 111; Machiavelli 1580: 123–4.

The meaning of Machiavelli's claim is profoundly transformed and resituated on a level that does not recognise the fracture between morality and politics.[16]

Finally, Tegli censors both the central passage of the fifth paragraph as well as the conclusion to the sixth paragraph. Here is the first passage he erases, which follows the claim of the necessity of deception [finzione]:

> Nay, I dare say this, that by having [the above-mentioned good qualities] and always observing them, they are harmful; and by appearing to have them, they are useful, as it is to appear merciful, faithful, humane, honest, and religious, and to be so; but to remain with a spirit built so that, if you need not to be those things, you are able and know how to change to the contrary. This has to be understood: that a prince, and especially a new prince, cannot observe all those things for which men are held good, since he is often under a necessity to maintain his state, of acting against faith, against charity, against humanity, against religion.[17]

And here is the second, which contains a disguised reference to King Ferdinand of Spain:

> A certain prince of present times, whom it is not well to name, never preaches anything but peace and faith, and is very hostile to both. If he had observed both, he would have had either his reputation or his state taken from him many times.[18]

Concerning the implicit interpretation underlying Tegli's translation, we can thus observe his intervention much less in the suppression of references to the historical-political panorama of the epoch than in the translation of Machiavelli's text on pacts (however, the reference to the deceiver Pope, Alexander VI, is conserved, which is clearly not a coincidence for a Calvinist persecuted at home). The meaning of Machiavelli's proposition actually establishes a de facto dependence of respect for pacts on the conjuncture and the relations of force that traverse it, while the meaning imposed by Tegli moves in the direction, however banal, that one should carefully reflect before agreeing to a pact.[19]

---

[16] Gerber also emphasises that this passage 'is essentially different' (Gerber 1962: 66).

[17] The Prince XVIII; Machiavelli 1985: 70.

[18] The Prince XVIII; Machiavelli 1985: 71.

[19] In chapter sixteen, regarding the vices necessary to rule, Machiavelli writes that being

Whatever exceptions are made for this particular case, which is not without importance, the more polemical passages that confront the theological-political power of Machiavelli's epoch are accurately translated. One example is the well-known opening of chapter fifteen. After translating the alternative between effectual truth and the imagination of the thing with the terms *veritas rei* and *simulacrum vel imago rei*, he proposes again in all of its force the thesis that derives from having chosen to treat men as they are and not as how they should be:

> For a man who wants to make a profession of good in everything must come to ruin among so many others who are not good. It is therefore necessary for a prince, if he wants to maintain himself, to learn how to not to be good, and to use this learning and not use it according to necessity. [*Qui enim se virum bonum omnibus partibus profiteri studet, eum certe inter tot non bonos periclitari necesse est. Necessarium est itaque principi, ut perceptum habeat (si se salvum velit) qua ratione possit esse non bonus, idque pro rei necessitate, in suum convertat, vel non convertat usum.*][20]

Another very eloquent example is provided by the passage from chapter seventeen where Machiavelli, after affirming that for the prince it is better to be feared than to be loved, shows his anthropology:

> For of men one can generally say this: they are ungrateful, fickle, simulators and dissemblers, avoiders of danger, and pursuers of gain. As long as you do them good, they are all yours, offering you their blood, their goods, their lives, and their children, when the need for these things is far away; but when it is close, they turn away. [*Nam de hominibus universe haec affirmari possunt, eos ingratos esse, inconstantes, simulatores, periculorum fugitantes, lucri cupidi: dumque de eis benemeritis, ac necessitas procul abest, tui omnes sunt studiosi, sanguinem pro te effundendum offerunt, fortunas, vitam, liberos. At ea premente, ut supra docuimus, confestim desciscunt.*][21]

We can add to this the passage that takes up this anthropological framework in terms of respecting pacts (the passage modified by Tegli that I mentioned above):

> called *mean* [*misero*] is 'one of those vices that enable [a ruler] to rule' (*The Prince* XVI; Machiavelli 1985: 64). Tegli translates, slightly modifying the meaning: '*Nam vitiorum id est unum, quo minime impeditur dominandi ratio*' (Machiavelli 1560: 102; Machiavelli 1580: 114).

[20] Machiavelli 1560: 97–8; Machiavelli 1580: 108–9.
[21] Machiavelli 1560: 106; Machiavelli 1580: 118.

And if men were all good, this precept would not be good, but because they are not all good, their wickedness must be carefully avoided [*Atqui, homines si probi fuissent, omnes, praeceptum hoc plane fuisset inutile: verum cum improbi sint, diligenter eorum improbitas perfidiaque erit eludenda*].[22]

Thus we can conclude that Tegli's edition is a good translation that manages the substantial risks of betrayal in this kind of work within acceptable limits, except for the passage on pacts in which Machiavelli's thought is smoothed over by a contractualist ideology entirely foreign to it.

Machiavelli's Image and Presence within Spinoza's Library

Analysing the books in Spinoza's library can provide us with other useful information to complete and also clarify the framework through which Spinoza presumably developed his reading of Machiavelli. We can find more traces of Machiavelli's reception in Spinoza's political texts than in his philosophical ones. This is clearly but a small part of the great debate that tormented Europe, first opposing Machiavellians and anti-Machiavellians, and then later the monarchic and republican interpreters of Machiavelli. However, we might say that the texts in Spinoza's library provide an *in vitro* example of these debates. Within them we can find the most important examples of Machiavelli's overall thought, both in the form of commentaries or rewritings of certain passages, and as independent discussions inspired by certain Machiavellian claims.

The following books in Spinoza's library concern Machiavellian thought in one of these forms:

> Among the books *in-quarto* n. 7 Descartes *Brieven*, n. 11 *Politike discoursen*. 1662. Leyden, n. 12 *Obras* de Quedevo, n. 16 *Corona Gothica. Hisp.* 1658.
> Among the books *in-octavo* n. 11 *Politieke Weegschaal* door V. H. 1661, n. 17 *Las Obras* de Perez. 1664, n. 34 *El Criticon* vol. 3.
> Among the books *in-dodicesimo* n. 10 Clapmarius *de arcanis Rerump.*, n. 21 Verulamii *Sermones fideles*, n. 22 *Le visioni Politique*.

These books include the following works:

> Renatus Des Cartes, *Brieven* [. . .], tr. Jan H. Glazemaker, t'Amsterdam, T. Houthaak voor Jan Rieuwertst, 1661, 2 vols.

[22] Machiavelli 1560: 111; Machiavelli 1580: 124.

[Pieter van de Hove (de la Court)], *Politike Discoursen* [. . .], Leyden, P. Hackius, 1662.

Francisco de Quevedo, *Obras* [. . .], Brusselas, F. Foppens, 1660–70, 2 vols.

Diego de Saavedra Fajardo, *Corona Gothica Castellana, y Austriaca*, politicamente ilustrada [. . .], Amberes, J.B. Verdussen, 1658.

[Jan van Hove–Jean de la Court], *Consideratien van Staat ofte Politieke Weegschaal* [. . .], t'Amsterdam, J. Volckertsz Zinbreker, 1661.

Antonio Perez, *Las Obras y Relaciones* [. . .], Genevae, J. de Tornes, 1644.

P. Balthasar Gracian, *El Criticon*, Madrid 1650–53.

Arnold Clapmarius, *De Arcanis Rerumpublicarum Libri sex* [. . .], Amsterodami, L. Elzevirius, 1641.

Franciscus Bacon de Verulamio, *Semones Fideles, Ethici, Politici, Oeconomici* [. . .], Lugduni Batavorum, F. Hackius, 1641.

Gregorio Leti, *Le visioni politiche sopra gli interessi più reconditi, di tutti i prencipi e repubbliche della Christianità, Divise in varij sogni, e ragionamenti tra Pasquino, e il Gobbo di Rialto. Il tutto data dalla luce per la commodità de' curiosi*, s.e., Germania 1671.

Bacon

The *Sermones fideles* is the second Latin translation of Francis Bacon's *Essayes*.[23] This text contains numerous references to Machiavelli's political theory,[24] references that are for the most part laudatory, despite the intellectual climate of the time.[25] Beyond these individual issues, however, what is most theoretically interesting in Bacon's work is his taking up the Machiavellian theme of the memory of things and its contingency in the chapter 'Of Vicissitude of Things':

> Solomon saith, *There is no new thing upon the earth.* So that as Plato had an imagination, *that all knowledge was but remembrance,* so Solomon giveth his sentence, *that all novelty is but oblivion.* Whereby you may see that the river of Lethe runneth as well above ground as below. [. . .] Certain it is, that the matter is in a perpetual flux, and never at a stay. The great winding-sheets, that bury all things in oblivion, are two: deluges and

---

[23] Bacon 1641; Bacon 1985. For a critical analysis of the different drafts and translations of the *Essayes*, see Melchionda 1979: 3–56.

[24] On the relationship between Machiavelli and Bacon, the most important and exhaustive work is without doubt Orsini 1936.

[25] On this, cf. Raab 1965; Praz 1962.

earthquakes. As for conflagrations and great droughts, they do not merely dispeople and destroy. [. . .] But in the other two destructions, by deluge and earthquake, it is further noted, that the remnant of people which hap to be reserved are commonly ignorant and mountainous people, that can give no account of the time past, so that the oblivion is all one as if none had been left. [. . .] As for the observations that Machiavel hath, that the jealousy of sects doth much extinguish the memory of things, traducing Gregory the Great, that he did what in him lay to extinguish all heathen antiquities, I do not find that those zeals do any great effects, nor last long: as it appeared in the succession of Sabinian, who did revive the former antiquities. [. . .] But to leave these points of nature, and to come to men. The great vicissitude of things amongst men is the vicissitude of sects and religions. For those orbs rule in men's minds most. The true religion is *built upon the rock*; the rest are tossed upon the waves of time.[26]

Bacon adjusts Machiavelli's arguments at several levels. First, he funda-mentally alters the beginning of the chapter by asserting the perfect symme-try of memory and oblivion, a claim that takes distance from Machiavelli's specific conception of the contingency of memory, cleaving instead to the Platonic idea of the eternal return of the same, in the sense that for Bacon nothing ever falls definitively into the void, but every memory lies dormant in the soul, waiting to be reawakened. Second, while he conserves Machiavelli's distinction about the causes that lead to oblivion, namely causes due to men and causes due to the heavens, he introduces some differ-ences at the level of the causes themselves. According to Machiavelli, the causes that come from the heavens, which 'eliminate the human race and reduce the inhabitants of part of the world to a few', are 'plague, famine, or an inundation of waters'.[27] For Bacon, the only causes that have the power to bury all things in oblivion are floods and earthquakes. In this way, he takes up the Machiavellian idea, which is incidentally also Platonic, that the only survivors of these types of catastrophes are coarse mountain men who are unable to transmit the memory of antiquity. In terms of the causes that come from men, Bacon erases Machiavelli's suggestion regarding the 'variation of languages',[28] in order to linger briefly on the causes that come from the conflict between different religious sects, taking into consideration Machiavelli's example of Gregory VII's rage in destroying every form of

[26] Bacon 1985: 472–81.
[27] *Discourses on Livy* II, 5; Machiavelli 1996: 139.
[28] Ibid.

paganism. Bacon finds the example unconvincing and also contradictory, in its universal sense, because of the fact that Gregory the Great's successor, Sabinian, restored previous antiquities to honour. However, Bacon's most important manoeuvre, prepared by his earlier moves, particularly the symmetry between memory and oblivion, consists in establishing Christianity over other religions, positioning it as an Archimedean point of history, whereas Machiavelli inscribes its narrative, its symbolisation of the world, in the aleatory necessity of historical events and relations of force: 'The true religion', Bacon concludes, echoing Matthew 16:18, 'is built on the rock; the rest are tossed upon the waves of time'.[29]

Clapmar

Although he is not one of its main sources,[30] Machiavelli is mentioned several times in Arnold Clapmar's *De arcanis rerumpublicarum*.[31] This text is divided into six parts, each of which corresponds to one of six facets of power: I) The Right of Sovereignty, II) The Mysteries of Sovereignty, III) The Mysteries of Domination, IV) The Right of Domination, V) The Depravity of Domination, and finally VI) The Semblances [*simulacri*] of Sovereignty. Clapmar uses Machiavelli in several ways: as a historical source, as a term of dialectical confrontation, as an authority [*auctoritas*], and also occasionally as a veiled source. In each case, he is held in high regard, as is evident in the labels *acutissimus*, *prudentissimus scriptor et popularis* and *acutus scritor ab Hetruria*. However, this does not prevent Clapmar, at several important points in the fifth part of the text, from tracing the relationship between religion and reason of state in contrast to Machiavelli, through citing Scipione Ammirato:

> And because, Scipione Ammirato says, as we have said, religion is the best thing, concerning reason of state, and its phases which are different from those of men, and not given in proportion by temporal things to eternal things: for these questions, one should turn first to religion and see what it is opposed to; because in such a case, reason of state needs to be accommodated to religion, and not religion to reason of state.[32]

[29] For a commentary on this chapter, see Rossi 1999: 21–43.
[30] For a confrontation between the two models of political theory, see Senellart 1995: 261.
[31] Clapmar 1641. On the relation between Spinoza and Clapmar, see Gebhardt 1923.
[32] Clapmar 1641: 229.

Indeed, as Clapmar writes several pages earlier, 'divine law, when contrary to religion'[33] is unworthy of being called right [*jus*]. In this way, he poses the fundamental distinction in moving towards his treatment of the depravity of domination [*flagitia dominationis*], which Clapmar significantly calls Machiavellian advice [*consilia machiavellistica*]. One speaks of depravity when the ruler, itself an intermediary form between the civil rule [*imperium civile*] and tyranny, no longer rests on theological-moral foundations: 'it is no longer', Clapmar writes, 'Domination, [*Dominatio*], Right [*Ius*], nor Sovereignty [*Imperium*], but rather the height of injustice and extreme tyranny'. Clapmar restages the classic distinction between good and evil reason of state with his own distinction between the right of domination [*iura dominationis*] and the depravity of domination, 'whose principles, as far as possible, should be avoided':

> The rights of domination are different from the depravities of domination, and even opposed to them. First, because the latter tend only to private utility, while the former tend to public utility as much as private utility. The depravities of domination are made to satisfy cruelty and sensual desire; the rights of domination are for conserving public peace. Finally, in the rights of domination, there is the reason of divine authority, honesty, faith and modesty, while in the depravities of domination, all of these are betrayed and trampled upon. However, both are dependent on secret and occult ways of consolidating and increasing their rule.[34]

As Clapmar would affirm in Thesis L of his *Conclusiones de iure publico*, Machiavelli's error lies precisely in having confused the mysteries of domination [*arcana dominationis*][35] and the right of domination, a distinction clearly summarised by Senellart: 'the *arcana* are to sovereign right what walls are to a fortress, in accordance with the etymology (*arcanum* derives from

---

[33] Clapmar 1641: 227.
[34] Clapmar 1641: 233–5.
[35] 'The *arcana imperii* relate to the conservation of the current form of the republic. They are divided into six categories: a) the regime that implements them (aristocracy, democracy, or monarchy); b) the opponent who is fought (people, prince, or nobility): aristocratic mysteries against the people or royalty, democratic mysteries against the nobility or royalty, royal mysteries against the people or the nobility. The *arcana dominationis* relate to the security of those who govern the city. They also differ according to the form of government. [. . .] *Arcana imperii* and *arcana dominationis*, without being confused, derive from the right of domination, which is, so to speak, the specification of the right of sovereignty in each government' (Senellart 1995: 267–8).

arx, fortress, or from *arca*, coffer, treasure chest [. . .]). Thus they cannot be confused with right, which constitutes their foundation' [*fundamentum huius doctrinae*].[36]

However, Clapmar's reading of Machiavelli is possible by means of a sim-plification, which is clearly exemplified in Thesis XLIV, where Machiavelli's political theory is summed up by an exercise of cruelty aimed at 'keeping the people in a perpetual state of fear'.[37] Clapmar's simplification and mis-understanding of Machiavelli consists in mistaking the affirmation of the necessary use of cruelty and violence for a praise of cruelty and violence. In this way, Clapmar eliminates the distinction between badly and well-used cruelty. Well-used cruelty involves acts that 'are done at a stroke, out of the necessity to secure oneself, and then are not persisted in but are turned to as much utility for the subjects as one can', whereas badly used cruelty involves those acts 'used which, though few in the beginning, rather grow with time than are eliminated'.[38] The former reinforce power, the latter weaken it, and in the long run, lead it to ruin. In not perceiving the importance of this distinction, Clapmar attributes to Machiavelli the politics of 'let them hate, so long as they fear' [*oderint dum metuant*], whereas Machiavelli argues instead in *The Prince* XVII that whoever holds power should be feared, but never hated, because hate brings sedition, and eventually, the loss of power.

The nature of the relation between religion and politics is therefore clearly an essential strategic location for Clapmar's skirmish with Machiavelli. In this sense Clapmar cannot avoid confronting one of the historical examples of this relationship that had become classic in treatises at the time, that of religion as an instrument of power in Roman history. Significantly, in approaching the question of atheism, Clapmar is preoccupied with refuting Machiavelli's thesis that the Romans were blasphemous and used religion in purely instrumental terms,[39] again relying on the authority of Scipione Ammirato.[40]

Clapmar refers here to *Discourses on Livy* I, 11–15, but misunderstands the meaning of these chapters. Far from affirming the impiety of the Roman people, Machiavelli emphasises their religiosity several times, in particular in chapter eleven, where he claims that 'for many years there was never so

---

[36] Senellart 1995: 262.
[37] Clapmar 1641: 17.
[38] *The Prince* VIII; Machiavelli 1985: 37–8.
[39] Clapmar 1641: 241
[40] Clapmar 1641: 242.

much fear of God as in that republic'.[41] It is very likely that what Clapmar hears as an accusation of impiety is Machiavelli's conception of religion as an essential component in the political make-up of a people, his insistence on its ordinary power, the fact that it 'served to command armies, to animate the plebs, to keep men good, [and] to bring shame to the wicked'.[42] It is in no case a claim about the impiety of the Roman people, but rather a claim about religion, insofar as it causes and guarantees order. Clapmar's interpretation proves useful, however, because it shows us the inability of comprehending the complexity of Machiavellian thought, which is irreducible to the antithetical schema of 'good' vs. 'evil' reason of state, or religion as the foundation of politics vs. religion as a mere instrument, a facade of power.

One of Clapmar's contemporaries, Christopher Besold, also took up the question of the relation between religion and politics in Machiavelli in an appendix to Clapmar's text. He specifies the difference between the conceptions of politics in Clapmar and Machiavelli, showing that Clapmar poses limits to the mysterious through the triple exigency of religion, faith, and modesty (Religio, fides, pudor), while Machiavelli does not recognise any moral limit to the prince's actions.[43] And, returning to the distinction between a reason of state that is not 'against religion',[44] and an 'evil reason of state', he identifies the latter completely with Machiavellian theory. Cesare Borgia would be a perfect example of this, since he acted 'under the very careful influence of Machiavelli' [sub Magisterio Machiavelli providissimo].[45]

However, in chapter three, devoted to the depravity of domination, Besold himself, after defining this as Machiavellian advice in continuity with Clapmar, introduces an element of doubt regarding Machiavelli's true intentions. Probably referring to the Discourses on Livy, Besold concludes that it is necessary to take into account the fact that Machiavelli did not only write The Prince, and that its scope must be called into question (considerandus est scopus, ad quem ille collimavit),[46] going as far as suggesting an indirect reading. And a reinforcement of the thesis of a democratic Machiavelli, only doubtfully implied by Besold, can be found in Wolfgang Heinrich Ruprecht's Theses de Iure Publico, which is also printed as an appendix to Clapmar's text. These theses, which inquire into the best form of government,

---

[41] Discourses on Livy I, 11; Machiavelli 1996: 34.
[42] Discourses on Livy I, 11; Machiavelli 1996: 34–5.
[43] Clapmar 1641: 10.
[44] Clapmar 1641: 7.
[45] Clapmar 1641: 13.
[46] Clapmar 1641: 45

openly take the side of monarchy, contrasting only Machiavelli (of the *Discourses on Livy*) as a theoretician of democracy.[47]

What I think is most important in the group of texts collected in Clapmar's work is that the entire interpretative spectrum of Machiavelli's work is deployed within them. This runs from his image as the wicked father of Machiavellianism and evil reason of state, who in *The Prince* teaches the disgraceful to conquer and conserve power against morality and religion, to the image of the only author who has openly taken sides for a form of democratic power in the *Discourses on Livy*, all the way to an indirect interpretation of *The Prince*, which questions the true meaning of the work, asking whether, as Ugo Foscolo said paradigmatically in *Dei Sepolcri*, 'that greatness, [. . .] strengthening the scepter of the rulers, / then removes, and reveals to the people / from whom tears pour and from whom blood pours'.

Leti

Gregorio Leti's *Le visioni politiche*, anonymously published in 1671, certainly offers the least interest among the books in Spinoza's library concerning Machiavelli.[48] Leti was an adventuring Milanese man who converted to Calvinism, and in the book he undertakes a general analysis of the European political situation at the time. Machiavelli's name appears as a symbol of an evil politician who has forgotten Christian values: his spectre simply evokes the devil, or Old Nick (although this would not spare Leti from being expelled from Geneva, precisely under the accusation of Machiavellianism). In Leti's political theory, which is entirely and strictly based on theology – defining God as the eternal craftsman [*eterno fabro*] and kings as his 'appearance [*simulacri*] on earth'[49] – Machiavelli embodies the separation of politics from theology, the inscription of politics in the field of immorality.

In the first *Ombra*, using the form of an exhortation by the king of France, Leti labels Machiavelli the theorist of evil reason of state who reduces religion to an instrument of power, basing his theory on the systematic destruction of dogmatic Christianity. Machiavelli sketches a world in which there

---

[47] Clapmar 1641: 101.

[48] Leti 1671.

[49] Leti 1671: 39. The following passage is also significant in this regard: 'Do not dreams, as always liars, deserve to be told with such care to rulers, who are satisfied with the truth, but not with lies, already participating in being divine, as referees over the life and death of others, Gods of the earth if not the Royalty of Heaven? And Empires that are real abhor, even for their own conservation, the shadow that negative things are' (Leti 1671: 50).

is no place for God or the soul, and lacks any other 'apprehension of divine things other than those which beasts have'.[50] In precise contrast to a theory that conceives the real as the place of simple relations of force, Leti puts forward the medieval idea of the moral exemplarity of the prince,[51] and rejects point by point the model of strategic politics that Machiavelli provides in *The Prince*.

Regarding the establishment of a new principality, Leti takes distance from Machiavelli's idea of well-used cruelty:

> A new Prince in particular must never cast the first stones from his Government among the foundation of rest, because in order to ascend the throne, confusing the spectre with the sword, giving preference to the arrogant, and the vindictive, always provokes the people to suspect, to changes, and even to tumults; military licence also gives military licence against the Prince to the subjects.[52]

The rejection of the political use of cruelty leads to the refusal of the idea that it is better for the prince to be feared than loved:

> On a par with perfidy, it is the ignorance of the impious Machiavelli which counsels the Prince to make himself more feared than loved. Fools, how foolish! Do they not know that the Cruelty of the Prince is the trumpet that calls for seditions from the people and awakens the nobles to conspiracies. [. . .] It is to love and not fear that we owe the preservation of a Prince, because a lenient Prince makes his subjects more attentive to his health than to the desire for his death.[53]

Reinserting the action of the sovereign into the fundamental principles of sovereignty leads Leti to distance himself from two Machiavellian teachings to which political action must conform in order to be efficacious: the necessity of appearing, that is, of an image that coheres with faith, kindness, religion, and humanity without being required actually to conform with them; and the idea that the prince does not need to respect pacts once the reasons for entering them no longer exist:

[50] Leti 1671: 12, II.
[51] Senellart 1995: 260.
[52] Leti 1671: 29.
[53] Leti 1671: 107–10.

And a wise man affirms that living without simulation is the touchstone that distinguishes the tyrant from the legitimate prince, but also that breaking the promised peace is very bad reason of state, because this carelessness and instability are likely to discredit the Prince and consequently deprive him of allies and friends.[54]

However, it should be noted that for Leti, the reasons to respect pacts are inscribed in a double register. The first is a moral order concerning divine judgement on the monarch, that is, its legitimacy (which differentiates the monarch and the tyrant). The second is a strategic-political level, and highlights the negative consequences of breaking pacts on a temporal level – the mistrust of allies.

For us, the image of Machiavelli that emerges in Leti's pages is much more interesting as a sociological indicator than anything else: it is an ordinary portrait deprived of any interpretative nuance, simply obtained as the inverse of the Christian prince.

Quevedo, Perez, Saavedra and Gracian

Among the Spanish section of Spinoza's library, references to Machiavelli are much less numerous and for the most part indirect.[55] In Antonio Perez there are but distant echoes,[56] while the more precise reference that appears in Saavedra is nothing but a polemical stereotype.[57] Indeed, the formula 'religion must not be governed by reason of state, but reason of state by religion',[58] evidently directed against Machiavelli insofar as he is the father of evil reason of state, is nothing more than Saavedra repeating a contemporary cliché.

We can find a similar cliché in a passage from Gracian's *Criticon*, where Machiavelli is associated with Bodin and contrasted to Aristotle and Giovanni Botero:

> This *Prince* of Machiavelli and this *Republic* of Bodin must not appear among men: let them not be called 'reason' because they are totally contrary to it. And I warn you that these two politicians show the baseness

---

[54] Leti 1671: 30.
[55] On Machiavelli and Spanish political thought, see Marvall 1955.
[56] Perez 1644: 1033–5.
[57] Saavedra 1681.
[58] Saavedra 1681: 111.

of those times, the wickedness of those centuries, and to what level the world had fallen. That [work] of Aristotle's is a good, old [reason]. For a prince who is just as Catholic as he is prudent, I recommend a work full of pearls and precious stones: Botero's *The Reason of State*.[59]

Similarly, the only passage in Quevedo on Machiavelli simply transposes contemporary prejudices. In *Fortuna con seso, y la hora de todos, fantasia moral*,[60] Quevedo writes:

Pacas Mazo, disguising his rapacity with a white dove, said that the delay was sufficient, the decision prudent, but that it was appropriate that the secret was deaf and mute. Then, pulling out a sheepskin-bound book with various woollen ornaments, he offered it to Rabbi Saadias and said, 'We give you this as a pledge.' The author took it and asked, 'whose works are these'? Pacos Mazo responded, 'They are our words.' The author is Nicolas Machiavelli, who composed the plainsong of our counterpoint. As the Jews looked at the book with great attention, particularly its sheepskin binding, Rabbi Asapha, the delegate of Oran, exclaimed: Here is the wool that the Spanish say is shorn from the back of who comes to shear it! Thereupon, they parted ways, each projecting to meet again, like stone and steel, to fight, collide, smash, and spit fire against the whole world; and thus was founded a new sect of moneyism [*Dinerismo*], changing their name from Atheists to *Dineranos* or *Dineristas*.[61]

The reference to Machiavelli is inserted in a text hostile to Portuguese Marranos, descendants of Jews who were expelled from Spain in 1492, who had gained freedom to trade in Spain on 7 December 1629. Recognition of juridical equality provoked a significant immigration of Marrano traders, and although it is not easy to determine the figures, this immigration took the form of a veritable invasion to some contemporary eyes.[62] Taking a position against the Jews, Quevedo inscribes them within 'an intense economic-political-religious battle which took place between the supporters

---

[59] Gracian 1653: 105. On the opposition of Machiavelli and Botero in terms of the question of reason of state, Senellart's work is interesting because it tends to show a more complex historical framework than that of Meinecke's continuist interpretation: 'in the sixteenth century, two distinct forms of rationality faced off, one war-like, the other economic' (Senellart 1989: 11).

[60] Quevedo 1660.

[61] Quevedo 1660: 358.

[62] Quevedo 1980: 150.

and opponents of the Marranos'.[63] In order to emphasise the spirit of revolt, lack of discipline, ingratitude, egotism, calculation and duplicity, he finds no better way than to accuse them of being disciples of Machiavelli.

The van Hove Brothers

Two works by the van Hove brothers, *Politike Discoursen* and *Politieke Weegschaal*, can be considered the ideological manifestos of the ruling Dutch mercantile class, which held power in the United Provinces between 1650 and 1672.[64] In these texts, the brothers take a twofold political position. First, they take a position against monarchy and for the republic, of which democracy and aristocracy are particular species (the phrase *Principes mortales, respublicae aeternae* is repeated almost obsessively in *Politieke Weegschaal*). Second, they argue in favour of a peaceful state that allows for a maximum development of commerce and industry.[65] Although no reference to Machiavelli with regard to the latter is possible in positive terms,[66] in the struggle against monarchy outlined in *Politieke Weegschaal* we can find a clear reference to the Machiavellian thesis about the influence of power over historiography: 'And if anyone should doubt these thoughts, consider the cruel and cursed tyrant, Emperor Augustus, whom all the historians feared.'[67] Machiavelli's judgment of Caesar echoes here: the celebration and praise given to him by writers was the effect of his power. 'Those who praise him are corrupted by his fortune and awed by the duration of the empire that, ruling under that name, did not permit writers to speak freely of him.'[68]

---

[63] Ibid.

[64] Machiavelli is used as a historical source on almost every page in *Politike Discoursen*. Among other texts, *The Prince*, *Florentine Histories* and *Discourses on Livy* are referenced at great length.

[65] A key analysis of the image and use of Machiavelli in seventeenth-century Holland is Mulier 1990. Following the work of Pocock on the Anglo-Saxon tradition, Mulier shows how, beside the image of Machiavelli as 'Old Nick', there is an equal, if not greater, importance to Machiavelli read 'as a republican': it is 'in the works of the de la Court brothers and Spinoza' that we find, according to Mulier, 'the first unequivocal expression of republicanism, based among other things on what Machiavelli had said' (Mulier 1990: 254). On the same themes, cf. also Visentin 1998.

[66] In another work by P. van Hove, there is an implicit reference to Machiavelli in negative terms (De Witt 1669: 252).

[67] van Hove 1662.

[68] *Discourses on Livy* I, 10; Machiavelli 1996: 31–2.

Descartes

Although Descartes wrote no work dedicated to politics, his correspondence contains two extremely important letters on Machiavelli, both addressed to Princess Elisabeth of Bohemia. The first was written after Descartes' July 1646 encounter with Elisabeth in The Hague. It contains a broad commentary on *The Prince*, which Descartes had read at Elisabeth's request.[69] Descartes' reading of Machiavelli, which we will analyse, is characterised by a strong ambivalence, the symptom of attraction and disorientation that elicits, in a reader that we certainly cannot suspect of dogmatism, the idea that the foundation of politics rests on the shifting sands of conflict instead of the solid stones of morality.

Descartes finds some good maxims in Machiavelli, such as those in chapters nineteen and twenty, which declare that 'a Prince should always avoid the hatred and contempt of his subjects' and that 'the love of the people is worth more than fortresses'.[70] However, there are others that he resolutely refuses to take up. Descartes' first critique of Machiavelli's work concerns the distinction between legitimate and illegitimate princes, which he finds insufficient. Machiavelli's distinction between hereditary and new princes actually concerns the level of the factual conditions under which the political action of the prince unfolds, but Descartes maintains that such action must be examined on a juridical-moral level:

> I think that the author's greatest fault is that he does not sufficiently distinguish between princes who have come to power by just means and those who have usurped it by illegitimate methods; and that he recommends indiscriminately maxims that are suitable only for the latter. If you are building a house on foundations insufficient to support high thick walls, the walls will have to be low and insubstantial; and similarly, those who have gained power by crime are usually compelled to continue their course of crime, and would be unable to remain in power if they took to virtue.[71]

---

[69] 'I have read the book [*The Prince*] which Your Highness commanded me to discuss' (AT IV: 486; Descartes 1991: 292). For more analysis of Descartes' letters to Elisabeth, as well as their French context, cf. Canziani 1980; Gouhier 1973. For Glazemaker's Dutch translation from Spinoza's library, see Des Cartes 1641: 42–6.

[70] AT IV: 486; Descartes 1991: 292. Cf. *The Prince* XIX; Machiavelli 1985: 71–86.

[71] AT IV: 486; Descartes 1991: 292. Regarding this letter, Namer writes that 'Descartes, preoccupied by personal problems, seemed to be reserved and was content to reiterate the opinion of Juan de Mariana' (Namer 1961: 212).

As the text unfolds, there is a displacement from the juridical to the factual level, and it is precisely at this second level that the practical uselessness of Machiavelli's prescriptions for legitimate princes, and their usefulness for usurpers, is revealed: virtue calls for virtue and vice calls for vice.

Descartes thus moves to summarising the precepts that are useful for usurpers,[72] each of which, in short, unanchors politics from morality. To this point, Descartes' argument is very clear. He divides those who hold power into two categories (legitimate and usurpers), and rejects Machiavelli's maxims, which he considers as only applicable to the usurpers. Descartes suggests that this is actually a terrible approach for a book written for princes, since as Machiavelli himself admits, 'princes cannot protect themselves from the first fellow who is willing to risk his own life to take revenge on them'.[73]

However, Descartes adds several lines that seem to respond to a clearly urgent question that remains implicit about the nature of the legitimacy of princes. He asks which signs allow us to distinguish and grasp the legitimacy of the prince (a question which, at root, is analogous to asking for the signs that allow us to distinguish the true idea). It is precisely the ability to respond to this question that establishes the validity of the division of those who hold power into two categories. Descartes' answer seems to radically oppose the terms of the problematic opened by Machiavelli:

> It seems to me that quite contrary maxims should be proposed for the instruction of good princes, however newly they may have come to power; and it should be presupposed that the means which they have used to gain that power have been just.[74]

Therefore, if one wants to instruct a prince, even a prince who ascended to the throne only recently, it is necessary to supply them with a hypothetical *Anti-Prince* (actually nothing other than one of several texts in the tradition of the mirror of princes), obviously assuming that he has taken power through just means. However, the use of the verb 'to suppose' [*supposer*] opens a chasm in Descartes' argument, putting its foundations back into question. What are these just means for taking power, and consequently, how can a good prince be distinguished from a usurper? Descartes' answer is surprising:

---

[72] Des Cartes 1641: 50.
[73] AT IV: 487; Descartes 1991: 292.
[74] Ibid.

Almost always, I think, they are just, provided the princes who use them think them to be; for justice between sovereigns does not have the same bounds as justice between individuals. It seems to me that in this instance God gives the right to those to whom he gives power. But of course the most just actions become unjust when those who do them think them so.[75]

The signs that distinguish just means are therefore not exterior signs, corresponding to a set of values that transcend the prince's conscience, but are on the contrary interior, corresponding to how the prince considers the means he uses. Whatever the prince considers to be just, in the interiority of his conscience, is also objectively just. In other words, he becomes the measure of justice and injustice: something is just if it appears as such to him. However, this means that the prince would be able to consider the means he used to take power to be just, even if he was unsuccessful. In order to respond to this problem, Descartes introduces the idea that victorious force is founded *de jure* on a divine guarantee. The path of Descartes' thought can be reconstructed in these terms: with him who has the force to take power lies the right to take it, by divine grace, and also the right to consider his actions as just and therefore to use violence with the aura of an eternal right (through a sort of pre-established harmony between right and force). Thus, to the prince's force there corresponds, in the order of providence, the conscience of the justice of the actions produced by force, a conscience that is given for us to suppose by our faith in divine providence, but not our knowledge of it.

Here Descartes' Augustinianism reveals itself: we can see it in the conception of language as the impoverishment and misunderstanding of noetic truth, whose originary place is in the conscience.[76] There is no moral evaluation of political action unless it is by the subject of this action and the unintelligible divine will. This is a typical structure of Descartes' metaphysical discourse. The fact of the clarity of the *cogito*, its force, establishes divine clarity, but only divine clarity guarantees the truth and clarity of the *cogito*.[77] The equation 'right or force' [*droit ou force*] cannot but evoke

---

[75] Ibid. As Padovani notes, 'with this subjective criterion of intention and the economy of force for judging the legitimacy of a conquering power, any conquest can easily be justified, even the most unjust' (Padovani 1937: 4).

[76] Cf. Robinet 1978: 79–103.

[77] Here I follow François Regnault's acute suggestion: 'The essential text is the one [. . .] which confers the right to use force and legitimacy on the prince who thinks himself as legitimate (I think myself just, therefore I am: the comparison with the Cogito is inevitable)' (Regnault 2012: 235).

Spinoza's formula 'right or power' [*jus sive potentia*]. The difference between the two formulas lies in their insertion into different theoretical frameworks, particularly Spinoza's negation of free human and divine will. However, we can perhaps claim that Spinoza's redefinition of Cartesian metaphysics finds its entry-point to the political terrain through this formulation.[78]

But let us return to Descartes' text. The equation *droit* = *force* seems to be a version of Machiavellianism *post festum*: through this formula all violent actions capable of establishing a new juridical and political order are declared legitimate. However, after hinting that this violence does not have limits, as long as it is blessed with divine grace (which points to a political version of the Protestant ethic), Descartes introduces a restriction. This violence cannot be unleashed against anyone without distinction, but must take into account the differences among the *subjects*, that is, those subjects who are *friends or allies*, and those who are *enemies*.

When confronting enemies,[79] Descartes maintains that common moral laws cannot have any validity, and therefore that Machiavelli's teaching, in this case alone, is applicable in all of its starkness. Indeed, provided that some utility is drawn for oneself or the subjects, 'almost everything is permitted', even what unites 'the fox and the lion, combining artifice with force'.[80] However, this *almost* [*quasi*] also reveals a moral limit in this case, not so much in the force of the lion as the cunning of the fox. Descartes condemns certain behaviour, approved by Machiavelli 'in several places', which Descartes thinks tears up society and negates its fundamental laws: 'pretending to be a friend of those one wishes to destroy, in order to take them by surprise'.[81] Friendship is actually *too holy* a thing because it can be used instrumentally. Whoever feigns such a feeling in view of a betrayal will therefore deserve not to be trusted, and even to be hated whenever they hold out a sincere feeling.

Descartes' argument becomes more complex and layered when he considers allies. He begins with an unequivocal moral claim: 'As for allies, a prince

---

[78] Regarding the Cartesian equation *droit* = *force*, Faraklas writes that 'Spinoza expands this definition to right in general' (Faraklas 1997: 85–6). This seems too simplified: between the two conceptions of politics there is a true change of metaphysical terrain, which confers a greatly different meaning to the term 'right'.

[79] Descartes provides some details in order to further specify this category: 'I include among enemies all those who are neither friends or allies, because one has a right to make war on such people when it is to one's advantage and when their power is increasing in a suspicious and alarming manner' (*AT* IV: 488; Descartes 1991: 293).

[80] Ibid. Translation modified.

[81] Ibid.

should keep his word to them strictly, even when it is to his own disadvantage.'[82] At first glance this statement seems to repeat Grotius's imperative that 'pacts are to be kept' [pacta sunt servanda]. But the moral character of Descartes' claim shifts in the following argument and a utilitarian calculus intervenes: it is not so much the violation of the moral law in itself that is inadvisable as the effects that such a violation would have on the reputation of the prince, who would end up being considered untrustworthy. The prince must therefore accept the eventual inconveniences that follow from concluded pacts, not out of respect for his word, but because in calculating advantages and disadvantages it is difficult to think that the advantages of breaking a pact could be greater than the disadvantages of the image that follows from breaking it. Precisely for this reason the prince is exempt from keeping pacts 'in situations where he would be altogether ruined': 'the law of nations', Descartes writes, 'dispenses him from his promise'.[83] In each case, Descartes maintains that 'it is necessary to use much circumspection in promising if one is to be able always to keep faith'.[84]

Moving on to the symmetrical question of loyalty to allies, Descartes emphasises the utility of maintaining good relations with the majority of one's neighbours, but also advises the formation of close alliances only with those who are less powerful. His explanation again recalls the calculation of advantages and disadvantages:

> For however loyal one intends to be oneself, one should not expect the same from others; one should count on being betrayed whenever one's allies find it to their advantage. Those who are more powerful may find it to their advantage to do so whenever they wish; not so those who are less powerful.[85]

Descartes' argument allows us to glimpse an oscillation between the level of right and the level of fact or relations of force. The discussion of loyalty to pacts concerns the level of what should be, in which, however, one cannot have confidence. For this reason, alliances must be based on the utilitarian calculus of advantages and disadvantages, and as such it becomes necessary to choose allies for whom betrayal would be disadvantageous.

Finally, Descartes turns to subjects [sujets], whom he divides into two

---

[82] Ibid.
[83] Ibid.
[84] Ibid.
[85] AT IV: 489; Descartes 1991: 293.

categories, the nobles and the people, which correspond to two different political strategies for the prince. Regarding the nobles, whom Descartes identifies as 'all of those who can form parties against the prince', one must try 'to be very sure of their loyalty'. Otherwise, 'all politicians agree that he should employ all his efforts to bring them low, and if they show any tendency to rock the ship of state, he should treat them as he would his enemies'.[86] In this way, the argument concerning nobles, like the discussion of allies, goes beyond the moral discourse of friendship and loyalty, and affirms the truth of relations of force: whoever among the nobles has the force necessary to destroy the state, regardless of their intention, must be considered an enemy of the prince. After all, the French Wars of Religion in the sixteenth century and the still open wounds of the St Bartholomew's Day massacre demonstrated the validity of this statement in action.

For the second category of subjects, the people, Descartes advises the avoidance of 'their hatred and their disdain' above all. This is not difficult as long as the prince sticks to a strict code of conduct:

1. Enforce the justice that the subjects are accustomed to, that is, justice in accordance with 'the laws with which they are familiar – without excessive rigour in punishment or excessive indulgence in pardoning'.
2. Do not hand over all duties to ministers, but rather 'leave them to pronounce the most odious condemnations, and he should display his own concern with everything else'.
3. Be careful to guard his own dignity, 'not [waiving] a jot of the honour and deference the people think due to him', without ever asking for more.
4. Only perform actions in public 'that everyone can approve, enjoying his own pleasures in private'.
5. Finally, be open to accepting the advice of counsellors for decisions and at the same time be immovable regarding decisions already made, even if these brought about harm for him: nothing could be 'as harmful to him as the reputation of being irresolute and inconstant'.[87]

For these reasons Descartes objects to the maxim in *The Prince* XV that 'since the world is very corrupt, a man who tries always to be good is bound to come off badly' [*si l'on veut estre tousiours homme de bien*]. Machiavelli would be right if the one who tries to be good is a superstitious person or fanatic, but

[86] Ibid.
[87] AT IV: 490; Descartes 1991: 294.

if understood as one who always follows the dictates of *true reason*, then the best thing 'is certainly to always try to be good'.[88] Descartes also rejects the maxim that 'one may be hated for good actions as much as for bad ones'. This could only be true if it referred to envy, 'a species of hatred',[89] but that is not the case for Machiavelli. Indeed, hatred sustained by envy rests on the recognition of a pre-existing order of moral values, while Machiavelli separates the level of political action from morality (without ignoring the efficacy of morality in politics), unmooring hate from evil and making it the possible effect of both good and bad actions.

Let us return to Machiavelli's argument. The envy created by the prince's virtue is not found in the people, but rather in the nobles and the neighbours, and creates fear at the same time;[90] 'therefore no prince should ever abstain from doing good in order to avoid that sort of hatred'.[91] The only type of hatred that the prince should fear is the hatred arising 'from the injustice or arrogance which the people judge him to have'. There will thus be no problems for the prince if he acts according to justice, whose measure resides in what the people believe to be just. Difficulties arise instead when two conceptions of justice appear and confront one another 'such as when the Roman emperors had to satisfy both citizens and soldiers'.[92] In this situation, one must concede something to both. In each case the people must be led [*condotto*] towards reason through persuasion and not violence, because the people accept everything that they consider just and reject as hateful 'the arrogance of princes, that is, the usurpation of some authority or rights or honours thought undue',[93] precisely because these are considered as a sort of injustice.

Finally, Descartes returns more explicitly to the problem of political epistemology that he confronted earlier, showing his disagreement with Machiavelli's claim in the Dedication to *The Prince* that 'just as one needs to be in the plains, in order to better see the silhouette of the mountains,

---

[88] *AT* IV: 491; Descartes 1991: 294.

[89] Ibid. Descartes defines envy in sections 182 and 183 of *Passions of the Soul*. Taking distance from common sense, he affirms that it is a passion, a sadness mixed with hate, and not exclusively vicious. It is justified when it emerges from seeing someone unworthy rewarded by fortune (*AT* XI: 466–8; Descartes 1985: 394).

[90] 'Princes are not commonly envied by the majority of their subjects but by great people or by their neighbours, among whom the same virtues which cause envy cause fear' (*AT* IV: 491; Descartes 1991: 294).

[91] Ibid.

[92] Ibid.

[93] Ibid.

if one wants to trace their outline, so also the condition of a private citizen is the best in order to understand well the tasks of a Prince'.[94] Descartes maintains that the political action of the prince is the effect of circumstances from such a particular point that, without being a prince or without having shared secrets for a long time, it is impossible even to imagine. Here again the methodological principle is affirmed that it is only possible for a theory of history and politics to be produced by the subjects of history and politics. This is precisely what Machiavelli denies in conceiving the prince's action not as a transcendent decision, but rather as an intervention into the conjuncture of the habits and passions of the people. Political science thus does not have the action of the prince as its object, but concerns instead the dynamic of the passions of the people, or more precisely, the encounter of political action and these passions.

Elisabeth's response to Descartes' letter is exceptionally lucid. She claims that in order to lay the foundation of political science, Machiavelli deliberately opted to consider a limit-case, believing that only an extreme situation would allow him to penetrate the structure of power: the most difficult state to govern, where 'the prince is a recent usurper, at least in the eyes of the people'. In such a case, Elisabeth says, not without irony towards Descartes, 'his opinion of the justice of his own cause could serve to ease his conscience', but it will not ease his security, facing a situation of general hostility 'where the laws oppose his authority, the great undermine him, and the people curse him'. And it is in the context of such a situation that the following directions of Machiavelli can be understood: 'great violence is less harmful than small violence'. And like the consideration of power, Elisabeth maintains that Machiavelli made use of a limit-case for allies, a case in which such allies are 'as evil as they can be' and the situation at a point such that 'it is necessary either to lose an entire republic or to break one's word to those who keep it only so long as it is useful to them' [qu'il faut perdre toute une republique, ou rompre sa parôle a ceux qui ne la gardent qu'aussi long tems qu'elle leur est utile].[95] If there is an error in Machiavelli's argument, it consists in making these maxims 'from those cases which occur in practice on very few occasions', an error that, according to Elisabeth, Machiavelli

---

[94] Descartes 1991: 45. Cf. The Prince: 'Just as those who sketch landscapes place themselves down in the plain to consider the nature of the mountains and high places and to consider the nature of low places place themselves high atop mountains, similarly, to know well the nature of the peoples one needs to be a prince, and to know well the nature of princes one needs to be of the people' (Machiavelli 1985: 4).

[95] AT IV: 520–1; Elisabeth of Bohemia and Descartes 2007: 145. Translation modified.

would have in common with 'almost all the Holy Fathers and ancient philosophers',[96] which comes from the taste for paradox.

In his response to Elisabeth, Descartes corrects the position he took
earlier:

> Your Highness has noted his faults – and mine – perfectly. For it is true
> that it was his plan to laud Cesare Borgia that led him to lay down gen-
> eral maxims in order to justify particular actions which may be difficult
> to excuse. I have recently read his discourse on Livy, and found nothing
> bad in it. His main precept, to eliminate one's enemies completely or
> else make them into one's friends, without ever taking the middle way, is
> undoubtedly always the safest. But when one has no reason to be fearful,
> this is not the most generous way to proceed.[97]

The oscillation between what is and what should be, between utilitarian calculus and moral matters, between security and generosity, which articulates
the rhythm of Descartes' two letters from beginning to end, reaches its highest level in the final phrase. Here, as elsewhere, the imbalance takes place
at what is, namely at the fact of relations of force: indeed, if Machiavelli's
alternative – that enemies must either be destroyed or made into allies – is
judged by Descartes as the safest, but not the most generous move, this
means that generosity, whose exercise presupposes the metaphysical horizon
of free will and therefore the alternative between good and evil which underlies morality,[98] is itself subordinated to calculation at the moment when
Descartes associates it with fear. An enemy from whom one has nothing to

---

[96] AT IV: 521; Elisabeth of Bohemia and Descartes 2007: 145.

[97] AT IV: 531; Descartes 1991: 297–8.

[98] Generosity is the passion that causes 'a person's self-esteem to be as great as it may
legitimately be'. It consists in the knowledge that 'nothing truly belongs to him but
this freedom to dispose his volitions, and that he ought to be praised or blamed for
no other reason than his using this freedom well or badly', as well as 'feeling within
himself a firm and constant resolution to use it well'. The generous man is identified
with the virtuous man: 1) generosity naturally leads him to do great deeds, but nothing
of which he does not feel capable; 2) he esteems nothing more than the fact of doing
good for others ('courteous, gracious and obliging to everyone'); and 3) he is master
of his own passions: desire, jealousy, envy, because nothing that does not depend on
himself is deemed sufficiently valuable to desire intensely; hatred because he esteems
everyone, insofar as he recognises that there is the same free will in others as there is
in him; and anger because he does not give any importance to things that depend on
others ('so they never give their enemies any advantage by acknowledging that they
are injured by them'). AT XI: 445–7; Descartes 1985: 384–5.

fear is clearly not an enemy, and in this case the exercise of generosity no longer encounters an obstacle.

* * *

To conclude this analysis of Machiavelli's image in Spinoza's library, it is necessary to caution against the implicit application of a naïve metaphysics, an inevitable risk in this kind of work: imposing on to Spinoza the reader what the contemporary reader who undertakes an analytic search for the clues to Machiavelli's presence finds in every line of every book in 'Spinoza's library'. We have already distanced ourselves from the error of reducing Spinoza's reading to the catalogue of archives in The Hague. Another danger would be to consider the prism of readings, on the basis of which a plural image of Machiavelli is elaborated, as an atemporal object facing an equally atemporal subject – Spinoza – taken as an eternal instant who contains within himself the key to the duration of his life and his encounters. A lexical analysis of the search for clues cannot tell us anything about the practical reality of reading, multiple and variegated, differently according to the times, of the object and the disposition of the subject. The encounter of a book with its reader produces variable effects; the degree of attention changes from one book to another, and even in the course of reading the same book. For example, abstracting from the subjective condition of the reader, it is likely that the reading of Descartes' letters provoked greater interest than the pages of Leti, just as Bacon's rewriting of the chapter on memory must have interested Spinoza much more than Quevedo's prejudices. And yet no one can rule out that the pages that we would think would have been most interesting to Spinoza, in the intricate paths of his studies, were not even encountered by him. However, despite the intrinsic limits of this kind of labour, I have considered it preferable to a general reconstruction of the history of Machiavellianism and anti-Machiavellianism, which would have assumed Spinoza's thought as a *pars totalis* of the history of European spirit in the sixteenth and seventeenth centuries. To a fresco permeated by the expressive and teleological unity of the Hegelian *Zeitgeist*, I have preferred reconstructing the acentric and aleatory materiality of languages and different traditions, without trying to reduce their complexity.

Spinoza's Strategy of Citation

Before we examine texts containing a direct reference to Machiavelli, it is necessary to remark on the general strategy of citation in Spinoza's texts. In Spinoza's work, proper names are in fact extremely rare, a sign that his own argumentation is founded on the clarity of conceptual construction rather on authorities. While Descartes, for example, plays a distinguished role in the elaboration of Spinoza's philosophy, he is only cited on two occasions, the preface to *Ethics* III and the preface to *Ethics* V. In both cases, Spinoza cites him in order to show how he has posed philosophical problems in the wrong way (the relationship between mind and affects[99] and the pineal gland),[100] despite emphasising his intelligence and astuteness. If we look at Hobbes, whose influence on Spinoza's political thought it is superfluous to underscore, we never find him cited in the two political works or the *Ethics*, and the only references we have are in Letter L, as a response to a specific question by Jelles,[101] and in a marginal note of the *TTP* ('NB. aliter Hobbium').[102] In both cases where Spinoza cites proper names, he clearly distances himself from those he cites.

For other cases, Spinoza substitutes individual citations with general references. What actually interests him is much less the precise reference to a particular author than the possibility of evoking a problematic field that an author represents, the specific way of posing questions that they have in common with other philosophers.[103] In this way, Maimonides and Jehuda Alfakhar are named at the beginning of *TTP* XV solely as an example of the debate that opposes sceptics and dogmatists, that is, as a way of contrasting two antithetical theses about the relationship between philosophy and theology, reason and scripture. In the appendix to *Ethics* I, Spinoza mentions the 'Theologians and Metaphysicians'[104] and the distinction between the end of need [*finis indigentiae*] and the end of assimilation [*finis assimilationis*], which refers to a scholastic problematic. Another example is the opposition between *Philosophers* and *Politicians* in the first chapter of the *TP*, which recalls the scholastics and the treatises on reason of state. Finally, in *Ethics* IV, 35 Spinoza maintains, against the *Satirists*, *Theologians* and *Melancholics*,

---

[99] *Ethics* III, Praef.; CWS I, 491–2.
[100] *Ethics* V, Praef.; CWS I, 594–7. On this point, we can also recall the well-known letter in in which Spinoza distances himself from Bacon as well as Descartes (*Ep.* II [to Henry Oldenburg]; CWS I, 167–8).
[101] *Ep.* L [to Jarig Jelles]; CWS II, 406–7.
[102] Cf. Vol. III, 263 in Spinoza 1925.
[103] In this sense, I agree fully with Pierre-François Moreau: 'When individuals are aimed at by Spinoza, it is in the capacity of victims of a certain way of thought and not as the authors themselves of these thoughts. Thus, if Spinoza's first trait is to reject, his second is to reject not a theoretician, but an entire space; he does not reject the words, but what governs and organises them' (Moreau 1975: 35–6).
[104] *Ethics* I, App.; CWS I, 442.

the necessity for humans to live together.[105] Clearly Spinoza privileges generic references in order to cordon off the theoretical field to which he opposes his conceptual system in the widest possible way, both in the form of a strict demarcation and through the discovery of a third way that renders obsolete the initial dilemma brought to the attention of the reader.

On the other hand, both Spinoza's direct references to Descartes and Hobbes and his evocations of impersonal figures in the philosophical tradition are always the occasion for carrying out rebuttals. The only example of a positive reference[106] concerns less a particular philosopher than what we could call, following Althusser's striking image, *the underground current of materialism*. This reference is found at the end of an interesting exchange of letters with Hugo Boxel about the existence of ghosts:

> To me the authority of Plato, Aristotle, and Socrates is not worth much. I would have been amazed if you had mentioned Epicurus, Democritus, Lucretius, or any of the Atomists, or defenders [*defensores*] of invisible particles. But it's no wonder that the people who invented occult qualities, intentional species, substantial forms, and a thousand other trifles contrived ghosts and spirits [*Spectra, & Lemures*], and believe old wives' tales, to lessen the authority of Democritus, whose good reputation they so envied that they had all his books burned, which he had published with such great praise. If you're willing to put your faith in them, what reason do you have for denying the miracles of the Virgin Mary and of all the Saints, which so many famous philosophers, theologians, and historians have described that I can cite a hundred of the latter to one of the former?[107]

The line of demarcation that Spinoza traces in the Western philosophical tradition therefore does not separate Platonism and Aristotelianism, the friends of heaven and friends of earth in Raphael's famous painting, but rather opposes both of these currents to materialism, with which he openly

---

[105] *Ethics* IV, 35 Schol.; CWS I, 564.

[106] Spinoza's reference to the Aristotelian and Scholastic theory of man as a social animal has an entirely different significance: 'If this is the reason the Scholastics want to say that man is a social animal – because in the state of nature men can hardly be their own masters – I have nothing to say against them' (*TP* II, 16; CWS II, 514). It is clear that the kind of agreement Spinoza finds with this tradition is merely verbal, while on the conceptual level there is a strict distance marked by his rejection of teleology.

[107] *Ep.* LVI [to Hugo Boxel]; CWS II, 423–4.

takes sides. Machiavelli, we will see, belongs to the same philosophical *Kampfplatz*.

Spinoza's Direct References to Machiavelli

Now that we have analysed the meaning of Spinoza's citations in general, we can turn to the two references to Machiavelli in the *TP* as well as to ana-lysing, in contrast, the absence of any reference to Machiavelli in Spinoza's other great political work, the *TTP*. According to Menzel, this absence can be explained by the fact that Spinoza still ignored Machiavelli's work at the time he was preparing the *TTP*. However, such a thesis is ruled out by the subterranean references to Machiavelli's texts in the *TTP*. I will devote part of the next chapter to a study of these references. For the moment, it is nec-essary to focus on the presence of Machiavelli's name in the *TP*.

The *TP* contains two explicit references to Machiavelli, who in both cases is the object of a relatively expansive treatment. Machiavelli is first named in the final paragraph of *TP* V, which is dedicated to 'the best situation for any type of state'.[108] Second, Machiavelli is named in the first paragraph of *TP* X, which takes up the causes of the dissolution of aristocracies. In both cases the citation is not in any way a happenstance, but on the contrary, is required in the argumentative strategy of the chapter.

Let us consider the first passage:

Machiavelli, ever shrewd, has shown in detail the means a Prince must use to stabilize and preserve his rule [*imperium*], if all he craves is to be master [*libero dominandi*]. Why he did this may not be clear. If his purpose was good, as we must believe of a wise man, it seems to have been to show how imprudent many people are to remove a Tyrant from their midst, when they can't remove the causes of the prince's being a Tyrant. On the contrary, they give the prince more reason to fear, and so more reason to be a Tyrant. When a multitude has made an example of their prince, and glories in his assassination, as in a deed well done, they give the new prince such reasons. Perhaps Machiavelli also wanted to show how much a free multitude [*libera multitudo*] should beware of entrusting its well-being absolutely to one person. Unless the prince is so vain that he thinks he can please everyone, he must fear treachery every day. So he's forced

---

[108] Commenting on this first passage, Cassirer writes: 'None of the great modern thinkers has done more to revise the judgment on Machiavelli and to purge his name from obloquy than Spinoza' (Cassirer 2007: 120).

to look out for himself, and to set traps for the people, rather than to look out for their interests. I'm more inclined to believe this about that very prudent man because it's clear he was on the side of freedom [*pro libertate fuisse*], and gave very good advice for protecting it.[109]

An initial conclusion that this text compels us to recognise is that the hypothesis of Machiavelli as being included among Spinoza's description of politicians in *TP* I, 1 must be discarded. This description is clearly modelled on Bacon's *New Organon*, which opposes spiders and ants, or beyond the metaphor, dogmatists and empiricists,[110] who are both characterised negatively. Here we should recall the exact terms of this text, which as Gallicet Calvetti notes, takes up a 'thematic treated at length by the Florentine secretary':

By contrast, Political Practitioners are thought more inclined to set traps for men than to look after their interests. They're judged to be shrewd rather than wise. Experience, of course [*nimirum*], has taught them that as long as there are men, there will be vices. So they try to anticipate men's wickedness, using the arts experience and long practice have taught them, arts that men usually practice more from fear than because they're guided by reason. In this way they seem to be opposed to Religion – especially to the Theologians, who believe the supreme powers ought to treat the public business by the same rules of Piety private men are bound by. Still, there can't be any doubt that Political Practitioners have written much more successfully about Political affairs than Philosophers have. Since

[109] *TP* V, 7; CWS II, 531. Translation modified. Proietti provides a general contrast between the Latin and Dutch editions of the *TP* in Proietti 1995 and Proietti 1997. In terms of the content of this passage, Mugnier-Pollet maintains that by refusing to make Machiavelli a political theorist who founds his theory on violence and deceit, Spinoza unconsciously expresses the meaning of his own philosophy, namely that 'the preservation of the state must not be done at the expense of the freedom of its citizens' (Mugnier-Pollet 1976: 216). Laurent Bove's interpretation is closer to the complexity of Spinoza's text: 'If Machiavelli believes that the prince, in his situation and according to his desire for domination, can identify the absolute power that allows him to possess an absolute right, he deceives himself. If Machiavelli solely wants to provide the theory of practical reason of a prudent prince [. . .] within the limits of his situation and a sole desire for domination, that would be completely correct. But if he believes that this circumstantial strategy and instrumental reason enables him to identify the rational strategy of the political body itself, i.e., to identify this with his own absolute right, then he commits a serious error' (Bove 1999: 61).

[110] Bacon 2000: 79.

they've had experience as their teacher, they've taught nothing remote from practice.[111]

The expression 'shrewd rather than wise' [*potius callidi quam sapientes*], through which Spinoza seems to give credence to the 'common opinion' [*communis opinio*] about politicians [*aestimantur*], and even further, the characterisation of their practice as guided more by fear than reason [*artes quas homines magis metu quam ratione ducti*], is in strident contrast with the wise and very prudent man [*vir sapiens* and *prudentissumus vir*], referring to Machiavelli. Gallicet Calvetti claims that *sapiens* should not be understood in a rigorous way.[112] However, the use of the second adjective confirms and reinforces the choice of the first adjective; indeed, according to the universally accepted Thomistic definition, 'prudence is wisdom in human affairs' [*prudentia est sapientia in rebus humanis*].[113] Thus, the fact that the adjective *sapiens* was used rigorously is also confirmed for us by the conclusive formula, otherwise censored in the Dutch translation of the *Opera Posthuma*, that Machiavelli was a clear advocate of freedom [*pro libertate fuisse constat*].[114] For Spinoza, a wise man is one who, thanks to the power of his reason, takes up the path of freedom, a path that has a collective dimension. Indeed, 'a man who is guided by reason is more free in a state, where he lives according to a common decision, than in solitude, where he obeys only himself'.[115]

A second conclusion that we can draw from *TP* V, 7 concerns a more important point. The passage on Machiavelli occupies a key theoretical position in the strategy of the *TP*. It closes the first five theoretical chapters, chapters in which Spinoza forges the conceptual instruments that allow him

---

[111] *TP* I, 2; *CWS* II, 504.

[112] Gallicet Calvetti 1972: 18. Cristofolini, in continuity with his general interpretation of the third kind of knowledge, maintains that the term must be understood in a rigorous way (Cristofolini 2003).

[113] Wuellner 1956: 100. It is clear that in both Spinoza and Machiavelli, prudence takes on a different meaning from the Aristotelian-Thomistic definition. '[Spinoza's definition] expresses a partisanship [*prise de parti*] for the integral rationality and intelligibility of the real in its different individuation; a rationality and intelligibility also of action and history, outside of any belief in their natural teleology' (Bove 1999: 56).

[114] *TP* V, 7; *CWS* II, 531. This suppression is noted by Francès, who attributes it to a 'reticent attitude which appears to have been adopted by certain editors, in light of the fundamentally democratic inspiration of the *TP*' (Spinoza 1954: 1495–6). Francès emphasises other analogous operations, particularly the translation, in the subtitle of *TP* VIII, of the Latin term *libertas* with the Dutch term *veligheit*. Cristofolini persuasively notes the weakness of Francès's arguments in Cristofolini 1996.

[115] *Ethics* IV, 73; *CWS* I, 587.

to build models of different forms of power (in this sense the refusal of naïve empiricism, the *experientia sive praxis* as direct source of political wisdom, could not be more radical). But not only this. These five chapters, which culminate with praise of Machiavelli, were themselves initiated in pure Machiavellian spirit. Let us recall the first paragraph of the first chapter of the *TP*:

> Philosophers conceive the affects [*affectus*] by which we're torn as vices, which men fall into by their own fault. That's why they usually laugh at them, weep over them, censure them, or (if they want to seem particularly holy) curse them. They believe they perform a godly act and reach the pinnacle of wisdom when they've learned how to praise in many ways a human nature which doesn't exist anywhere, and how to bewail the way men really are. They conceive men not as they are, but as they want them to be [*ut sunt, sed, ut eosdem esse vellent*]. That's why for the most part they've written satire instead of ethics, and why they've never conceived a politics which could be put to any practical application, but only one which would be thought a fantasy, possible only in utopia, or in the golden age of the poets, where there'd be absolutely no need for it. In all the sciences which have a practical application, political theory is believed to be out of harmony with political practice. No men are thought less suitable to guide public affairs than theorists, *or* philosophers.[116]

It would be difficult, in reading these lines, not to think of the programmatic pages in chapter fifteen of *The Prince*, in which Machiavelli poses the distinction between political theory and utopia:

> Since my intent is to write something useful to whoever understands it, it has appeared to me more fitting *to go directly to the effectual truth of the thing than to the imagination of it*. And many have imagined republics and principalities that have never been seen or known to exist in truth; for *it is so far from how one lives to how one should live* that he who lets go of what is done for what should be done learns his ruin rather than his preservation. For a man who wants to make a profession of good in all regards must come to ruin among many who are not good.[117]

Spinoza's text clearly echoes the praise Bacon gives to Machiavelli in *De augmentis*: 'We are much beholden to Machiavel and others, who write what men do and not what they ought to do.'[118]

---

[116] *TP* I, 1; CWS II, 503–4. Translation modified.
[117] *The Prince* XV; Machiavelli 1985: 61. My emphasis.
[118] Bacon 1861: 201.

The beginning and end of the general part of the *TP* both refer to Machiavelli. Between *TP* I, 1 and *TP* V, 7, Spinoza expresses his metaphysics of politics, conceptually building the specific object of the science of politics, without which the modelisation of different forms of power would be impossible and experience would be blind, or better, traversed by the moral-theological imagination. At this point, I think it is useful to reconstruct the argument of the first five chapters, saving the subterranean references to Machiavelli in the *TP* for the next chapter.

After rejecting the opposing errors of philosophers and politicians, Spinoza suggests treating the history of hitherto existing societies as a field of empirical analysis. According to Spinoza, this is a matter of demarcating the true from an imaginary that thinks politics on the basis of an inexistent human nature, instead conceiving history as a process in which the interweaving of passions gives rise to determinate political forms: monarchy, aristocracy, democracy. In chapter two, Spinoza rewrites the concept of natural right in terms of power of existing [*potentia existendi*] and power of acting [*potentia agendi*]. The right of each person is identical to her power: the equation *jus sive potentia* means that the question that torments and characterises the modern epoch is resolved in a purely factual way, that is, in each individual's singular mode of operation. However, Spinoza adds that the very conception of an isolated individual is also the result of the confusion of reality and imagination: individuals are not capable of exercising their right singularly, but rather join in community in order not to be overwhelmed by the immense power of nature. Natural right [*jus naturale*] is therefore thinkable in an adequate way only as common right [*jus commune*], and common right cannot be determined except by the power of the multitude [*multitudinis potentia*].

In the third chapter, Spinoza shows how civil right is not an interruption of natural right, but rather its prolongation. The state [*imperium*] is thus nothing but a determinate figure of the power of the multitude, and therefore the right of sovereignty [*summa potestas*], that is, power [*potestas*], is not at all a right, but rather the fact of a relation of force. Given these premises, Spinoza concludes in chapter four that if the state cannot be subject to civil laws, because civil laws do not exist within it, it is, however, subject to natural laws, whose prohibition is best represented by the medical metaphor of sickness, and not the moral metaphor of sin or the penal metaphor of crime (the necessity, to borrow a German distinction, is one of *müssen* rather than *sollen*). Power [*potestas*] is indeed defined both by the power of acting and the ability to undergo [*aptitudo patientis*]. This means that material conditions govern the exercise of power, which is not an attribute of the sovereign but a relation between the sovereign and the multitude, a relation founded not on civil legislation but the right of war. From this theoretical basis, chapter five poses the fundamental question of the true goal of the state, which for Spinoza resides in peace and security. The latter do not depend on the goodness or wickedness of citizens, but rather on the laws of the state. The best form of government is, then, that in which men live by reason, the true power of the life and mind [vera Mentis virtus, & vita], but this form of government is not possible except for a free multitude [libera multitudo].

Along this path, Spinoza addresses two questions to Machiavelli. First, 'what is the object of political philosophy?', that is, in the last analysis, 'what is political theory'? And second, 'what is the purpose of political theory'? Machiavelli unequivocally responds to this double question: the specific object of political theory, which can be produced only by tracing a line of demarcation against the illusions of morality and utopia, is made up of the weave of human passions that compose and traverse society, while the purpose of political theory lies in the attempt to produce effects of freedom on the basis of the knowledge of this interweaving order. Invoking Machiavelli as the alpha and omega of the metaphysics of politics clearly has an acute symbolic meaning. For Spinoza, Machiavelli embodies the discovery of a new theoretical continent, that of politics. The praise he gives Machiavelli (acutissimus, prudentissimus, sapiens) is the homage to an exemplary path that has brought him to a theoretical solitude[119] similar to his own: the solitude of one who has sailed the ocean in search of new lands to break away from religious superstition.

Returning to the concluding paragraph of the first part of the TP (V, 7), we can note that it summarises Spinoza's entire political proposal in the form of an interpretation of Machiavelli's thought. Initially, in affirming that the proposal of The Prince is to expose the means through which a prince, moved by a pure will to dominate [libido dominandi], can establish and maintain his rule, Spinoza questions the real purposes of the work. Practically, rendering such a text public involves revealing these means to the people and thus, in part, neutralising them, as Alberico Gentili had already emphasised: 'it was not his purpose to instruct the tyrant, but by revealing his secret counsels to strip him bare, and expose him to the suffering nations'.[120]

Spinoza fully grasps the paradoxical character of the political theory expressed by The Prince. For Spinoza, however, contrary to the majority of interpretations, the paradox is not the dilemma of monarchy vs. republic,

---

[119] See Althusser 1999: 115–30.
[120] Gentili 1964: 156.

requiring a position taken in the abstract in favour of one form of government or the other. According to him, Machiavelli's thought is much more subtle, founded not on the illusion of the best possible regime, but on the hypothetical stoic syllogism 'if . . ., then . . .'.[121] Political solutions must be thought on the basis of this syllogism by departing from the real conditions of a people's existence:

1. If there are structural causes that lead a prince to behave like a tyrant, tyrannicide is useless and devoid of any meaning, since it is an act that cannot improve the situation and likely risks making it worse.[122]
2. In the case of a free people, the same structural causes make putting all the power in the hands of only one man meaningless; indeed, a prince, not being able to be loved by everyone, will have the constant fear that a part of the people will rebel.[123]

The logic presiding over Machiavelli's political theory is one that affirms the primacy of the necessity of the historical conjuncture: no form of government exists in the absolute. What does exist is a form of government adapted to the habits and laws of a determinate people in an irreducibly singular history. The logic presiding over Machiavelli's political theory is therefore the logic of the cogency of the structure of habits, customs and laws that comprise the historical existence of a people. In a more far-reaching way, such a logic is the structure of the relations of ideas and passions that traverse the singular existence of a people in order to determine the unavoidable horizon of political action.

The two models of strategy that Spinoza attributes to Machiavelli – the renunciation of tyrannicide if it is impossible to eliminate the causes of tyranny, and the refusal to confer all power on a single man in the case of a free people – refer to two essential chapters in the *Discourses on Livy*. The same two chapters are also referred to in the concluding part of the paragraph, wherein Spinoza considers Machiavelli as a partisan of freedom [*pro libertate fuisse constat*].

The first model of strategy is a summary of the arguments in *Discourses on*

---

[121] Cf. Althusser 1997: 14–19. Defining Spinozist politics as *realist*, or better, *possibilist*, Peña Echevarría is close to Machiavelli on this point (Peña Echevarría 1989: 49–50).

[122] Commenting on Livy, de la Court makes the same point in *Politieke Weegschaal* (van Hove 1662: 188).

[123] The same argument is found in *TTP* XVIII, 27–35; *CWS* II, 328–31, although Spinoza does not mention Machiavelli. Cf. also Clapmar 1641: 91.

Livy I, 16 ('A People Used to Living Under a Prince Maintains Its Freedom with Difficulty, if by Some Accident It Becomes Free'). The opening of this chapter is decisive:

> Infinite examples read in the remembrances of ancient histories demonstrate how much difficulty there is for a people used to living under a prince to preserve its freedom afterward, if by some accident it acquires it, as Rome acquired it after the expulsion of the Tarquins. Such difficulty is reasonable; for that people is nothing other than a brute animal that, although of a ferocious and feral nature, has always been nourished in prison and in servitude. Then, if it is left free in a field to its fate, it becomes the prey of the first one who seeks to rechain it, not being used to feed itself and not knowing places where it may have to take refuge.
>
> The same happens to a people: since it is used to living under the government of others, not knowing how to reason about either public defense or public offense, neither knowing princes nor known by them, it quickly returns beneath a yoke that is most often heavier than the one it has removed from its neck a little before.[124]

It is thus habit that constitutes the essence and historical form of a people, and not the *libido dominandi* of a prince. The prince and the tyrant are nothing other than the effect of an encounter of political action with the structure of customs, passions and ideas of the people.

As for the second model, just as for Machiavelli it is useless for a people accustomed to slavery to kill its prince, it is also dangerous for a people accustomed to living freely to be submitted to a prince, because 'for as much as it is difficult and dangerous to wish to make a people free that wishes to live servilely, so much is it to wish to make a people servile that wishes to live free'.[125] Therefore there is not an absolute position to take about the best form of power, but there is a relation of political action with given historical conditions in which a people exist, which determines what Spinoza calls the form of the commonwealth [*civitatis facies*].[126]

Spinoza's second citation of Machiavelli also occupies a strategic position in his argument. It is found in *TP* X, 1, where Spinoza analyses the causes

---

[124] *Discourses on Livy* I, 16; Machiavelli 1996: 44.

[125] *Discourses on Livy* III, 8; Machiavelli 1996: 239. Machiavelli takes up the same concept concerning the conquest and occupation of foreign territories in *The Prince* V; Machiavelli 1985: 20–1.

[126] *TP* VI, 2; CWS II, 532.

of the alteration or destruction of aristocratic government. It is preceded by
two chapters on the aristocratic state (the simple, Venetian model and the
federal, Dutch model), and followed by two chapters on monarchy. What is
at stake here, once more, is the very essence of political theory insofar as it
is the instrument of knowledge useful for intervening in the conjuncture:

> Now that we've explained and shown the foundations of each kind of
> Aristocratic state, it remains to ask whether they can, from some inherent
> defect, be dissolved or changed into another form [*dissolvi, aut in aliam
> formam mutari*]. The primary cause for the dissolution of states of this kind
> is the one that that most acute Florentine noted in Bk. III, Disc. i, of his
> *Discourses on Titus Livy*, namely that in the state, as in the human body,
> 'something is added daily which eventually requires treatment'. So it's
> necessary, he says, that at some time something happens which returns a
> state to the principle on which it was established [*imperium ad suum prin-
> cipium redigatur*]. If this return doesn't happen when it should, the defects
> [of the state] increase to the point where they can't be removed unless
> the state itself is removed with them. The return, he says, can happen by
> chance or by the judgment and wisdom either of the laws or of a man of
> outstanding excellence [*vel casu contingere potest, vel consilio, & prudentia
> legum, aut viri eximia virtutis*]. We can't doubt that this is a matter of the
> greatest importance. If there's been no provision for dealing with this
> problem, the state won't be able to last by its own virtue [*virtus*], but only
> thanks to fortune [*fortuna*]. On the other hand, when a suitable remedy
> for this evil has been adopted, not only will it not fall by its own defect, it
> will fall only by some inevitable fate [*inevitabilis aliquis fatus*].[127]

Using Machiavelli as an intermediary, Spinoza establishes a parallel between
states [*imperia*] and the human body, which, as he writes in the *Ethics*, '[in
order to be preserved], requires many other bodies, by which it is, as it were,
continually regenerated'.[128] Now, this regeneration is not possible unless the
same proportion or relation among the different parts of the individual is
maintained, as lemmas four, five and six of *Ethics* II indicate.[129] This ratio,
which is constitutive of the form of a body, can be modified by sickness and
destroyed by death, which Spinoza thinks by using the model of poisoning,

---

[127] *TP* X, 1; CWS II, 596. Translation modified. On the return to principles, cf. Clapmar
1641: 79.
[128] *Ethics* II, Post. 6; CWS I, 462.
[129] *Ethics* II 13, Lem. 4–6; CWS I, 461.

as Deleuze has shown.[130] This happens when the intervention of one or more bodies modifies the ratio of movement and rest among the parts that compose each individual.

In the same way that medical practice combats the changes in ratio that constitute the human body, political practice combats the changes in ratio that constitute the social body. It is very significant that, through the metaphor of the human body, Spinoza puts us in a condition to read the Machiavellian concept of principle [*principio*] in terms of a relation of force rather than an originary peace.[131] Indeed, Spinoza does not confer an axiological value on the origin of the state, but rather a simply ontological value. In other words, Spinoza gives the origin of the state a value in terms of cause, or, more precisely, Spinoza thinks the origin of the state as the stabilisation of a determinate ratio of movement and rest among the parts that constitute it.

We can now consider Machiavelli's text which Spinoza summarises in *TP* X, 1:

> It is a very true thing that all worldly things have a limit to their life; but generally those go to the whole course that is ordered for them by heaven, that do not disorder their body but keep it ordered so that either it does or does not alter or, if it alters, it is for its safety and not to its harm. Because I am speaking of mixed bodies, such as republics and sects, I say that those alterations are for safety that lead them back toward their beginnings. So those are better ordered and have longer life that by means of their orders can often be renewed or indeed that through some accident outside the

---

[130] Deleuze 1988: 30–43.

[131] The model of this latter conception is without doubt the Platonic myth of 'the life of men in the time of Chronos' in contrast to 'the time of Zeus' (Plato 1997: 314). In the time of Chronos there was 'a form of government and administration which was a great success, and which served as a blueprint for the best run of our present-day states'. The reason for this success was that Chronos appointed not men but spirits as the kings and rulers for states: 'The story has a moral for us even today, and there is a lot of truth in it: where the ruler of a state is not a god but a mortal, people have no respite from toil and misfortune. The lesson is that we should make every effort to imitate the life men are said to have led under Chronos; we should run our public and our private life, our homes and our cities, in obedience to what little spark of immortality lies in us, and dignify these edicts of reason with the name of "law"' (Plato 1997: 1399–400). Esposito rightly notes that 'in no way does the Machiavellian "return to principles" repeat the Platonic *topos* of "originary pacification" as the absence of passions'; for Machiavelli, on the contrary, 'the origin is the place in which passions live and encounter one another with the most intensity' (Esposito 1984: 200–1).

said order come to the said reversal. And it is a thing clearer than light that these bodies do not last if they do not renew themselves.

The mode of renewing them is, as was said, to lead them back toward their beginnings. For all the beginnings of sects, republics, and kingdoms must have some goodness in them, by means of which they may regain their first reputation and their first increase. Because in the process of time that goodness is corrupted, unless something intervenes to lead it back to the mark, it of necessity kills that body. Speaking of the bodies of men, these doctors of medicine say 'that daily something is added that at some time needs cure'. Speaking of republics, this return toward the beginning is done either through extrinsic accident or intrinsic prudence. [. . .] As to the latter, it must arise either from a law that often looks over the account for the men who are in that body or indeed from a good man who arises among them, who with his examples and his virtuous works produces the same effect as the order.[132]

This text, which Spinoza summarises so accurately, is not just any section from the *Discourses on Livy*: it is an essential passage in which Machiavelli presents the key concepts of his political ontology. Spinoza synthesises its central argument, which delineates the different modalities whereby a republic returns to its principles, and even mimics Machiavelli's style: '*vel casu contingere potest, vel consilio, & prudentia legum, aut viri eximae virtutis*' ('this can happen by chance or by the judgment and wisdom either of the laws or of a man of outstanding excellence'). A state can return to its principles either because of foreign conquest, as happened when the Gauls took Rome in 390 CE, or by the prudence of laws, thanks to legislation that cyclically calls for the re-establishment of the relation of forces that saw to the birth of the state; or a state can return to its principles by the example of virtue given by a single man capable of instilling his own values in the entire people. The fundamental distinction is thus *aut virtus, aut fortuna* – either virtue, or fortune. Virtue in a state arrangement or a single citizen, fortune in the form of chance that brings a state back to virtue thanks to an event external to it, or in person, as a weave of favourable events that make a state survive until then without virtue, or yet also as *fatus aliquis inevitabilis*, as a hostile destiny, a weave of unfavourable events, which destroys a state even though it is full of virtue. Spinoza bases the entire chapter dedicated to the protection of the aristocratic state on this ontology. The formula *aut virtus, aut fortuna* must be considered the unavoidable horizon of politics, a

---

[132] *Discourses on Livy* III, 1; Machiavelli 1996: 209–10.

horizon that radically excludes any pagan or Christian philosophy of history, inscribing human action in a necessity that is aleatory and yet completely intelligible.

2

Machiavelli's Implicit Presence in Spinoza's Texts

Machiavelli in the *Theological-Political Treatise*

In his analysis of the Spinoza–Machiavelli relation at the outset of the twentieth century, Menzel speculated that Spinoza had not read Machiavelli's work until after writing the *TTP*. For Menzel, only the *TP* bears clear signs of the Florentine thinker. However, as we have seen, more than one scholar has demonstrated the weakness of this hypothesis, albeit in fragmentary ways. In fact, despite the absence of direct references to Machiavelli (a necessary precaution in order to avoid the aura of infamy that surrounded his name), numerous key arguments in the *TTP* are based on Machiavellian themes. I will now turn to a precise reconstruction of Spinoza's implicit use of Machiavelli, first in the *TTP*, and then in the *TP*, before considering whether and how these uses hang together.

TTP III's Ontology of History and its Debt to Machiavelli

In its project of demonstrating the imaginary status of the concept of election, a keystone of Jewish religion, *TTP* III forms one of the essential axes of the entire work. As he does elsewhere, Spinoza begins by defining fundamental concepts, simultaneously undermining the ground on which his theological-political adversary stands. Spinoza proposes definitions for five terms: 'God's guidance' [*directio Dei*], 'God's external aid' [*Dei auxilium externum*], 'God's internal aid' [*Dei auxilium internum*], 'God's election' [*electio Dei*] and 'fortune' [*fortuna*]. The first four terms come from the Judeo-Christian tradition while the last comes from the pagan tradition, although Boethius had claimed it for Christianity by interpreting it as the 'servant of God' [*ancilla Dei*] in *The Consolation of Philosophy*.[1] Spinoza draws his rational concept of election from within the play of the identification and differentiation of the meaning of these terms. Spinoza begins by claiming that he understands God's guidance, that is, divine rule, as 'the fixed and immutable order of nature or the concatenation of natural things' [*fixus & immutabilis naturae ordo, sive naturalium concatenatio*],[2] because the universal laws of nature are nothing other than the eternal decrees of God, which entail truth and necessity. Having established this identity of natural and divine power, it follows that the internal and external assistance of God should be understood as nothing other than, respectively, the human *conatus*, persevering in its own being, and whatever nature spontaneously offers as the means for this conservation:

> Whatever human nature can furnish for preserving its being from its own power alone, we can rightly call *God's internal aid*, and whatever in addition turns out for his advantage from the power of external causes, we can rightly call *God's external aid.*[3]

'God's guidance' is therefore a fixed and unchanging order that permeates both the human *conatus* (internal aid) and external causes (external aid). Fortune, then, is simply 'God's guidance' insofar as it 'directs human affairs through external and unforeseen causes' [*quatenus per causas externas & inopinatas res humanas dirigit*].[4]

The oxymoron with which Spinoza concludes his conceptual construction, *directio Dei sive fortuna*, produces a radical redefinition of the traditional concept of election. Spinoza first considers this in general terms, as *vocatio*:

> For since no one does anything except according to the predetermined order of nature, i.e., according to God's eternal guidance and decree, it follows that no one chooses any manner of living for himself, or does anything, except by the special calling of God, who has chosen him before others for this work, or for this manner of living.[5]

Each natural being is called to be and act in a given manner of *vocatio Dei*, which is nothing other than the unfolding of the causal order. From this general discursive level Spinoza moves secondly to his definition of political

---

[1] Boethius 1990: 94–5.
[2] *TTP* III, 7; CWS II, 112. Translation modified.
[3] *TTP* III, 9; CWS II, 113.
[4] *TTP* III, 11; CWS II, 113.
[5] *TTP* III, 10; CWS II, 113.

election, the particular election that is the *vocatio* of a people. The construction of this concept as the encounter of 'God's internal aid' and 'fortune' is at the same time a genealogy of its religious form:

> To form and preserve a society, no small talent and vigilance [*ingenium & vigilantia*] is required. So a society which for the most part is founded and directed by wise and vigilant men [*prudentes & vigilantes*] will be more secure, more stable, and less subject to fortune [*fortuna obnoxia*]. Conversely, if a society consists of men of untrained intelligence, it will depend for the most part on fortune and will be less stable. If, in spite of this, it has lasted a long time, it will owe this to the guidance of another, not to its own guidance. Indeed, if it has overcome great dangers and matters have turned out favorably for it, it will only be able to wonder at and revere the guidance of God. Since nothing has happened to it except what is completely unexpected and contrary to opinion [*praeter opinionem*], this can even be considered to be really a miracle.[6]

There is an inversely proportional relationship between 'God's internal aid' of a people and the possibility that 'God's external aid' has influenced its destiny. If a society is founded and directed by wise men, it will be less vulnerable to the blows of fortune. If a society is comprised of men of untrained intelligence, then it is abandoned to the variable currents of fortune as if it were a boat without a rudder. However, if these currents randomly conspired such that this society overcame innumerable dangers and achieved a certain level of material well-being, chance (i.e., the *causae latentes externae*) will come to be adored as a sign of divine intervention, as an election. The theological-political conception of election is thus nothing other than the imaginary effect of a repeatedly beneficial intervention of fortune in a society – a repeated intervention that, through its extreme improbability, can appear miraculous.[7] Given these premises, Spinoza concludes:

> The only thing which distinguishes one nation from another, then, is the social order and the laws [*societas & leges*] under which they live and by which they are directed. So the Hebrew nation was not chosen by God before others because of its intellect or its peace of mind, but because of its

---

[6] *TTP* III, 14–15; CWS II, 114. Translation modified.

[7] Moreau demonstrates clearly that 'the term fortune refers to the hazardous consequences of this absence of chance', as well as how 'the natural tendency to sacralise History takes root' within such consequences (Moreau 1994: 479–80).

social order and the fortune [*societas & fortuna*] by which it came to have a state, and kept it for so many years.[8]

Spinoza's argument subverts the traditional meaning of the terms. By identifying the Hebrew concept of election with the pagan concept of fortune, Spinoza at once neutralises the imaginary content of both and constructs a new concept, one that allows him to think the history of a people as the simultaneously necessary and aleatory encounter of the social structure and external order of causes. With this conceptual operation, Spinoza incorporates several of Machiavelli's theoretical moves.

Machiavelli affirms the idea that 'God's direction' is identical to the unchanging order of nature – of which the human is nothing but a part, on the same footing as all other parts of nature (and therefore unable to constitute a kingdom within a kingdom [*imperium in imperio*]) – in several places. In the preface to *Discourses on Livy* I, aiming to establish a knowledge of history that can be translated into practice, Machiavelli declares the immutability of the natural order that underlies the continuous variation of events:

> From this it arises that the infinite number who read [histories] take pleasure in hearing of the variety of accidents contained in them without thinking of imitating them, judging that imitation is not only difficult but impossible – *as if heaven, sun, elements, men had varied in motion, order, and power from what they were in antiquity.*[9]

The unchanging order of nature to which Spinoza refers is the effect of the immutability of the Cartesian God whose eternal decrees are the natural laws themselves. However, there is an essential similarity between Spinoza's and Machiavelli's positions concerning the place of humanity in the universe: it is a cause among causes proceeding from one and the same necessity. These causes do not, however, follow a parallel path,[10] but rather concern continuous and unpredictable intersections, as Machiavelli maintains in *The Prince* XXV with regard to the influence of fortune on human affairs.[11]

---

[8] *TTP* III, 16; CWS II, 114. Translation modified.

[9] *Discourses on Livy* I, Preface; Machiavelli 1996: 6. My emphasis.

[10] Gerbier rightly argues that fortune 'is not a celestial influence but rather the combination of multiple encounters' (Gerbier 1999: 78). Gerbier articulates a sharp polemic against the cosmological version of Machiavelli argued for by Parel (Parel 1992).

[11] Droetto argues that 'the pure and simple *auxilium Dei externum*, to which society owes its own conservation, corresponds to what Machiavelli [. . .] calls simply fortune' (Spinoza 1972: 96). We find the same point in Pires Aurélio's translation (Spinoza

Here, after confessing to elsewhere being inclined towards a fatalistic position, he concedes only part of the determination over human destinies to fortune, reserving the other half, 'or perhaps a bit less', for virtue. He uses the famous metaphor of the raging river:

> I liken [fortune] to one of these violent rivers which, when they become enraged, flood the plains, ruin the trees and the buildings, lift earth from this part, drop in another; each person flees before them, everyone yields to their impetus without being able to hinder them in any regard. And although they are like this, it is not as if men, when times are quiet, could not provide for them with dikes and dams so that when they arise later, either they go by a canal or their impetus is neither so wanton nor so damaging. It happens similarly with fortune, which demonstrates her power where virtue has not been put in order to resist her and therefore turns her impetus where she knows that dams and dikes have not been made to contain her.[12]

Machiavelli therefore proposes a theory of history conceptualised through the terminological couple virtue and fortune, wherein the former term, which he calls free will [*libero arbitrio*], is nothing other than the necessary inclination of the agent,[13] and the second term is the continuous variation of times. The powerful metaphor of the river represents fortune as a force

2004: 388). Moreau claims that in the semantic field evoked by the term fortune for a seventeenth-century reader, there is, among other senses, one that 'can be read along with Machiavelli, and what is not far removed from what is now desginated as conjuncture: fortune as occasion [*occasio*] and not only as chance [*casus*]. It is the possibility of being active towards history rather than observing that one undergoes it' (Moreau 1990: 301).

12 *The Prince* XXV; Machiavelli 1985: 98–9. Cf. Machiavelli's *Di Fortuna*: 'As a rapid torrent, swollen to the utmost, destroys whatever its current anywhere reaches / and adds to one place and lowers another, shifts its banks, shifts its bed and its bottom, and makes the earth tremble where it passes / so Fortune in her furious onrush many times, now here now there, shifts and reshifts the world's affairs' (Machiavelli 1958: 748).

13 'On this also depends the variability of the good: for if one governs himself with caution and patience, and the times and affairs turn in such a way that his government is good, he comes out happy; but if the times and affairs change, he is ruined because he does not change his mode of proceeding. *Nor may a man be found so prudent as to know how to accommodate himself to this, whether because he cannot deviate from what nature inclines him* or also because, when one has always flourished by walking on one path, he cannot be persuaded to depart from it' (*The Prince* XXV; Machiavelli 1985: 100, my emphasis). Almost the exact same words are found in *Discourses on Livy* III, 9; Machiavelli 1996: 239–40. Cf. also Machiavelli 1958: 745–8.

that sometimes runs parallel to human affairs, and sometimes runs through them with a violence that modifies their form. Virtue is simply the resistance of an individual or a people who oppose themselves to these violent interruptions in order to maintain their own form. From Machiavelli to Goethe, passing through Spinoza, we can find a line of thought for which singular things, within an acentric and asystematic nature, exist in the open conflict between the continuous variation of times and the effort that the individual opposes to this variation in order to persevere in its own being.[14]

The encounter between these two orders renders the model of transitive causality useless for historical knowledge; indeed, because human action is exercised over times that are in continuous variation, the same conduct can bring about success as much as failure, and two antithetical behaviours can both bring about success. The only rule consists in conforming each action 'to the quality of the times'.[15] History is the conjugation of two necessities: the necessity of virtue, and the necessity of times which in their incessant variation are presented by Machiavelli in the form of the ancient pagan divinity of fortune, free from any idea of distributive regularity.[16]

Spinoza's schema *directio Dei* = *[auxilium internum* + *(auxilium externum* = *fortuna)]* thus translates Machiavelli's political schema *history* = *virtue* + *fortune* on an ontological level. Given this proximity in the conception of history, a new question can then be posed: is the concept of election, as Spinoza develops it concerning the ancient Hebrews – namely, the effect of

---

[14] I have elaborated on this further in Morfino 1997: 157–66.

[15] 'But restricting myself more to particulars, I say that *one sees a given prince be happy today and come to ruin tomorrow without having seen him change his nature or any quality.* This I believe arises, first, from the causes that have been discussed at length in the preceding, that is, that the prince who leans entirely on his fortune comes to ruin as it varies. I believe, further, that he is happy who adapts his mode of proceeding to the qualities of the times; and similarly, he is unhappy whose procedure is in disaccord with the times. *For one sees that in the things that lead men to the end that each has before him, that is, glories and riches, they proceed variously:* one with caution, the other with impetuosity; one by violence, the other with art; one with patience, the other with its contrary – and with these different modes each can attain it. *One also sees two cautious persons, one attaining his plan, the other not;* and similarly two persons are equally happy with two different methods, one being cautious, the other impetuous. This arises from nothing other than from the quality of the times that they conform to or not in their procedure. From this follows what I have said, that two persons working differently come out with the same effect; and of the two persons working identically, one is led to his end, the other not' (*The Prince* XXV; Machiavelli 1985: 99–100, my emphasis).

[16] Cf. *Di Fortuna*: 'Fortune times events as suits her; she raises up, she puts us down *without pity, without law or reason*' (Machiavelli 1958: 746, my emphasis). Translation modified.

'God's external aid', the fortune that influences human affairs in an unpredictable way – suggested by Machiavelli's thought?[17] In *Discourses on Livy*
II, Machiavelli contests Plutarch's thesis from *On the Fortune of the Romans*
that the victories of the Roman people were due to the favour of fortune
rather than their virtue, where by fortune Plutarch does not understand the

---

[17] In any case, it is an open question whether the material election of the Hebrews
derives only from fortune or also from a good arrangement of their society. While
in *TTP* III, Spinoza implies that the election is only due to fortune, in *TTP* XVII he
emphasises the economic and political structures that 'could moderate people's hearts,
and restrain both the rulers and the ruled, so that the ruled did not become rebels and
the rulers did not become Tyrants' (*TTP* XVIII, 212; CWS II, 310). Among these
institutions, there was first of all the institution of a national army (*TTP* XVII, 212–13;
CWS II, 312–13). Another extremely important institution was the economic equality of all citizens (*TTP* XVII, 215–16; CWS II, 314–15). The link between these two
institutions and the freedom of a people is Machiavellian as well. Machiavelli weaves
in praise for the idea of a national army across his work (for example, cf. *The Art of
War*, Machiavelli 1958: 590–2). As for economic equality, Machiavelli writes the
following about the Swiss in his *Ritratto delle cose della Magna*: 'The Swiss are not only
enemies to the princes, like the communes, but they are also hostile to the Gentiles,
because in their country they have neither of these. Instead they enjoy, without any
distinction among them, outside of those who sit in the magistrates, a free freedom'
[*una libera libertà*] (Machiavelli 1971: 69). See also *Discourses on Livy* I, 55; Machiavelli
1996: 109–13. However, it should be noted that between Spinoza and Machiavelli,
there is a powerful mediation in this case: Harrington's *The Commonwealth of Oceana*.
Taking up and developing Machiavelli in a framework of what we could call, following
Macpherson, possessive individualism, Harrington poses two fundamental conditions
as indispensable for the survival of the republic of Oceana, which is the imaginary
transfiguration of England in his time. First, a citizen must bear arms, and only on this
condition can the citizen be considered an active political subject. Second, a certain
equality must be maintained among the owners who make up the *demos*. Even more
significant is the fact that in elaborating on the history of political power, Harrington
presents Moses (with Lycurgus, Solon and Romulus) as author of an agrarian legislation which allowed for the founding of a state of warriors and free owners, conceiving
the Hebrew theocracy not as a monarchy (as Hobbes did), but as a republic ('demo-
cratical' or 'popular') in which all of the citizens were capable, under divine sovereignty, of equivalent freedom (for his analysis of the Hebrew people, see Harrington
1977: 174–7). Cf. also the following passage, where Harrington limits the equality of
the Hebrew state to its foundation: it lacks equality in the 'superstructures', i.e., in the
rotation, or the 'equal vicissitude in government, or succession unto magistracy conferred for such convenient terms, enjoying equal vacations, as take in the whole body
by parts, succeeding others through the free election or suffrage of the people. [. . .]
Israel and Lacedaemon [. . .] were each of them equal in their agrarian and unequal
in their rotation, especially Israel, where the Sanhedrin or senate, first elected by the
people, as appeareth by the words of Moses, took upon them thenceforth without any
precept of God to substitute their successors by ordination' (Harrington 1977: 180–4).

aleatory necessity of Machiavelli and Spinoza, but rather a divinity open to praise ('[the Roman people] built more temples to Fortune than to any other god').[18] In this passage, Machiavelli provides Spinoza the means for undoing the concept of election:

> For if there has never been a republic that has made the profits that Rome did, this arose from there never having been a republic that has been *ordered so as to be able to acquire as did Rome*. For the armies' virtue made them acquire the empire; and the *order of proceeding* and its own mode found by its first lawgiver made them maintain what was acquired.[19]

With this specific case, Machiavelli contests a conception of history that superimposes a transcendent level over the relations of force immanent to virtue and fortune. Fortune is therefore not the personified divinity that directs worldly affairs, but rather the continuous variation of times within which new encounters with virtue – and from these encounters, new conjunctures – are produced. The corollary to this 'materialism of the conjuncture' is that nations differ among themselves by means of their sociopolitical arrangement and not by means of some divine privilege accorded to them.[20] Consequently, no definitive hierarchy between societies exists, because any ordering of societies derives from an unstable and complex relation between the spiritual and material constitution of a state (its regulations, laws and customs), and the power of causes external to it. Confronting the theological-political problem *par excellence* of election (whose archetype is, after all, the concept of the fatherland), Spinoza once again meets Machiavelli in his assertion of the absolute immanence of the political and its independence from the theological field, that is, from an order that at the same time transcends and hypostasises relations of force.

The Utility of Ceremonies in the Hebrew and Roman States

Spinoza devotes *TTP* V to explaining the meaning of ceremonies [*cerimoniae*] within the economy of states in general, and the history of the Hebrew people in particular. This chapter complements but stands in opposition to the preceding one, in which Spinoza had established the universal value of

---

[18] *Discourses on Livy* II, 1; Machiavelli 1996: 125–6.

[19] *Discourses on Livy* II, 1; Machiavelli 1996: 126. My emphasis.

[20] Gebhardt underlines the proximity of Machiavelli and Spinoza on this point in his commentary in Vol. V (Spinoza 1925: 98).

divine law for the knowledge of true life.[21] Ceremonies, on the contrary, are merely devices aimed at producing obedience, which lose all meaning if they are considered outside of the historical-political conjuncture of the Hebrew people.[22] The efficacy of ceremonies is thus limited to the political level, to the sphere of temporal prosperity [*temporanea fœlicitas*], and does not rise to the level of virtue [*beatitudo & virtus*]. This means that ceremonies are good not in themselves, but only through an institution.[23]

However, Spinoza does not simply say that ceremonies aim at temporal prosperity. In order to show the meaning of temporal prosperity and the political function of ceremonies, he must first explain what a society is (*quomodo et qua ratione caerimoniae inserviebant ad imperium Hebraeorum conservandum, & stabiliendum*). Society is 'extremely useful, and even most necessary', Spinoza writes, both for living safely away from enemies as well as for acquiring many other advantages [*compendium multarum rerum*], that is, because of the division of labour within it. The laws that regulate social life are necessary because of the fact that men seek their own interest, not by following the dictates of sound reason but rather on the basis of desire [*libido*] and passion:

> That is why no society can continue in existence without authority and force, and hence, without laws that moderate and restrain [*moderentur & cohibeant*] men's immoderate desires and unchecked impulses. Nevertheless, human nature does not allow itself to be compelled in everything. As the Tragic poet Seneca says, no one has sustained a violent rule for long [*violenta imperia nemo continuit diu*]; moderate ones last [*moderata durant*].[24]

The fear elicited by a violent power brings men to desire and seek ways of destroying this power, because they cannot withstand being ruled by their

---

[21] On the concept of law as the *pars construens* of the *pars destruens* constituted by *TTP* III, see Tosel 1984: 169–206; Mugnier-Pollet 1976: 127–33.

[22] On the way in which this conjuncture is transformed by the passionate structure of humans, cf. *Ethics* III, 36; *CWS* I, 515: 'He who recollects a thing by which he was once pleased desires to possess it in the same circumstances as when he was first pleased by it.' Spinoza's use of the term *circumstantiae* is important here, as a term emphasising the contingency of origin, in order to understand the interweaving of the natural and historical characteristics in the constitution of the fabric of the ideas and passions of the multitude.

[23] *TTP* V, 5; *CWS* II, 139: '*ex solo instituto, & non ex natura sunt bona*'.

[24] *TTP* V, 22; *CWS* II, 144. Translation modified.

equals or losing their liberty 'once it has been conceded' [*libertas semel concessa*]. On the basis of this presupposition, Spinoza proposes an alternative: either an entire society collegially exercises its power together, or whoever exercises power must possess supernatural qualities (or at least convince the people that this is the case). Society therefore arises from the necessity for humans to unite in order to cooperate on both the level of the division of labour and defence against enemies. Such cooperation, however, is traversed and unsettled by the passions. The survival of a society thus requires a power that is both capable of reining in human desire [*libido hominum*] and boundless impulse [*effraenatus impetus*].

It is precisely in relation to the question of social order and the necessity of constraint that the political function of ceremonies becomes clear. Spinoza here abandons the general level of analysis in order to arrive at the singular object of his theological-political discourse: the history of a people, namely the Hebrews, who after the exodus from Egypt, had the power to establish laws and occupy new territories. A people, however, who because of their rough nature, were incapable of collegially exercising power. The Hebrews had to put this power in the hands of a single man whose virtue, divine in their eyes, permitted him to command and compel with force, and prescribe and interpret the laws. This man, Moses, introduced religion into the state precisely with the purpose of rendering docile a people who were 'obstinate':

> So through a virtue in which he was distinguished, he established legislation and prescribed it to the people. But in these matters he took the greatest care in that the people should do their duty, not so much from fear, as spontaneously. Two things in particular forced this on him: the obstinate character of the people (which does not allow itself to be compelled solely by force), and the threat of war. For if war is to go well, it is better to encourage the soldiers than to frighten them with penalties and threats. In this way they will be eager to distinguish themselves for excellence and nobility of spirit than merely to avoid punishment.
>
> That's why Moses, with his virtue [*virtus*] and by divine command, introduced religion into the republic [*religionem in Rempublicam introduxit*], so that the people would do their duty not so much from fear as from devotion. He also placed them under obligation with benefits, and in the name of God promised them many things in the future. Moreover, the laws he enacted were not too severe. [. . .] And finally, in order that the people, who were not capable of being their own masters, should hang on the words of its ruler, he did not permit these men, accustomed as they were to bondage, to act just as they pleased. For the people could do

nothing without being bound at the same time to remember the law, and to carry out commands which depended only on the will of the ruler. For it was not at their own pleasure, but according to a fixed and determinate command of the law, that they were permitted to plow, to sow, to reap. Likewise, they were not permitted to eat anything, to dress, to shave their head or beard, to rejoice, or to do absolutely anything, except according to the orders and commandments prescribed in the laws. This was not all. They were also bound to have on the doorposts, on their hands, and between their eyes, certain signs [*signa*], which always reminded them of the need for obedience.[25]

To use anachronistic terminology, what Spinoza sees at work in the history of the Hebrew people is a microphysics of power. The introduction of religion into the state cannot be reduced to a simple belief in the divine inspiration of Moses on the part of the people, but occurs instead as the construction of a pervasive and diffuse network [*reseau*] that directs religious imagination down to the very granules of society. Ceremonies produce discipline by inscribing the law and its meaning in the daily practices of bodies, and by imposing signs of obedience that at the same time cement the community.[26]

We can now consider the Machiavellian origin of Spinoza's arguments. It is worth noting that, concerning the double necessity presiding over the birth of society in Spinoza – defence from enemies and the division of labour – in Machiavelli only the former is present.[27] And these societies, which arise in order to defend themselves from external enemies, can have different political forms, which find their reasons in the particular historical circumstances of their foundation and the material conditions that have made them possible. 'Of these', Machiavelli writes:

among many others, were Athens and Venice. The first was built for like causes by the dispersed inhabitants under the authority of Theseus. The

---

[25] *TTP* V, 28–30; CWS II, 145–6.

[26] 'This, then, was the purpose of introducing ceremonies: that men should do nothing by their own decision, but everything according to the command of someone else, and that they should confess, both by constantly repeated actions and by meditations, that they were utterly nothing on their own, but were completely subjected to someone else's control' [*Hic igitur scopus caeremoniarum fuit, ut homines nihil ex proprio decreto, sed omnia ex mandato alterius agerent, & contiinuis actionibus, & meditationibus faterentur, se nihil prorsus sui, sed omnino alterius juris esse*] (*TTP* V, 31; CWS II, 146). Translation modified.

[27] *Discourses on Livy* I, 1; Machiavelli 1996: 7.

other consisted of many peoples reduced to certain small islands at the tip of the Adriatic Sea, who began among themselves, without any other particular prince who might order them, to live under the laws that appeared to them most apt to maintain them, so as to flee the wars that arose every day in Italy because of the coming of new barbarians after the decline of the Roman Empire.[28]

The examples of Athens and Venice correlate to the two types of rule [*imperia*] Spinoza mentions: power held by only one man, Theseus, who imposes the law on the people, and power exercised *collegialiter* by society in its entirety.

The question of the alternative between monarchic and democratic power attests to Spinoza's extensive adherence to a fundamental conceptual pair in Machiavellian political ontology: violence and habit. This pair could perhaps even be considered as a restatement, from a different angle, of the pair virtue and fortune. Indeed, virtue designates the efficacy of human action, invariable in its necessity, insofar as it is opposed to the variations of the times, to the aleatory nature of fortune, while violence refers to the efficacy of human action in opposition to the persistence of the singular structure of a people that has been durably constituted and reinforced by habit, manifested in its institutions, laws and customs. Only violence is then capable of breaking the order established by habit, provided it is succinct and severe: Spinoza's citation of Seneca that no one has maintained a violent regime for long (*violenta imperia nemo continuit diu*)[29] echoes *The Prince* VIII, in which, regarding the political use of cruelty, Machiavelli defines as well-used only that cruelty that is exercised *at one stroke*, and that immediately afterwards is converted into something *advantageous for the subjects*.[30] Only a punctually exercised violence can establish a new order, given that the preceding order was powerfully consolidated by habit (clearly *de facto* and not *de iure*), whether it was an order of slavery or freedom, 'because as much as it is difficult and dangerous to wish to make a people free that wishes to live servilely, so much is it to wish to make a people servile that wishes to live free'.[31]

Spinoza's reprise of Machiavellian political ontology as defined by the

---

28 Ibid.

29 *TTP* V, 22; CWS II, 144.

30 *The Prince* VIII; Machiavelli 1985: 38. Cf. also *Discourses on Livy* I, 45; Machiavelli 1996: 94.

31 *Discourses on Livy* III, 8; Machiavelli 1996: 239.

violence–habit pair circumscribes the framework in which he poses the problem of the political use of religion. The monarchic state, in order to be durable, must establish an imbalance within the natural equality of humans, who detest serving their equals (a problem not posed by the democratic state, in which each person, in obeying the laws, obeys themselves). The imaginary transcendence of the discourse of the law generates a real hierarchy. Belief in the divinity of the legislator makes a people act by the power of another [*alterius iuris*] as if it were their own [*sui iuris*], or better yet, as the impassioned tone of the *TTP* puts it, it makes humans fight for their servitude as if they were fighting for their own survival.[32]

Having thus taken up an ontological framework that coincides with Machiavelli, Spinoza describes the establishment of Moses' power by utilising *Discourses on Livy* I, 11–15 as a model.[33] Moses, Spinoza claims, having taken into account the rough nature [*ingenium rude*] of his people, which was the consequence of many years of slavery in Egypt, needed to make the establishment of a collegially held power impossible. Moses succeeded in convincing the people of his virtue and imposed laws upon them in such a way that they performed their duties [*officia*] not because of fear, but rather because of their own initiative [*sed sua sponte*]. In *Discourses on Livy* I, 11 Machiavelli describes the introduction of religion into Rome by Numa in analogous terms:

> As [Numa] found a *very ferocious people and wished to reduce it to civil obedience with the arts of peace, he turned to religion as a thing altogether necessary if he wished to maintain a civilization*; and he constituted it so that for many centuries there was never so much fear of God as in that republic, which made easier whatever enterprise the Senate or the great men of Rome might plan to make. [. . .] Whoever considers well the Roman histories

---

[32] *TTP*, Praef., 7; CWS II, 68: '*ut pro servite, tanquam pro salute pugnent*'.

[33] Indeed, Machiavelli himself had considered the establishment of power for Moses and Romulus in tandem: 'But, to come to those who have become princes by their own virtue and not by fortune, I say the most excellent are Moses, Cyrus, *Romulus*, Theseus, and the like. *And although one should not reason about Moses, as he was a mere executor of things that had been ordered for him by God, nonetheless he should be admired if only for that grace which made him deserving of speaking with God*. [. . .] *It was necessary then for Moses to find the people of Israel in Egypt, enslaved and oppressed by the Egyptians, so that they would be disposed to follow him so as to get out of their servitude*' (*The Prince* VI; Machiavelli 1985: 22–3, my emphasis). See also *Discourses on Livy* I, 9; Machiavelli 1996: 29–30. On the differences between Moses in Machiavelli and Moses in Spinoza, see Caporali 2000: 109.

sees how much religion served to command armies, to animate the plebs, to keep men good, to bring shame to the wicked.[34]

Numa, as an 'orderer of extraordinary laws', had recourse to the divine by pretending 'to be intimate with a nymph' in order to receive counsel so that he could 'put new and unaccustomed orders in the city'.[35]

Spinoza's repetition of Machiavelli's schema is clear: the introduction of religion into the state has the same condition, the rough nature of the people, and the same objective, civil obedience and command of the army. For this reason, we should underscore Spinoza's claim that 'if war is to go well, it is better to encourage the soldiers than to frighten them with penalties and threats',[36] which repeats Machiavelli's description of the Roman auguries in *Discourses on Livy* I, 14:

> Not only were the auguries the foundation, in good part, of the ancient religion of the Gentiles, as was discoursed of above, but also they were the cause of the well-being of the Roman republic. Hence the Romans took more care of them than of any other order in it and used them in consular assemblies, in beginning enterprises, in leading out armies, in making battles, and in every important action of theirs, civil or military; nor would they ever go on an expedition unless they had persuaded the soldiers that the gods had promised them victory.[37]

The religion of the Romans, according to Machiavelli, like the religion of the Hebrews according to Spinoza, is a source of hope rather than fear for the army. Machiavelli provides a counter-example to the positive use of religion. The religion that gives rise to terror in the spirits of soldiers actually prepares defeat, as in the historical example of the Samnites, who were defeated by the Romans after being terrorised by the ceremonies of their religion.[38] Thus, there is a good and a bad use of religion: the former is founded on hope, the latter on fear (if it is true that fear and hope are always linked, it

---

[34] *Discourses on Livy* I, 11; Machiavelli 1996: 34–5. My emphasis. Cf. *TTP* XVII, 11–28; *CWS* II, 298–302 on the necessity for kings to convince the people of their divine origin.

[35] *Discourses on Livy* I, 11; Machiavelli 1996: 35.

[36] *TTP* V, 28; *CWS* II, 145.

[37] *Discourses on Livy* I, 14; Machiavelli 1996: 41.

[38] 'To weaken the opinion his soldiers had of the enemy, he said the oath [the Samnites] had taken *represented their fear and not their strength, for they had to have fear of the citizens, gods, and enemies at the same time*' (*Discourses on Livy* I, 15; Machiavelli 1996: 43).

is, however, in an inversely proportional way). The former reinforces the army, the latter weakens it, as demonstrated by the antithesis between fear and strength that Machiavelli constructs in the speech attributed to the Samnites' priest Paccius.[39]

Finally, regarding Spinoza's analysis of Moses' political use of religion as conducive of civil obedience,[40] we can find the archetype in Machiavelli at the beginning of *Discourses on Livy* I, 12:

> Those princes or those republics that wish to maintain themselves uncorrupt have above everything else to maintain *the ceremonies of their religion* uncorrupt and hold them always in veneration; for one can have no greater indication of the ruin of a province than to see the divine cult disdained. This is easy to understand once it is known what the religion where a man is born is founded on, for every religion has the foundation of its life on some principal order of its own. The life of the Gentile religion was founded on the responses of the oracles and the sect of the diviners and augurs. All their other ceremonies, sacrifices, and rites depended on them; for they easily believed that that god who could predict your future good or your future ill *could* also grant it to you. From these arose the temples, from these the sacrifices, from these the supplications and every other ceremony to venerate them; through these the oracle of Delos, the temple of Jupiter Ammon, and other celebrated oracles who filled the world with admiration and devotion.[41]

For Machiavelli and Spinoza, the good use of religion is therefore founded on hope, which is generated by *devotion* (as Spinoza writes, 'Moses [. . .] introduced religion into the Republic so that the people would do their duty not so much from fear as from devotion').[42] Within this theoretical horizon, the category of possibility becomes central, and possibility, despite Spinoza's determinism, is what the passionate life of the multitudes hinges upon. Indeed, as Spinoza writes, 'for practical purposes it is better, indeed necessary, to regard things as possible';[43] we are dealing with a necessity of possibility.

---

[39] *Discourses on Livy* I, 15; Machiavelli 1996: 43–4.
[40] Mugnier-Pollet emphasises the proximity of Machiavelli and Spinoza with respect to the concept *religio patriae* (Mugnier-Pollet 1976: 213).
[41] *Discourses on Livy* I, 12; Machiavelli 1996: 36–7. My emphasis.
[42] *TTP* V, 29; CWS II, 145–6.
[43] *TTP* IV, 4; CWS II, 126.

While the concept of rite, as a reference to a microphysics of power that inscribes obedience to the sovereign in the daily habits of the people, is absent from Machiavelli, there is an idea of cultural ceremonies generating order and union within society. This is shown clearly by chapter five of *The Golden Ass*:

> There is assuredly need for prayers; and altogether mad is he who forbids people their *ceremonies and their devotions* / because in fact it seems that from them may be reaped *union and good order*; and on them in turn rests good and happy fortune.[44]

In order to conclude these reflections, we should note one complication in the conceptual pair violence and habit. Religion constitutes the alternative to violence in political action, acting on the habits of the people in a way that is certainly kinder but no less powerful. It depends on a different temporality: violence is of the order of discontinuity, an improvised and instantaneous break (*at a stroke*, Machiavelli would say), while religion is of the order of continuity and duration. Religion, therefore, is an alternative to violence, and yet it is also complementary to it in the way in which, on the one hand, it secures the new order established by violence, and on the other, in how it also uses violence to reinforce its message.[45]

Miracles

Nowhere in Machiavelli's work is there a theoretical discussion of the subject of miracles. The only occurrence of the term from which some implicit suggestions can be drawn is *Discourses on Livy* I, 12. However, it is necessary to state preliminarily that it would be incorrect to speak of continuity between Machiavelli and Spinoza on this question. Their emphasis on the

---

[44] Machiavelli 1958: 764. My emphasis.
[45] 'From this it arises that all the armed prophets conquered and the unarmed ones were ruined. For, besides the things that have been said, the nature of peoples is variable; and it is easy to persuade them of something, but difficult to keep them in that persuasion. And thus things must be ordered in such a mode that when they no longer believe, one can make them believe by force. Moses, Cyrus, Theseus, and Romulus would not have been able to make their peoples observe their constitutions for long if they had been unarmed, as happened in our times to Brother Girolamo Savonarola. He was ruined in his new orders as soon as the multitude began not to believe in them, and he had no mode for holding firm those who had believed nor for making unbelievers believe' (*The Prince* VI; Machiavelli 1996: 24).

political use of miracles is something closer to harmony than identical notes. Within his analysis of the introduction of religion into the Roman state, Machiavelli offers the following reflections:

> Princes of a republic or of a kingdom should maintain the foundations of the religion they hold; and if this is done, it will be an easy thing for them to maintain their republic religious and, in consequence, good and united. All things that arise in favor of that religion they should favor and magnify, even though they judge them false; and they should do it so much the more as they are more prudent and more knowing of natural things. Because this mode has been observed by wise men, the belief has arisen in miracles, which are celebrated even in false religions; for the prudent enlarge upon them from whatever beginning they arise, and the authority then gives them credit with anyone whatever.[46]

At first, Machiavelli seems to consider the miracle only from the point of view of its political effects and power of persuasion within a given political and religious order, without posing the question of its truth or falsity. But a closer look shows that, while it is true for Machiavelli that the miracle arises from ignorance, the wise man, 'knower of natural things', should prudently confirm this ignorance with his own authority, because it has the effect of reinforcing the political order.[47]

This is very clear if we consider the example Machiavelli uses in order to confirm his thesis:

> There were very many of these miracles at Rome; among them was that when Roman soldiers were sacking the city of the Veientes, some of them entered the temple of Juno and, drawing near her image, said to it, 'Do you want to come to Rome?' It appeared to someone that he saw her not and to someone else that she said yes. For, being men full of religion (which Titus Livy demonstrates, for in entering the temple they entered without tumult, all devoted and full of reverence), *it appeared to them [that] they heard* the response to their question that they had perhaps

---

[46] *Discourses on Livy* I, 12; Machiavelli 1996: 37.

[47] Regarding this theme, Gallicet Calvetti writes that 'the supernatural economy of miracles seems to escape Machiavelli' (Gallicet Calvetti 1972: 87). If we read the passage closely, however, we can realise that the 'much the more' strengthens the political use of miracles for the 'knowers of natural things', which clearly underlies the opinion that they consider them false and yet they must use them.

presupposed. *That opinion and credulity were altogether favored and magnified by Camillus and by other princes of the city.*[48]

Machiavelli thus regards miracles as distorted perceptions of reality sustained by religious faith, and thinks that rulers should be sure only to indulge them and not produce them, since they are generated spontaneously.

It is well known that Spinoza's analysis of the concept of miracles is one of the strategic points of the *TTP*. Spinoza articulates his analysis around four fundamental hinges. First, he shows that nothing happens in nature that violates its fixed and unchanging order [*ordo aeternus fixus, & immutabilis*]. Second, he demonstrates that miracles provide no knowledge of God's essence or existence, which is on the contrary displayed through the fixed and unchanging order that he has established. Third, he claims that what the Sacred Scriptures mean by divine providence is the order of nature and the eternal laws that follow from it. Finally, fourth, Spinoza demonstrates how miracles must be interpreted by means of several examples.

With the first two points, Spinoza attempts to dismantle the theological discourse on miracles from within. This explains why he seems to allow for a legislator God in discussing miracles, despite rejecting the idea in *TTP* IV as an image that was *human, all too human.*[49] Taking up and reworking the arguments of Juan de Prado,[50] Spinoza demonstrates that the word miracle only has meaning in relation to human ignorance of the order and knowledge of nature, and that true knowledge of God resides in the knowledge of this order rather than in miracles. He develops these two arguments on the basis of the idea that the miracle would consist in a singular volition or intellection in contradiction to the volition or intellection inscribed *ab aeterno* by the creation of natural laws.

With the third point Spinoza seeks to demonstrate that when Scripture speaks of 'this or that thing made by God', it must be understood that it was made 'according to the laws and order of nature' [*secundum leges et ordinem*

---

[48] *Discourses on Livy* I, 12; Machiavelli 1996: 37. My emphasis.

[49] On the metaphorical application of the term 'law' to natural things, cf. *TTP* IV, 5: 'the word *law* seems to be applied metaphorically to natural things' [*nomen legis per translationem ad res naturales applicatum videtur*] (CWS II, 126, translation modified). Cf. also *Ethics* I, 31: 'The actual intellect, whether finite or infinite, like will, desire, love, etc., must be referred to *Natura naturata*, not to *Natura naturans*' (CWS I, 434, translation modified).

[50] Cf. Vol. 5 of Spinoza 1925: 39. Yovel, on the contrary, maintains that 'Spinoza's encounter with Prado may have been more important from a pragmatic and psychological perspective than it was ideologically' (Yovel 1989: 80).

naturae], even though this is not explicitly stated, because the scope of Scripture is not to explain things through their natural causes, but rather to narrate events in a way that strikes the imagination and impresses devotion in the spirit of the common people [*vulgus*]. But it is in the fourth point that we find, certainly here with a more thorough elaboration, Machiavelli's perspective regarding miracles:

> It is quite rare for men to relate to a thing simply, just as it happened [*ut gesta est*], without mixing any of their own judgment into the narration [*ut nihil sui Judicii narationi immisceant*]. Indeed, when they see or hear something new, unless they take great precautions against their preconceived opinions, they will, for the most part, be so prejudiced by them that they will perceive something completely different from what they see or hear has happened, especially if the thing which has been done surpasses the grasp of the narrator or the audience, and most of all if it makes a difference to his affairs that the thing should happen in a certain way. This is why in their chronicles and histories men speak more about their opinions than the actions they're reporting, and one and the same event can be so differently narrated by two persons with different beliefs that they seem to be reporting two different events. And finally, why it is often not very difficult to understand the opinions of the chroniclers and historians just from their histories.[51]

The opinions of men influence the way they perceive reality: in the perception of natural events in the form of miracles – that is, in the form of events that interrupt the usual course of nature – religious imagination plays an essential role, constituting the framework in which it is possible to confer meaning upon them. As in the case of Machiavelli, Spinoza's example is informative:

> In the time of Joshua, the Hebrews [. . .] commonly believed that the sun moves, as they say, with a daily motion and that the earth is at rest. They adapted the miracle which happened to them when they fought against the five kings to this preconceived opinion. For they did not relate simply that that day was longer than usual, but that the sun and the moon stood still, *or ceased their motion. This could also have been quite advantageous to them* [*non parum inservire poterat*] at that time in overcoming the pagans, who worshipped the sun, and in proving to them by experience that the

---

[51] *TTP* VI, 53–4; CWS II, 164. Translation modified.

sun is under the control of another divinity [*solem sub alterius numinis imperio esse*], according to whose command it is bound to change its natural order. So partly because of religion and partly because of preconceived opinions they conceived and recounted the affair differently than it really could have happened.[52]

For Spinoza as well as for Machiavelli, the interpretation of a natural phenomenon as a miracle requires three conditions:

1. Ignorance of the natural order.
2. The force of the religious belief of the people.
3. The political use of the miracle in terms of a sign indicating the direction of history. In other words, the conviction, to use an apt description of Benjamin's, of swimming in the direction of the current.[53]

The Social Pact

In *TTP* XVI, Spinoza re-examines and reformulates the question of the foundations of the state within the horizon of natural law theory. We find here the essential terms of political theory at that time, but they have a new arrangement.[54] It is Machiavelli's conception of the pact that allows Spinoza to trace a line of demarcation with regard to the theoretical instrumentation of natural law theory. Let us examine the moves that permit Spinoza to construct this new ontology in more detail.

For Spinoza, what defines each individual's right of nature [*jus & institutum naturae*] are the natural rules [*regulae naturae*] according to which the individual is determined to exist and act. This is because when nature is taken in its totality [*absolute considerata*], it has the right to do everything that it can do (that is, its right and power are equivalent), and because the power of nature is the same as God's power, it follows that 'the right of each thing extends as far as its determinate power does' [*jus uniuscujusque eo usque se extendere, quo usque ejus determinata potentia se extendit*].[55] Spinoza thus defines the natural right of each individual on the basis of the fact of its

---

[52] *TTP* VI, 55; CWS II, 164–5. My emphasis. Translation modified.

[53] Cf. Benjamin 1968.

[54] Walther provides a fine description of the strategy Spinoza uses against natural law ideology (Walther 1985: 74). On Spinoza's strategy of transforming the semantic content of language, see also Moreau 1985: 189–94.

[55] *TTP* XVI, 3; CWS II, 282.

power. And on this basis, he rejects both differences between humans and the other parts of nature, as well as differences between humans endowed with reason and humans *who do not know true reason*, or alternatively, between the sane and fools or deviants [*fatui et delirantes*]. This means that both the wise and the ignorant have the right to live in their own way: 'as long as humans are considered as living only according to the rule of nature, no sin can be acknowledged' [*nullum peccatum agnoscit*].[56]

In other words, individual natural right is not determined by reason, but rather by desire [*cupiditas*] and power [*potentia*]. This means that each person can do anything useful for herself, whether moved by reason or by the passions, and can try to realise her desires by any means [*sive vi, sive dolo, sive precibus, sive quocunque demum modo facilius poterit*],[57] considering anyone who tries to get in the way as an enemy. Since nature is not limited by the laws of human reason, natural right does not exclude 'disputes or hatred or anger or deceptions or anything at all that the appetite urges'.[58] However, since it is unquestionable that humans aspire to live in security [*secure extra metum*], protected from the dangers that characterise the natural state, and since only reason tends towards actual utility, humans have in unison [*in unum conspirare*] to make sure that the right to all things [*jus ad omnia*], which they have by nature, is collectively held by all, no longer by the force and appetite [*vis et appetitus*] of each one, but as the power and will of all [*potentia et voluntas omnium simul*].

In order to ensure the duration of the pact, however, it is necessary to take into account a universal law of human nature whereby each person, when presented with two good things, will choose the greater, and when presented with two bad things, will choose the less bad (Spinoza emphasises that this is a choice for each person determined by their own judgement, which does not necessarily conform to reality).[59] In this way the pact, in order to last, must be founded on such a balance of *good* and *bad*, both real and imaginary, and capable of demonstrating the utility of society to the individual:

From this it follows necessarily that no one will promise to give up the right he has to all things [*jus in omnia*] except with intent to deceive, and that absolutely no one will stand by his promises unless he fears a

---

[56] *TTP* XVI, 6; CWS II, 283. Translation modified.
[57] '[. . .] by force, by deception, by entreaties, or by whatever way is, in the end, easiest' (*TTP* XVI, 8; CWS II, 284).
[58] *TTP* XVI, 9; CWS II, 283.
[59] *TTP* XVI, 15–20; CWS II, 285–6.

greater evil or hopes for a greater good. [. . .] From these considerations we conclude that a contract can have no force [vis] except by reason of its utility [ratio utilitatis]. If the utility is taken away, the contract is taken with it [qua sublatum pactum simul tollitur], and remains null and void. For that reason it's foolish to demand of someone that he keep faith with you forever [fides in aeternum], unless you try at the same time to bring it about that breaking the contract you're entering brings more harm than utility to the one who breaks it. This is especially applicable to the institution of the Republic [in Republica instituenda].[60]

Therefore, there is no juridical guarantee of the pact. Its only guarantee is a *de facto* guarantee deriving from relations of force both real, and – this is essential – imaginary. This means that the utility of the pact can also be only imaginary; the pact can be upheld or broken by hopes or fears of illusory events, which nonetheless provoke powerful, real effects. If humans were guided by reason, no one would have recourse to fraud and everyone would abide by pacts with full integrity, but because 'everyone is guided by their own pleasure' [voluptas] and their minds are swept up 'by greed, glory, jealousy, [and] anger', even if people promise 'to keep faith by offering sure signs of sincerity', they cannot have confidence in each other's good faith. The pact that institutes society must therefore not be founded on utility and its necessity through reason, but rather on the passions of hope and fear that speak to the desire [voluptas] of the individual:

Because we've already shown that each person's natural right is determined only by his power, it follows that as much of his power as he transfers to another, whether spontaneously or because he's forced to [vel vi vel sponte], so much of his right does he also necessarily give up to the other person. It follows also that if a person has the supreme power [summa potestas], which enables him to compel everyone by force, and restrain them by fear of the supreme punishment (which everyone, without exception, fears), then that person has the supreme right over everyone. He will retain that right as long as he preserves this power of doing whatever his wishes. Otherwise his power will become precarious [precario imperabit], and no one stronger will be bound to obey him unless he wishes to.[61]

---

60 *TTP* XVI, 16, 20; *CWS* II, 285–6.
61 *TTP* XVI, 24; *CWS* II, 287. Translation modified.

Power [*potestas*] is therefore the effect of an equilibrium of passions, and the alienation of individual right as regards who governs is simply the temporary stabilisation of this equilibrium within each individual.

Just like the remarks on the genesis of society in *TTP* V, this fundamental passage in Spinoza's political theory suggests the strong presence of Machiavelli in the *TTP*. The Florentine's political theory is surreptitiously used in order to break with the ideological framework of natural law, within which Spinoza had situated himself, at least on a terminological level. The equation *jus sive potentia*, which after all fully belongs within the originality of Spinozist ontology, emphasises at once the anthropomorphism and utopianism of contractualist ideology. Its roots reach down to a fundamental passage in Machiavelli, which shortly afterwards will become a *topos* of European Machiavellianism and anti-Machiavellianism. However, before turning to this text, it is useful first to consider the two major positions on natural law in Spinoza's time, outlined by Hobbes and Grotius, in order to fully understand the singularity and force of the impact of this passage on the seventeenth-century reader.

In the prolegomena to *On the Law of War and Peace*, Grotius bases his political theory on the existence of an unchanging and absolutely natural right, whose ultimate roots he identifies as within human nature. The essence of this human nature is the desire for society, the *appetitus societatis, id est communitatis*,[62] from which it is possible to deduce the fundamental principles of natural right through reason. These principles would subsist unchanged even if God did not exist or did not care about human affairs: they are a dictate of proper reason [*dictatum rectae rationis*] that derive from a judgement of the human mind about whether an action is in the interest of the social nature of man or not. In the prolegomena to *The Rights of War and Peace*, Grotius holds that the following are rules or fundamental conditions that agree with peaceful living:

> This Sociability, which we have now described in general, or this Care of maintaining society in a Manner conformable to the Light of human Understanding, is the Fountain of Right, properly so called; to which belongs the Abstaining from that which is another's [*alieni abstinentia*], and the Restitution of what we have of another's, or of the Profit we have made by it, the Obligation of fulfilling Promises [*promissorum implendorum obligatio*], the Reparation of a Damage done through our own Default

---

[62] On the Grotian *appetitus societatis*, Costa importantly notes that Grotius stands at a distance from the Aristotelian-Thomistic model (Costa 1999).

[*damni culpa dati reparatio*], and Merit of Punishment among Men [*poenae inter homines meritum*].[63]

Among these principles of natural right, the commandment to respect promises is fundamental for Grotius. Civil right is in fact founded on an obligation to consent [*ex consensu obligatio*] that receives its force from natural right:

> Again, since the fulfilling of Covenants belongs to the Right of Nature [*ius naturae*] (for it was necessary there should be some Means of oblig-ing Men among themselves, and we cannot conceive any other more conformable to Nature) from this very Foundation Civil Rights [*iura civilia*] were derived. For those who had incorporated themselves to any one Man, or Number of Men, had either expressly, or from the Nature of the Thing must be understood to have tacitly promised, that they would submit to whatever either the greater part of the Society, or those on whom the Sovereign Power had been conferred, had ordained.[64]

The construction of a model of human nature whose essence is *appetitus societatis*, the tendency towards sociality, allows Grotius to deduce the rules of natural right through *recta ratio* that found the legitimacy of civil right: among these, the most fundamental is keeping agreements [*stare pactis*].

In Hobbes, the same theme is founded on opposite anthropological pre-suppositions. What is for Grotius finally a norm of natural right becomes for Hobbes a provision of natural law, that is, a prescription of reason aimed at exiting from a state of nature characterised by a war of all against all, in which there is no possibility of benefiting from the fruits of science and technology, those comforts of life deriving from progress. Instead, life in the state of nature is defined by the constant fear of a violent death: 'the life of man is solitary, poor, nasty, brutish, and short'. There can be no injustice in this state, because 'the notions of right and wrong, justice and injustice, have no place', just as property and control do not exist, 'but rather what belongs to each man is anything that can be taken by him for as long as he can hold it' [*ius in omnia*]. In the state of nature, men have the right to 'resort to any means, and carry out any actions, without which they could not preserve themselves' [*ius naturale*]: the cardinal virtues in a time of war are violence and fraud.

---

[63] Grotius 2005: 85–6.
[64] Grotius 2005: 93. Translation modified.

The fear of violent death pushes man to listen to the voice of reason, which suggests searching for peace, if possible, and foregoing the *ius in omnia* by channelling his own natural right into a pact that must be clearly respected.[65] In this way, Hobbes declares the second natural law in *De cive* III, 1: 'Stand by your agreements, or keep faith [*fidem observandam esse*].'[66]

In both cases the question of the agreement has no meaning outside of the juridical-moral framework. The use of the Latin gerundive by both Grotius and Hobbes highlights the deontological horizon, although in the case of Grotius we find an order that supports human inclination, whereas in Hobbes this order can be guaranteed only by establishing a coercive power whose transcendence to the state of nature is deeply aporetic.[67] Against this, if one affirms the identity of right and power, *ius* and *factum*, then the agreement loses its transcendence (it is less the case that Grotius's *ius naturale* emanates from God than Hobbes's *lex naturalis*, even while being valid independently from him) and is absorbed into the simple configuration of real or imaginary relations of force within a given time. Such a configuration does not offer any guarantees for the future, and is nothing but the product of the singular history of each people.

It is therefore within the theoretical horizon of *ius sive potentia* that the Machiavellian theory of agreements becomes decisive against the line of separation between the state of nature and civil society traced by natural law theories, particularly Hobbes. Clearly Machiavelli's passage on agreements refers to relations between princes rather than men in the state of nature. This is of little importance, however, if we keep in mind the fact that both Hobbes and Spinoza institute a strict parallelism between relations among men in the state of nature and relations between states.[68]

With this in place, let us reread the passage from Machiavelli that I alluded to above, whose meaning had escaped Tegli:

> A prudent lord, therefore, cannot observe faith, nor should he, when such observance turns against him, and the causes that made him promise have

---

[65] D'Andrea rightly observes that 'fear possesses in reason an instrument which projects the necessary correctives to its own inefficiency'; the instability of consent to the laws of nature produced by fear can be stabilised by creating a power through reason that will stably compel consent (D'Andrea 1997: 196).

[66] Hobbes 1998: 43. On Hobbes's terminology, which is eccentric to the tradition in which it is rooted, see Burot 1992.

[67] On this point, see the excellent collection of Schmitt's articles on Hobbes (Schmitt 1986). Cf. also Althusser 2006: 179–83.

[68] For Hobbes, see Hobbes 1994: 140. For Spinoza, see *TP* III, 11; *CWS* II, 522.

been eliminated. And if all men were good, this teaching would not be good; but because they are wicked and do not observe faith with you, you also do not have to observe it with them.[69]

This passage from *The Prince* XVIII immediately follows the theory of the prince's doubling as man and beast, that is, moving beyond the metaphor, the theory that breaks with the idea of politics as the kingdom of law. Indeed, Machiavelli maintains that laws are one of *two wellsprings of struggle [gener-azioni di combattere]*, the other being force. This means that politics cannot be the kingdom of reason, separated once and for all from the animality of the passions. On the contrary, politics is the *Kampfplatz* where reason, force and cunning face off in the absence of a juridical guarantee that could put an end to the struggle, as in Hobbes's political philosophy, or a cunning of reason that utilises the unchained brutality of force for its own ends, as in Hegel's philosophy of history.

We can perhaps hypothesise that it is by traversing the work of Machiavelli that Spinoza was able to starkly observe what separates his theory from Hobbes, as he paradigmatically expressed in Letter L to Jarig Jelles:

> As far as politics is concerned, the difference between myself and Hobbes, which you have asked me about, consists in this: I always preserve natural right [*ego naturale Jus semper sartum tectum conservo*] and affirm that the supreme power in any city has no more right over its subjects than it has power over them [*quodque Supremo Magistratui in qualibet Urbe non plus in subditos juris, quam juxta mensuram potestatis qua subditum superat*], as is always the case in the natural state.[70]

Man, therefore, in Machiavelli's metaphor, is never free of a part of animal-ity, just as men, according to Spinoza, continue to preserve their natural right even in the political state. Power [*potestas*] is not the transcendent

---

[69] *The Prince*, XVIII; Machiavelli 1985: 69. Cf. also *The Florentine Histories*: 'Force and necessity, not writings and obligations, are what make principles be observed' (Machiavelli 1971: 833). On this conception of politics, which is already at work in Machiavelli's *Del modo di trattare i popoli della Valdichiana ribellati*, Esposito writes: 'From here there originates a vector of reasoning that seems to invalidate the entire contractualist tradition *ante litteratum*: any pact, agreement or contract stipulated in foundational terms is itself politically founded. It already springs from politically determined relations of force, as is proved moreover by the *de facto* rather than *de jure* character that characterises the genesis of human societies' (Esposito 1984: 197).

[70] *Ep*. L [to Jarig Jelles]; CWS II, 406. Translation modified.

attribute of the sovereign, but rather the always reversible, open and aleatory product of relations of force immanent to the social body.

The Limits of the summa potestas

In the first paragraph of *TTP* XVII, Spinoza reconsiders the relation between natural and civil right in terms of the problem of the limits of state power. The definition of power as absolute power can function on a strictly theoretical level [*mere theoretica*], but it must also be reconsidered after a confrontation with the practical level:

> No one will ever be able to transfer to another his power [*potentia*], or consequently, his right, in such a way that he ceases to be a man. And there will never be a power so absolute [*summa potestas*] that can get everything to happen just as it wishes. [. . .] I think experience itself also teaches this very clearly. Men have never surrendered their right and transferred their power [*potentia*] to another in such a way that the people who received the right and power from them did not fear them, and that the state was not in greater danger from its own citizens than from its enemies (even though those citizens had deprived themselves of their right).[71]

Here Spinoza's use of Machiavelli against contractualist ideology is again noticeable. The revolt of subjects against the sovereign is not a formal right, as Locke would later conceive it, but an always possible fact, widely attested to by experience. On the subject of conspiracies, Machiavelli (who devotes *Discourses on Livy* III, 6 to a consideration of them) expresses himself in analogous terms:

> It did not appear to me that reasoning about conspiracies should be omitted, since it is a thing so dangerous to princes and private individuals; for many more princes are seen to have lost their lives and states through these than by open war. For to be able to make open war on a prince is granted to few; to be able to conspire against them is granted to anyone.[72]

The relation between sovereign and subjects is therefore a relation of force. However, Spinoza insists on the fact that the *potestas imperii* is not limited to the use of fear, 'but extends to absolutely everything it can use to it to ensure

---

[71] *TTP* XVII, 2–3; CWS II, 296. Translation modified.
[72] *Discourses on Livy* III, 6; Machiavelli 1996: 218.

obedience to its commands'.[73] The right of the *imperium* therefore extends to all of the means that are capable of forcing subjects to act in accordance with the commands of the *summa potestas*, including being pushed 'by love', compelled 'by fear', 'by fear and hope together' [*spes et metus simul*], 'by reverence [*reverentia*], a passion composed of mixed fear and admiration', or driven 'by any other reason'.[74] Finally because obedience is far more an internal state of mind than an external act, he 'who resolves wholeheartedly to obey all the other's commands' is subject to the *imperium* of others, and therefore 'that ruler has the greatest authority who reigns over the hearts of his subjects'. This is because, Spinoza concludes, 'if those who were most [*maxime*] feared had the greatest authority [*maximum imperium*], then the subjects of tyrants would surely have it. For they are most [*maxime*] feared by their tyrants.'[75]

Machiavelli devotes *Discourses on Livy* III, 19–23 to the problem of the best strategy for ruling on the basis of a statement that he attributes to Tacitus (*In multitudine regenda plus pœna quam obsequium valet*), although this passage does not occur anywhere in Tacitus' work.[76] On the basis of historical examples, Machiavelli takes up the question of whether, as he attributes to Tacitus, 'to rule a multitude, compliance is more necessary than punishment'.[77] He concludes that both compliance and punishment have shown themselves efficacious and should therefore be used as situations demand. What is new within Machiavelli's reflections on this theme, which we also find in Spinoza, is the fact that political action is analysed independently from any moral criteria: *pietas* and *crudelitas* are considered only on the level of political efficacy.[78] It is not therefore because of moral

---

[73] *TTP* XVII, 5; CWS II, 297. Translation modified.

[74] *TTP* XVII, 7; CWS II, 297.

[75] *TTP* XVII, 8; CWS II, 297–8.

[76] De la Court follows Machiavelli in attributing the line to Tacitus: 'For this reason and others, Tacitus says: *in multitudine regenda, plus pœna quam obsequium valet*, and to govern a community [*ein gemeente*] punishments are better than honesty and complacency' (de la Court 1662: 56). In the pages following this, de la Court discusses the examples of Manlius Torquatus, Hannibal and Valerius Corvinus (de la Court 1662: 56–61).

[77] *Discourses on Livy* III, 19; Machiavelli 1996: 260.

[78] Ibid. In chapter twenty-one Machiavelli shows how Scipio and Hannibal, the former with a comportment full of 'humanity and mercy', the latter 'with modes all contrary – that is, with cruelty, violence, robbery, and every type of faithlessness', produced the same effect. In fact, Machiavelli writes, 'men are driven by two principal things, either by love or by fear; so whoever makes himself loved commands, as does he who makes himself feared. Indeed, most often whoever makes himself feared is more followed and more obeyed than whoever makes himself loved' (*Discourses on Livy* III, 21;

reasons that Spinoza, following Machiavelli, rejects the idea of a power that is only supported by violence. Rather, it is because of political relations of force, since any people becomes an enemy if subjected to continuous violence. Such tyranny, precisely because it provokes hate and fear, is the weakest *imperium*,[79] the form of power that generates the most conspiracies and revolts.

Salus populi suprema lex

In *TTP* XIX, where Spinoza focuses on one of the questions that founds and characterises politics in modernity, the attribution of the right concerning sacred matters [*jus circa sacra*] to the *summa potestas*, we find a final theoretical passage inspired by Machiavelli. After demonstrating that the values of justice and religion have no force of law except as decrees from the authority of an *imperium*, Spinoza takes up an argument from *Discourses on Livy* I, 2:

> Since the inhabitants were sparse in the beginning of the world, they lived dispersed for a time like beasts; then, as generations multiplied, they gathered together, and to be able to defend themselves better, they began to look to whoever among them was more robust and of greater heart, and *they made him a head, as it were, and obeyed him. From this arose the knowledge of things honest and good, differing from the pernicious and bad.* For, seeing that if one individual hurt his benefactor, hatred and compassion among men came from it, and as they blamed the ungrateful and honored those who were grateful, and thought too that those same injuries could be done to them, to escape like evil they were reduced to making laws and ordering punishments for whoever acted against them: hence came the knowledge of justice.[80]

There is thus no justice prior to and outside of society: justice is always the emanation of a power that establishes it as such (this is also a fundamental assumption for Hobbes: there is no justice or injustice before the pact). But

---

Machiavelli 1996: 263). In the next chapter, Machiavelli reiterates this example, here regarding the toughness [*durezza*] of Manlius Torquatus and the kindness [*comità*] of Valerius Corvinus, and maintains that the former is more commendable in a republic, while the latter is more commendable in a monarchy (*Discourses on Livy* III, 22; Machiavelli 1996: 263).

[79] *Discourses on Livy* I, 2; Machiavelli 1996: 10–14.

[80] *Discourses on Livy* I, 2; Machiavelli 1996: 11–12. My emphasis. This passage also seems to influence *TP* II, 18–20.

here again, taking a cue from Machiavelli, Spinoza abandons legal positivist relativism, in order to anchor the concept of justice to the well-being of the people [*salus populi*]:

> It's certain that piety toward a person's country [*pietas erga patriam*] is the supreme piety that a citizen [*aliquis*] can render. For if the political institution is destroyed [*sublato imperio*], nothing good can remain, but everything is at risk. Anger and impiety rule, and everyone lives in the greatest possible fear. From this it follows that you can't do anything pious to your neighbor which doesn't become impious if some harm to the republic as a whole [*tota respublica*] follows from it. Conversely, you can't do anything impious to anyone which shouldn't be ascribed to piety if it's done for the well-being of the people [*salus populi*]. [. . .] That's why Manlius Torquatus is honored: because he valued the well-being of the people more than piety toward his son. Since this is so, it follows that the well-being of the people is the supreme law. All laws, both human and divine, must be accommodated to this.[81]

Spinoza is inspired here by a passage in *Discourses on Livy* III, 41, where Machiavelli writes, 'where one deliberates entirely on the safety of his fatherland, there ought not enter any consideration of either just or unjust, merciful or cruel, praiseworthy or ignominious', and one ought to 'follow entirely the policy that saves its life and maintains its liberty'.[82] The same episode regarding Manlius Torquatus is cited in several places throughout the *Discourses on Livy*; the most explicit passage is III, 34, where Machiavelli claims that 'by then of mature age, he killed his son for having engaged in combat without authorization, even though he had overcome the enemy'.[83]

The *salus populi* is beyond moral judgement. However, if it is left only to the sovereign to determine the real content of the *salus populi*, then there is the risk of falling into an aporia of legitimation. Hobbes falls victim to this risk in *Leviathan* XXX, where he claims that, indeed, 'the office of the sovereign (be it a monarch or an assembly) consisteth in the end for which he was trusted with the sovereign power, namely, the procuration of the

---

[81] *TTP* XIX, 22–4; CWS II, 336–7. Translation modified.

[82] *Discourses on Livy* III, 41; Machiavelli 1996: 301.

[83] *Discourses on Livy* III, 34; Machiavelli 1996: 288. Translation modified. Cf. also *Discourses on Livy* I, 16; Machiavelli 1996: 44–7; *Discourses on Livy* III, 1; Machiavelli 1996: 209–12; *Discourses on Livy* III, 22; Machiavelli 1996: 264–8.

safety of the people', but the *salus populi* is that 'to which he is obliged by the law of nature'. The sovereign therefore must 'render an account thereof to God, the author of that law, and to none but him'.[84] Spinoza dissolves the aporia with the help of Machiavelli, because he rejects thinking the pact as the place of the once-and-for-all alienation of the right of man in the state of nature. The evaluation of the *salus populi* is thus not a private question between God and the conscience of the sovereign, but rather concerns the relation between the sovereign and the people, in which the power itself of the sovereign is at stake.

Machiavelli in the *Political Treatise*

The first part of this chapter was dedicated to the implicit, although clearly identifiable, references to Machiavelli's thought in Spinoza's first political text. In the *Political Treatise*, Machiavelli is present to a greater extent. Indeed, Spinoza does not only explicitly refer to Machiavelli at two key points in his argument, but the entire work is traversed by a network of references that form, without any exaggeration, its skeletal structure.

Spinoza's Political Anthropology

After contrasting philosophers and politicians in the first two paragraphs of *TP* I, Spinoza states that he does not want to propose a new form of government, because everything compatible with experience [*experientia*] and practice [*praxis*] has already been 'discovered and tried'. Instead, he proposes to deduce the principles that 'agree best with practice [. . .] from the very condition of human nature'.[85] The novelty of Spinoza's project therefore does not reside in its content, which derives from experience, that is, pagan and sacred history as testified to by the Bible and classical histories,[86] but rather in the theoretical form that he will give to this content, a form that could not be elaborated except by means of the theoretical instruments forged in the *Ethics*. It is precisely from within this theoretical context that Spinoza can analyse the passions 'not as vices of human nature but as properties which pertain to it in the same way as heat, cold, storms, thunder, etc., pertain to the nature of air. Though these things are inconvenient, they're

---

[84] Hobbes 1994: 219.
[85] *TP* I, 2; CWS II, 505. Translation modified.
[86] Mugnier-Pollet speaks of Spinoza's Tacitus-like quality of recalling the eminently historical dimension of experience (Mugnier-Pollet 1976: 103–6).

still necessary, and have definite causes, through which we strive to understand their nature.'[87]

For political matters, the novelty thus resides in a new anthropology that Spinoza sketches in the fifth paragraph of *TP* I:

> For these things are certain (and we've demonstrated them in our *Ethics*): men are necessarily traversed by passions [*homines necessario affectibus esse obnoxios*]; they're so constituted that they pity those whose affairs are going badly, and envy those who are prospering; they're more inclined to vengeance than to mercy; moreover, everyone wants others to live according to his own way, approving what he approves and rejecting what he rejects. Since everyone wants to be first, they fall into quarrels and *strive as much as they can to overpower one another* [*quantum possunt, nitantur se invicem opprimere*]. Whoever turns out to be the winner prides himself more on harming the loser than on doing good for himself. Though everyone is persuaded that religion, on the contrary, teaches each person to love his neighbor as himself – i.e., that he should defend his neighbor's right as he would his own – still, we've shown that this persuasion has little power against the affects. It's strong, of course, at the point of death, when illness has conquered the affects and the man lies wasting away. It's strong also in houses of worship, where men have no dealings with one another. But it has no weight in public places or corridors of power [*in foro vel in aula* – Trans.], where it would be needed most of all. Moreover, though we've shown that reason can do much to restrain and moderate the affects, we've also seen that the path reason teaches us to follow is very difficult. So people who persuade themselves that a multitude, which may be divided over public affairs, can be induced to live only according to the dictates of reason are dreaming of the golden age of the poets or a fable.[88]

Believing that a politics governs by the rules of religious morality or even *the difficult path of reason* means falling into utopia. Politics is the place of the encounter and the clash of passions from which neither the multitude nor those managing public affairs are exempt. From this point of view, we can observe Spinoza's debt to Machiavelli, who paints the following fresco of the stormy sea of human passions in a famous passage of *The Prince*.

---

[87] *TP* I, 4; CWS II, 505.
[88] *TP* I, 5; CWS II, 505–6. My emphasis. Translation modified.

For one can say this generally of men: that they are ungrateful, fickle, pretenders and dissemblers, evaders of danger, eager for gain. While you do them good, they are yours, offering you their blood, property, lives, and children, as I said above, when the need for them is far away; but, when it is close to you, they revolt.[89]

And again, in the *Discourses on Livy*:

As all those demonstrate who reason on a civil way of life, and as every history is full of examples, it is necessary to whoever arranges a republic and orders laws in it *to presuppose that all men are bad*, and that they always have to use the malignity of their spirit whenever they have a free opportunity for it. When any malignity remains hidden for a time, this proceeds from a hidden cause, which is not recognized because no contrary experience has been seen. But time, which they say is the father of every truth, exposes it later.[90]

Politics is founded neither on a prescriptive morality nor an abstract rationality, but can be defined instead as the attempt to construct, on the basis of the concrete reality of human passions (which certainly in Machiavelli assume a gloomy hue,[91] unlike the *arduo cristal* carved by Spinoza),[92] a state that lasts. In the text that follows the passage I have just cited from the *Discourses on Livy*, Machiavelli recalls the tendency of the nobility to oppress the plebs, one example among many running throughout his work of the presence and clash of two *humours* within society. Spinoza says nothing different when he refers to the propensity of humans to overpower each other [*a se invicem opprimere*]. A rational politics, namely one that does not rest on the utopia of the rationality of the people or rulers, must take into account the inextinguishable conflict that rules among humans, not in order to suppress it, but rather to regulate it. Politics is thus not popular because it is rational, but it

---

[89] *The Prince* XVII; Machiavelli 1985: 66.

[90] *Discourses on Livy* I, 3; Machiavelli 1996: 15. My emphasis. Translation modified.

[91] Concerning this gloominess, however, Altini's considerations are worth keeping in mind: 'The theory of "natural" human wickedness does not so much have an ethical quality – much less a religious one, which, as such, refers to the idea of corruption, or better of sin – but rather a "factual" value that is strictly linked to the idea of dangerousness understood as the fruit of their instinctual vitality, which appears as an inextricable fabric of the insufficiencies of will and reason' (Altini 1998: 34).

[92] 'Free of metaphor and myth, he grinds / A stubborn crystal [*arduo cristal*]: the infinite / Map of the One who is all His stars' (Borges 1972).

is rational because it recognises the popular as being a factual condition of the duration of a state, that is, that it prevents the oppression of the people. In this sense Spinoza concludes that 'if [a state] is to endure, its public affairs [*res publicae*] must be so organized that, whether the people who administer them are led by reason to the affects, they can't be induced to be disloyal or to act badly'.[93]

The Constitution of Society

Spinoza's reference to Machiavelli occupies a central position in the argumentative structure of the second chapter. It appears in the twelfth paragraph (exactly the core of the chapter, which consists in twenty-four paragraphs), which at the same time governs what precedes and follows it. The objective of the paragraph is to express the illusory character of any juridical ideology that pretends to superimpose a right over the power and action of things, seeking to transpose on to an eternal level what only has existence in the aleatory interweaving of durations.

Let us consider the conceptual construction that allows Spinoza to deduce the Machiavellian conclusions of this paragraph (and this deduction, far from being a logical procedure, is nothing but a strategic device directed against the theoretical adversary of contractualism). Because every natural thing is contingent, its power of being and acting derives from God; the identification of power and, therefore, divine right, with the power and right of nature, implies that natural right is nothing other than the rule according to which each thing exists and acts.[94] Everything that a thing does according to the laws of its nature, it carries out in conformity with natural right: this means that natural right is not limited to reason, but extends to all actions, whether they are dictated by reason or desire [*cupiditas*]. For humans are not an *imperium in imperio*, but, on the contrary, it is 'no more in our power to have a sound mind than it is to have a sound body'.[95]

This point allows Spinoza to deconstruct the myth of an originary fall and the doctrine of free will, both founded on the belief in the will's absolute dominion over the passions: 'we conclude', Spinoza writes, 'that it is not in

---

[93] *TP* I, 6; CWS II, 506. Translation modified.

[94] Clearly, the identity of God and nature does not follow from the fact that the contingency of things is founded on the necessity of God: the latter is not therefore a deduction, as Spinoza says, but a rather a stance and a deconstruction of the discourse of natural law theory.

[95] *TP* II, 6; CWS II, 509.

anyone's power [in potestate uniuscuiusque] to always use reason and be at the highest peak of human freedom'.[96] It follows that 'the right and established practice of nature, under which all men are born and for the most part live, prohibits nothing except what no one desires and what no one can do'.[97] Each person is therefore in another's right [alterius juris] insofar as he remains in another's power [alterius potestas], and becomes in his own right[98] [sui juris] insofar as he is able 'to fend off every force and avenge an injury done to him, as seems good to him, and absolutely, insofar as he can live in his own way' [ex suo ingenio vivere].[99] However, power is not only exercised on the body (by imprisonment, or depriving another of weapons, etc.), but also on the body and mind at the same time (through fear and hope).

This is therefore the basic ontology that allows Spinoza to use Machiavelli: right is nothing but power [potenza], and power [potere] is nothing but a relationship between powers [potenze], real or imagined, that by means of one another produce the effects of reality. At this point, it is necessary to turn to the twelfth paragraph:

> An assurance [fides] given to someone by which someone has promised only in words that he will do something he could legitimately omit doing, or conversely [i.e., an assurance given where someone has promised not to do something he could legitimately do], remains valid just as long as the person who has given the assurance does not change. For if he retains the power [potestatem habet] to cancel his assurance, he really hasn't surrendered his right; he's only given his words. So if this person, who, by right of nature, is his own judge, has judged – whether rightly or wrongly (for since he's human, he may have erred) – that the assurance he gave will lead to more harm than good, he will think, in his own mind, that he ought to cancel his assurance [fidem solvendam esse]. And by the right of nature he will cancel it.[100]

It is on the basis of this conceptual articulation that, in the following paragraphs, Spinoza will describe the mechanisms that push the multitude to construct itself in society ('The right of nature [. . .] can hardly be conceived

---

[96] *TP* II, 8; CWS II, 510.
[97] Ibid.
[98] On the concepts of *alterius juris* and *sui juris*, see Cristofolini 1985.
[99] *TP* II, 9; CWS II, 511–12. Translation modified.
[100] *TP* II, 12; CWS II, 512–13.

except where men have common rights').[101] Really, however, society is always-already constituted. What Spinoza assembles by passing through Machiavelli, from whom he takes up the most scandalous position – the submission of faith to utility – are the conceptual instruments that enable an account of the notion of *imperium*. *Imperium* is not the attribute of a transcendent entity (whether king or assembly) as in Hobbes's *Leviathan*, but the result of a momentary equilibrium of forces belonging to a double register, real and imaginary. Here the project of political philosophy as an omnipotent project of the organisation of society is rejected, in order to leave room for a theory of politics in which such organisation is conceived as an intervention in the conjuncture.

The summa potestas

Just as *TP* II has its keystone in the silent repetition of Machiavelli on the question of pacts, *TP* III is indebted to several of the Florentine thinker's arguments involving public right, or external state right,[102] to use Hegelian terminology. In the first paragraph of this chapter, Spinoza defines the 'supreme right of the commonwealth, or the supreme powers' [*jus summarum potestarum seu imperii*], following the political ontology espoused in chapter two, as nothing but the 'power of the multitude, led as if by one mind' [*potentia multitudinis, quae una veluti mente ducitur*].[103] Just as each individual

---

[101] *TP* II, 15; *CWS* II, 513.

[102] The question of the *jus in reliqua* is actually a simple corollary of Spinoza's theory of *jus sive potentia*, because the relation between states corresponds to the relation between men in the state of nature (*TP* III, 11; *CWS* II, 522). It follows that an agreement [*fœdus*] remains valid only as long as the reasons of the promise persist; when taken away, nothing prevents breaking the pact (*TP* III, 14; *CWS* II, 523). *Discourses on Livy* I, 41 and *The Prince* XVIII reverberate throughout these paragraphs, as Mugnier-Pollet emphasises: 'Spinoza is situated well in line with the theorists of reason of state, particularly Machiavelli' (Mugnier-Pollet 1976: 157). *TP* IV, 35, then, seems to maintain the total absence of any moral rule in the foundation of the *jus in reliqua*. The same argument appears in *TP* IX, 13, which Cristofolini, correcting Gebhardt, renders as follows, according to the *Opera posthuma*: 'At urbes jure belli captae, et quae imperio accesserunt, veluti imperii Sociae habendae, et beneficio victae obligandae, vel Coloniae, quae jure Civitatis gaudeant, eo mittendae, et gens alio ducenda, vel omnino delenda est'. Gebhardt, following the *Nagelate Schriften*, softens it in this way: 'gens alio ducenda, vel *urbs* omnio delenda est'. Cf. also Cristofolini 1999. Cf. *The Prince* V and *Discourses on Livy* II, 23. Lucas treats a parallel between Spinoza and Machiavelli on this subject in Lucas 1988.

[103] *TP* III, 2; *CWS* II, 516. One must remember, against interpretations of the 'one mind' in the future anterior in terms of a general will (cf., for example, Francès 1951:

has much less power insofar as the state is greater than him, so also does the multitude, taken together, confer much more power on the state. The state therefore cannot concede that each individual can live in his own way [*ex suo ingenio*]: 'It can't be conceived in any way that each citizen should be permitted by the established practice of the commonwealth to live in whatever way he pleases.'[104] Living *ex suo ingenio*, as Spinoza specifies, counts by the established practice of the commonwealth [*ex instituto Civitatis*] and not by natural right, because natural right is not in any way abolished in civil order [*in statu civili*]. However, insofar as he is a citizen, each man ceases to be *sui juris* in order to become *civitatis juris*, and consequently does not have 'the right to decide what is fair or unfair'.[105] On the contrary, Spinoza writes,

> because the body of the state must be guided as if by one mind, and hence, the will of the commonwealth must be considered the will of all, what the commonwealth has decided is just and good must be thought of as having been declared by each [citizen]. So, though the subject may think the decrees of the commonwealth unfair, he's nevertheless bound to carry them out.[106]

Here Spinoza takes up Hobbes's legal positivism; for Hobbes, among the doctrines that lead to sedition we find one for which 'knowledge of good and evil is a matter for individuals' [*cognitionem de bono et malo pertinere ad singulo*].[107] But again it is Machiavelli who opens up a way for Spinoza to leave Hobbesian relativism behind, a route prepared, on the level of the construction of political ontology, by the retention of natural right in the civil state. Here we can read the entirety of paragraph nine which, not by chance, is situated at the centre of the chapter (consisting of eighteen paragraphs), comprising its theoretical core:

> The third and final consideration is that things most people resent are less within a commonwealth's [*Civitas*] right. For certainly men are guided by nature to unite in one aim, either because of a common fear, or because they long to avenge some common loss. Because the commonwealth's

61–84), the specificity of Spinoza's concept of *mens*, as well as the different theoretical-political frameworks of the two authors.
104   *TP* III, 3; *CWS* II, 518. Translation modified.
105   *TP* III, 5; *CWS* II, 518.
106   *TP* III, 5; *CWS* II, 518–19.
107   Hobbes 1998: 131.

right is defined by the common people of the multitude, it's certain that its power and right are diminished to the extent that it provides many people with reasons to conspire against it. Certainly the commonwealth [*Civitas*] has some things it must fear for itself. Like each individual citizen, or like a man in the natural state, the greater the reason for fear it has, the less it is its own master.[108]

The debt to Machiavelli is clear. In *Discourses on Livy* III, 6, regarding the causes of conspiracies, Machiavelli argues that the greatest 'is being hated universally':

> For it is reasonable that the prince who has excited this universal hatred against himself has particular individuals who have been offended by him and who desire to avenge themselves. This desire of theirs is increased by that universal bad disposition that they see to be excited against him. A prince, thus should flee these private charges [. . .] because if he guards himself from this, simple particular offenses will make less trouble for him. First, because one rarely meets men who reckon an injury so much that they put themselves in so much danger to avenge it; the other, because if they were even of the spirit and had the power to do it, they are held back by the universal benevolence that they see a prince has.[109]

In other words, the right of the *summa potestas* is absolute insofar as it is civil right, because it is the state that declares what is just and unjust, but it is relative insofar as it is natural right, because it is founded on the relations of force that constitute society. The power of sovereigns rests on the network of passions that traverse the people; there is no power more secure than that which has the support of the people, and no more uncertain that that which has aroused its hatred.[110]

---

[108] *TP* III, 9; *CWS* II, 521. Translation modified. Therefore, as we saw in the *TTP*, the weakest state is tyranny, because it has the greatest reason for fear.

[109] *Discourses on Livy* III, 6; Machiavelli 1996: 219. In *The Prince*, Machiavelli equally poses the avoidance of popular hatred as a condition for the duration of a principality (*The Prince* XIX; Machiavelli 1985: 71–82). He repeats this in his reflections on the usefulness of fortresses: 'Therefore the best fortress there is, is not to be hated by the people, because although you may have fortresses, if the people hold you in hatred fortresses do not save you; for to peoples who have taken up arms foreigners will never be lacking to come to their aid' (*The Prince* XX; Machiavelli 1985: 87).

[110] 'In interpreting Machiavelli', Gramsci writes, 'it is forgotten that in those times absolute monarchy was a form of popular rule, and it supported the bourgeoisie against the nobility and the clergy' (Gramsci 1966: 118).

The Relations between the Individual and Power

As in the two preceding chapters, Machiavelli also serves an important purpose in the argumentative structure of *TP* IV. Indeed, after having formulated the definition of the right of the supreme power in the first two paragraphs,[111] Spinoza claims that 'only the supreme power possesses the right to handle public affairs, or to choose ministers to do so':

> If a subject, by his own decision, without the knowledge of the supreme council, undertakes some public business – even if he believes that what he intends to do will be best for the commonwealth [*Civitas*] – he is laying claim to political authority.[112]

This paragraph immediately evokes the case of Manlius Torquatus, who Spinoza indeed cites explicitly in *TTP* XIX. After his son engaged in battle without permission and won, Torquatus sent him to death. Spinoza therefore agrees with Machiavelli concerning the relationship between an individual and power: power is absolute vis-à-vis the individual, who is completely subjugated from the civil point of view.

But then what is there in natural right that, as Spinoza himself says, persists in civil society? In the fourth paragraph, Spinoza asks precisely whether sovereign power is bound by the laws and whether, consequently, it can be at fault [*peccare*] in violating these laws. Such a fault is understood as medical rather than juridical or ethical: 'in this sense we can say that a commonwealth does wrong when it does something contrary to the dictates of reason. For a commonwealth is most its own master when it acts according to the dictates of reason. Insofar as it acts contrary to itself, it fails itself or does wrong.' As such, power [*potestas*] must not be defined only on the basis of the power [*potentia*] of those who exercise it but also on the basis of the receptivity of those who are subjected to it:

> Even though we say that men are not their own masters, but are subject to the commonwealth [*Civitas*], we do not mean that they lose their human nature and take on a different nature. Nor do we mean that the commonwealth has the right to make men fly, or – and this is just as impossible – to make men honor those things which move them to laughter or disgust. No, what we mean is this, that *there are determinate*

---

[111] *TP* IV, 2; CWS II, 525–6.
[112] *TP* IV, 3; CWS II, 526.

circumstances that, if operative, entail that subjects will have respect and fear toward the commonwealth, while the absence of these conditions entails the annulment of that fear and respect and together with this, the destruction of the commonwealth [sed quod quaedam circumstantiae occurrant, quibus positis ponitur subditorum erga Civitatem reverentia, & metus, & quibus sublatis metus, & reverentia, & cum his Civitas una tollitur]. So for the commonwealth to be its own master, it's bound to maintain the conditions of fear and respect; otherwise it ceases to be a commonwealth. For it's as impossible for one who holds political authority (or those who do so) to run, drunken or naked, through the streets with prostitutes, to play the actor, to openly violate or disdain the laws he himself has made, and at the same time to preserve his authority, as it is to both be and not be at the same time. To slaughter and rob his subjects, to rape their young women, and actions of that kind turn fear into indignation, and consequently the civil order into a state of hostility [metum in indignationem, & consequenter statum civilem in statum hostilitatis vertunt].[113]

Like all natural things, the state has rules of operation, namely relations of movement and rest among the parts that compose it: its functioning is bound to the maintenance of such relations. The natural law that regulates the functioning of the state does not permit the summa potestas to arouse popular hate and indignation, the penalty for which is sedition,[114] which decomposes the social body in the same way that sickness decomposes the human body. It is precisely this law that Machiavelli describes in The Prince XVII:

[113] TP IV, 4; CWS II, 526–7. My emphasis. Translation modified. In correspondence, Laurent Bove pointed out to me that Spinoza's formulation reuses a phrase from The Prince XXIV. When Spinoza claims that 'insofar as the commonwealth acts contrary to reason, it fails itself', he takes up a passage in which Machiavelli claims that the new prince will be defended by his own men 'if he is not lacking in other things as regards himself' (Machiavelli 1985: 96).

[114] In a more recent article, Matheron has altered the explanation of the evolution from the TTP to the TP that he provided earlier (Matheron 1969), on the basis of the theory of affective imitation in Ethics III, taking a cue from the concept of indignation in the TP. Matheron thus thinks of indignation not only as the passion that produces the dissolution of the state, but also as the passion that re-establishes it: 'we have in both cases a pendular oscillation between an indignation against the established order [. . .] and an indignation against the enemies of order. [. . .] And fundamentally, this pendular oscillation manifests nothing but the conatus itself of political society: its stubborn and tenacious effort to persevere in its being against everything' (Matheron 1994: 160–1). See also Matheron 1990.

The prince should nonetheless make himself feared in such a mode that if he does not acquire love, he escapes hatred, because *being feared and not being hated can go together very well*. This he will always do if he abstains from the property of his citizens and his subjects, and from their women; and if he also needs to proceed against someone's life, he must do it when there is suitable justification and manifest cause for it. But above all, he must abstain from the property of others, because men forget the death of a father more quickly than the loss of a patrimony.[115]

In *Discourses on Livy* I, 45 Machiavelli further emphasises how it 'sets a wicked example [. . .] to make a law and not observe it, and so much the more as it is not observed by him who made it'.[116] But it is popular indignation that Machiavelli identifies as the main cause of revolts, as he repeatedly insists throughout his works.[117] In particular, this is shown in *Discourses on*

---

[115] *The Prince* XVII; Machiavelli 1985: 67. My emphasis.

[116] *Discourses on Livy* I, 45. Machiavelli 1996: 93.

[117] See *Discourses on Livy* I, 8; Machiavelli 1996: 27–8, where Machiavelli shows the social danger of calumnies as opposed to accusations, because calumnies are not subject to the control of institutions ('Men are accused to magistrates, to peoples, to councils; they are calumniated in piazzas and in loggias'): 'The Florentine army was in the field at Lucca, commanded by Messer Giovanni Guicciardini, its commissioner. Either his bad governance or his bad fortune willed for the capture of that city not to occur; yet, however the case stood, Messer Giovanni was faulted, as it was said he had been corrupted by the Lucchese. When that calumny was favored by his enemies, it brought Messer Giovanni almost to ultimate despair. Although to justify himself he wished to be put in the hands of the captain, nonetheless he could never justify himself because there were no modes in that republic to enable him to do it. On account of this there was great *indignation* among Messer Giovanni's friends, who were the larger part of the great men, and among those who desired to bring innovation to Florence. For this and other like causes, this affair grew so much that the ruin of the republic followed from it' (my emphasis). Cf. also *Florentine Histories* II, 13; Machiavelli 1988: 65–6: 'Fate then brought it about that a man of the people was killed in a brawl in which many nobles had taken part, among whom was Messer Corso Donati. As he was bolder than the others, the blame was put on him and he was therefore arrested by the Captain of the People. And however the thing should have gone, whether Messer Corso may not have erred or the Captain was afraid to condemn him, he was absolved. This absolution so displeased the people that they took up arms and ran to the house of Giano della Bella to beg him to be the one to see to it that the laws of which he had been the inventor be observed. Giano, who desired Messer Corso to be punished, did not make them put down their arms as many judged that he ought to have done, but encouraged them to go to the Signori to complain about the case and to beg them to provide for it. Thereupon the people were filled with *indignation*, and as it appeared to them that they had been offended by the Captain and abandoned by

Livy I, 7, whose purpose is to highlight the usefulness of institutions, specifically the popular magistrate (in the French case, the parliament), which has the function of regulating the violence generated by popular indignation:

> Coriolanus, enemy of the popular faction, counseled that the time had come when, by keeping it famished and not distributing the grain, they could punish the plebs and take from it the authority that it had taken to the prejudice of the nobility. When that judgment came to the ears of the people, it *aroused such indignation* against Coriolanus that as he emerged from the Senate they would have killed him in a tumult, had the tribunes not summoned him to appear to defend his cause.[118]

And here is the extraordinary description of the dynamic, triggered by the indignation of the Florentine people against Walter VI of Brienne, known as the Duke of Athens, which led to insurrection:

> Thus did citizens live full of *indignation* as they saw the majesty of their state ruined, the orders laid to waste, the laws annulled, every decent being corrupted, all civil modesty eliminated. [. . .] *Thus the indignation and hatred grew* to such a degree that they would have inflamed not only the Florentines, who did not know how to maintain freedom and are unable to bear slavery, but any servile people to recover their freedom. Wherefore many citizens of every quality resolved to lose their lives or get back their freedom.[119]

Giano, they went not to the Signori but to the Captain's palace, took it, and sacked it' (my emphasis). In *Florentine Histories* 2, XXXII; Machiavelli 1988: 88, Machiavelli presents the Bardi conspiracy as the effect of 'their indignation'. In *Florentine Histories* 3, XIII; Machiavelli 1988: 122, he writes regarding the tumult of Ciompi: 'Thus the men of the plebs, those placed under the Wool Guild as well as those under the other guilds, were, for the causes mentioned, *full of indignation*' (my emphasis). In *Florentine Histories* 5, IV; Machiavelli 1988: 191–2: 'When the Genoese saw how the duke had liberated the king without any regard for them, and that he had been honored through their dangers at their expense, that to him had gone gratitude for the liberation but to them the injury of the capture and the defeat, *they were all very indignant with him*. [. . .] [Francesco Spignola] decided to try his fortune again and with one stroke get back liberty for his fatherland and fame and security for himself, judging that there was no other remedy with his fellow citizens but to do a deed in which the medicine and cure would arise from what had been the wound. And when he saw the *universal indignation* engendered against the duke because of his liberation of the kind, he judged that the time was right for putting his plan into effect' (my emphasis).

[118] *Discourses on Livy* I, 7; Machiavelli 1996: 24. My emphasis.

[119] *Florentine Histories*, II, 36; Machiavelli 1988: 95. My emphasis. The expression

It is from this thematic that the final two paragraphs of *TP* IV derive, where Spinoza uses the term *contractus* for the first and last time in his work. However, he radically modifies the general meaning of this context as opposed to the natural law tradition, particularly its Hobbesian variant. Spinoza maintains that 'the contract, *or* the laws by which the multitude transfers its right to a council or a man, undoubtedly should be violated when their violation is in the protection of the common interest', and that, however, 'only he who rules the state has the right to judge whether or not their violation is in the protection of the common interest'. The violation of contracts and laws is thus subordinated by civil right to the interpretation of whoever governs. However, such interpretation is bound to social relations of force: there are cases in which the violation of these laws, although authorised by those holding power, 'weaken the commonwealth' and cause 'the common fear felt by the citizens to turn into indignation':

> By that very fact [of political weakness arising from general indignation] the commonwealth [*Civitas*] is dissolved, and the contract is inoperative. Thus the contract is not guaranteed by civil right but by the right of war. So the ruler is bound to observe the conditions of the contract for exactly the same reason as man in the natural state, in order not to be his own enemy, is bound to take care not to kill himself, as we said in the previous paragraph.[120]

The contract and laws (which we could translate with the Machiavellian phrase *ordini e leggi*) constitute the political structure of a state, and have validity not as civil rights [*jure civili*], but as rights of war [*jure belli*], in the sense that the supreme authority can violate them from the point of view of civil law, being the foundation from which they spring, and yet if in doing so the indignation of the multitude is provoked, it will respond with force.

The Primacy of the Law

Spinoza dedicates chapter five – which as we have indicated, he concludes by explicitly evoking and praising Machiavelli – to the question of the best organisation of the state [*de optimo cujuscunque imperii statu*].[121] According

---

'majesty ruined' [*maestà rovinata*] is echoed by the Spinozist impossibility of 'guarding majesty' [*majestas servare*].

[120] *TP* IV, 6; CWS II, 528. Translation modified.

[121] *TP* V, 1; CWS II, 529.

to Spinoza, the greatest possible regime can only be determined according to the purpose of its civil status, 'which is nothing other than peace and security of life'.[122] Consequently, 'the state is best where men pass their lives harmoniously and where the laws are kept without violation'.[123]

It is in this context that Spinoza introduces some arguments that are Machiavellian in form, such as this passage from paragraph two:

> For certainly we should impute rebellions, wars, and contempt for, or violation of, the laws not so much to the wickedness of the subjects as to the corruption of the state. Men aren't born civil; they become civil. Moreover, the natural affects of men are the same everywhere. If wickedness is more prevalent in one commonwealth than in another, and more transgressions [peccata] are committed there, this surely comes from the fact that this commonwealth hasn't set up its laws wisely enough, and so, hasn't obtained the absolute right of a commonwealth [Jus Civitatis absolutum].[124]

Spinoza offers a mirroring argument in the next paragraph:

> But just as the subjects' vices, and their excessive license and stubbornness, are to be imputed to the commonwealth [Civitas], so, on the other hand, their virtue and constant observance of the laws are to be attributed most to the virtue of the commonwealth and its absolute right. This is evident from II, 15. That's why it is rightly credited to Hannibal's exceptional virtue that there was never any rebellion in his army.[125]

A reference to the preface of *Discourses on Livy* I shines through here, where Machiavelli affirms the permanence, in space and time, of human passions. From this permanence derives the value of law and the education to the law, which is one of the essential elements of politics, as Machiavelli recalls in *Discourses on Livy* III, 29, explaining how 'the sins of the people arise from princes':

> Princes should not complain of any wrongdoing [peccato] that the peoples whom they have to govern commit, for it must be that such wrongdoings

---

[122] *TP* V, 2; CWS II, 529.
[123] Ibid.
[124] *TP* V, 2; CWS II, 529. Translation modified.
[125] *TP* V, 3; CWS II, 529–30.

[*peccati*] arise either by his negligence or by his being stained with like errors. Whoever reviews the peoples who in our times have been held full of robberies and of like wrongdoings [*peccati*] will see that it has arisen entirely from those who governed them, who were of a like nature.[126]

Spinoza likely takes up the very example of Hannibal from Machiavelli, who deploys it as follows in an explanation of the political use of cruelty:

But when the prince is with his armies and has a multitude of soldiers under his government, then it is above all necessary not to care about a name for cruelty, because without this name he never holds his army united, or disposed to any action. Among the admirable actions of Hannibal is numbered this one: that when he had a very large army, mixed with infinite kinds of men, and had let it fight in alien lands, no dissension ever arose in it, neither among themselves nor against the prince, in bad as well as in good fortune. This could not have arisen from anything other than his inhuman cruelty which, together with his infinite virtues, always made him venerable and terrible in the sight of his soldiers; and without it, his other virtues would not have sufficed to bring about this effect. And the writers, having considered little in this, on the one hand admire this action of his but on the other condemn the principal cause of it.[127]

However, even if the absolute power of the state is cruelly exercised, it must be in service of complying with the laws and not above the laws, because in this case it would provoke indignation, and consequently sedition, from the citizens.

The Machiavellian structure of Spinoza's argument is then completed by a reference, which was to become topical in modern political philosophy,[128] to the Turkish monarch:

A commonwealth [*Civitas*] whose subjects, terrified by fear [*metu territi*], don't take up arms should be said to be without war, but not at peace. Peace isn't the privation of war, but a virtue that arises from the strength

---

[126] *Discourses on Livy* III, 29; Machiavelli 1996: 277. Translation modified.
[127] *The Prince* XVII; Machiavelli 1985: 67. Machiavelli gives the same example in *Discourses on Livy* III, 21; Machiavelli 1996: 264.
[128] Cf. Procacci 1995: 171–83, which highlights Machiavelli's repetition, often disguised, of an opposition between the Turkish and French monarchies. Cf. Bacon 1641: 68–70.

of mind [*animi* – Trans.]. For it's obedience, a constant will to do what must be done in accordance with the common decree of the commonwealth. When the peace of a commonwealth depends on its subjects' passivity – so that they're led like sheep, and know only how to be slaves – it would be more properly called a desert than a commonwealth [*rectius solitudo, quam Civitas dici potest*].[129]

This paragraph is a reprise of Machiavelli's description of the Turkish government in *The Prince* IV, where he opposes this type of regime to the French monarchy:

The principalities of which memory remains have been governed in two diverse modes: either by one prince, and all the others servants who as ministers help govern the kingdom by his favor and appointment; or by a prince and by barons who hold that rank not by favor of the lord but by antiquity of bloodline. Such barons have their own states and subjects who recognize them as lords and hold them in natural affection. States that are governed by one prince and his servants hold their prince in greater authority because in all his province there is no one recognized as superior but himself; and if they obey someone else, they do so as a minister and official, and do not bear him any particular love.

In our times the examples of these two diverse kinds of government are the Turk and the king of France. The whole monarchy of the Turk is governed by one lord; the others are his servants. Dividing his kingdom into sanjaks (administrative units), he sends different administrators to them, and he changes and varies them as he likes. But the king of France is placed in the midst of an ancient multitude of lords, acknowledged in that state by their subjects and loved by them: they have their privileges, and the king cannot take them away without danger to himself. Thus, whoever considers the one and the other of these states will find great difficulty in acquiring the state of the Turk, great ease in holding it. So inversely, you will find in some respects more ease in seizing the state of France, but great difficulty in holding it.[130]

The opposition between these two models highlights the superiority of the institutions of the French monarchy, which, assuming the universality and

129 *TP* V, 4; CWS II, 530. Translation modified. What Spinoza associates here with the Turkish monarchy is made evident in *TP* VI, 4; CWS II, 533.
130 *The Prince* IV; Machiavelli 1985: 17–18.

irreducibility of human passions, strive to regulate them. Regarding the French parliament, which he considers as the cause of the security of the king and the kingdom, Machiavelli offers the following praise, which can be considered as an exemplary synopsis of the meaning of the entirety of *TP* V:

> Among the well-ordered and governed kingdoms in our times is that of France; and in it are infinite good institutions on which the liberty and security of the king depend. The first of these is the parliament and its authority. For the one who ordered that kingdom, *knowing the ambition of the powerful and their insolence*, and judging it necessary for them to have a bit in their mouths to correct them, and on the other side, *knowing the hatred of the generality of people against the great*, which is founded in its fear, and wanting to secure them, intended this not to be the particular concern of the king, so as to take from him the blame he would have from the great when he favored the popular side, and from the popular side when he favored the great; and so *he constituted a third judge to be the one who would beat down the great and favor the lesser side without the blame for the king.*[131]

Good institutions guarantee peace and security, and order and harmonise passionate forces of social life, without, however, seeking to annul them.

The Monarchic State and Aristocratic States

In the next five chapters of the *TP*, Spinoza deals with monarchic power (chapters six and seven), aristocratic power (simple aristocracies in chapter eight, confederate aristocracies in chapter nine), and the dissolution of aristocratic power (chapter ten). The historical models of these forms of power can be considered France for the monarchic power[132] (although the reference is disguised due to Dutch hostility against this invader country),

---

[131] *The Prince* XIX; Machiavelli 1985: 74–5. My emphasis. (I follow Vivanti's reading of this passage in Machiavelli 1997: 169.) See also the passage in the *Discourses on Livy* regarding the institution of the plebian tribunal in Rome: 'Nor can one in any mode, with reason, call a republic disordered where there are so many examples of virtue; for good examples arise from good education, good education from good laws, and good laws from those tumults that many inconsiderately damn. For whoever examines their end well will find that they have engendered not any exile or violence unfavorable to the common good but laws and orders in benefit of public freedom' (*Discourses on Livy* I, 4; Machiavelli 1996: 16).

[132] It should be noted that in the *Politietke Weegschaal*, de la Court opposes the Turkish monarchy with European monarchy, and within his treatment of the latter, devotes the most space to the French monarchy (van Hove 1662: 137–224).

Venice for the aristocracy in only one city, and the United Provinces for the confederated aristocracy. Given this schema of references, it is clear that Machiavelli is present in the construction of the monarchic model and entirely absent in the aristocratic model,[133] which he did not take up even in a negative way, simply considering it unfit for expansion.

In *TP* VI, 4 on the question of good institutions in a monarchy, Spinoza takes up even more explicitly the example of the Turkish state, which functions as an antithetical model to what he intends to propose:

> Experience seems to teach that it contributes to peace and harmony when all power is conferred on one man. No state has stood so long without notable change as that of the Turks. On the other hand, none have been less lasting than popular, *or* democratic states. Nowhere else have there been so many rebellions. Still, if slavery, barbarism, and being without protection are to be called peace, nothing is more wretched for men than peace. No doubt there are more, and more bitter, quarrels between parents and children than between masters and slaves. Nevertheless, it doesn't make for the orderly management of a household to change paternal right into mastery, and treat children like slaves. To transfer all power to one man makes for bondage, not peace. As we've said, peace does not consist in the privation of war, but in a union *or* harmony of minds [*animi* – Trans.].[134]

The positive models that inspire Spinoza seem to be the French monarchy and the Roman republic, wherein the passionate dynamics are not overwhelmed by the terror that tyrannical power imposes, but channelled and regulated by political institutions. The political institution intended for this purpose in Spinoza's model of monarchy is the council, which is elected because it consists of 'those whose personal situation and advantage depend on peace and the common well-being of everyone'. This means that 'it's clear that if some are chosen from each kind *or* class of citizens, that will be to the advantage of the majority of the subjects, because they'll have the greatest number of votes in this council'.[135]

---

[133] Spinoza seems to repeat Machiavelli in *TP* VIII, 12 when he describes the genesis of the aristocratic state: it arises from an originally democratic state in which, with the increase in population, the political rights of original citizens are not conceded to foreign immigrants. With this, Spinoza proposes in abstract terms the Machiavellian example of the rise of the Venetian aristocracy in *Discourses on Livy* I, 6; Machiavelli 1996: 20–1.

[134] *TP* VI, 4; CWS II, 533.

[135] *TP* VII, 4; CWS II, 546.

The council will be capable of providing the king with a map of the interests and requests that emerge from the multitude, which must be taken into account if he wants to preserve his power:

So whether the king is led by a fear of the multitude, perhaps to bind the greater part of the armed multitude to himself, or led by a nobility of spirit, to consult the public advantage, either he'll always endorse the opinion which has the most votes, i.e., which is most useful to the majority. [. . .] When he most looks after the common well-being of the multitude, he'll be most his own master, and will have the greatest control.[136]

Spinoza, in other words, does not presuppose the morality of the prince, although he does not exclude it. However, even the prince who lacks a generous spirit [*generositas animi*] will be pushed by the structure of the institutions to endorse the resolution favourable to the majority and therefore concretely occupy himself with the *salus populi*. In his model of the monarchic state, Spinoza reproduces the schema that Machiavelli puts forward in *The Prince* IX. Here Machiavelli claims that whether a prince takes power with the favour of the people or the favour of the nobles, in each case he must 'have the people friendly; otherwise he has no remedy in adversity', offering an institutional warning capable of protecting the sovereign from his own nature and from the political errors that can derive from it.[137]

Given this general model of popular monarchy,[138] namely a monarchy where, in order to maintain his power, the king must follow the dictates of the majority – that is, the people – it also becomes necessary to follow Machiavelli's teaching regarding the make-up of the army.[139] This must be a

---

[136] *TP* VII, 11; *CWS* II, 549.

[137] *The Prince* IX; Machiavelli 1985: 41.

[138] Here we can note that the concept of popular monarchy has roots in Machiavelli. In *TP* VII, 1, Spinoza writes: 'The most important point is that it's not at all contrary to practice for these laws to be so firmly established that not even the King himself can repeal them. [. . .] And nowhere that I know is a Monarch elected absolutely, without any explicit conditions. This is not contrary to reason, or to the absolute obedience owed to the King' (*CWS* II, 544). Cf. the following from *The Art of War*: 'The kingdoms that have good laws do not give absolute command to their king except in their armies; in this place alone sudden decision is necessary, so in it there must be one and only one authority. In other things he cannot do anything without consultation, and they are obliged to fear – those who give him advice – that he will have somebody near him who in time of peace will desire war, being unable to get his living without it' (Machiavelli 1958: 577); see also *Discourses on Livy* I, 35; Machiavelli 1996: 76–7.

[139] Commenting on *TP* VI, 10, Mugnier-Pollet notes how it 'begins, in a dialogue with

popular army, because in the other case, and here the negative model is once again the Turkish state, the monarchy 'is really in a condition of war, [and] only the military enjoys freedom, [while] the rest of the people are slaves'.[140]

> The army must be formed only from the citizens, without exception, and not from any others. [. . .] Furthermore, the leaders of companies and regiments are to be chosen for life. But whoever commands the entire army of a clan is to be chosen only in wartime, and is to have a supreme command for only a year. He cannot be continued in command or chosen again later. These commanders are to be chosen from the king's counselors or from those who've served as counselor. [. . .]
>
> No regular payments are to be made to the military in peacetime. In wartime a daily payment should be made only to those who make their living by daily work. The commanders and the other officers of units should expect no other pay than the spoils they get from the enemy.[141]

In *TP* VI, 10 and 31, Spinoza thus takes up Machiavelli's teaching that a wise prince should avoid the use of mercenary armies, '[preferring] to lose with his own [arms] than to win with others'.[142] Spinoza also invokes Machiavelli's warning about prolonging the position of the commander of the army,[143]

Machiavelli, to demonstrate the difference of opinion between those who favour a selective national army and those who prefer universal military service. Machiavelli, on the word of Fabrizio Colonna, envisaged rather a choice [*deletto*] made by the sovereign among all citizens. For Spinoza, all the citizens without exception served in the army because having one's own arms means having the power as well as the guarantee of one's own freedom. Not having one's own arms means transferring one's right to another absolutely, whether this other is a foreigner or an ambitious general' (Mugnier-Pollet 1976: 185). Del Lucchese points out that Mugnier-Pollet exaggerates this difference between Machiavelli and Spinoza (Del Lucchese 1999–2000: 99–102).

140 *TP* VII, 22; *CWS* II, 555. The roots of this point begin in paragraph 17. Compare this judgement of Machiavelli's: 'The whole monarchy of the Turk is governed by one lord; the others are his servants' (*The Prince* IV; Machiavelli 1985: 17). Cf. also 'Now it is necessary for all princes except the Turk and the Sultan to satisfy the people rather than the soldiers, because the people can do more than the soldiers. I except the thousand infantry and fifteen thousand horses on whom the security and strength of his kingdom depend; and it is necessary for that lord to put off every other regard and keep them his friends' (*The Prince* XIX; Machiavelli 1985: 81–2).

141 *TP* VI, 10, 31; *CWS* II, 535, 541.

142 *The Prince* XIII; Machiavelli 1985: 55. Translation modified.

143 See also *TP* VIII, 9; *CWS* II, 568–9. 'When a citizen remained commander of an army for a very long time, he would win it over to himself and make it partisan to him, for the army would in time forget the Senate and recognize that head. Because of this, Sulla and Marius could find soldiers who would follow them against the public

and finally his teaching that 'the practice of warfare shall be used in times of peace for exercise and in times of war for necessity and glory'.[144]

However, Spinoza's entire argument is based on a presupposition that emerges only in *TP* VII, 27. Here Spinoza rejects the prejudice that common people are nothing but an ignorant mob prone to violent excesses unless they are kept in a condition of fear:

> What we've written may be ridiculed by those who think the vices common to all mortals belong only to the plebeians [*plebs*] – those who think that 'there's no moderation in the common people; that they're terrifying, unless they themselves are cowed by fear'; or that 'the plebians either serve humbly or rule proudly, like despots'; and that 'there's neither truth nor judgment in [the plebian class], etc.' But nature is one and common for all – we're just deceived by power and refinement. That's why we often say 'When two people do the same thing, it's all right for one to do it, but not for the other' – not that the act itself is different, but that the one who does it is. Pride is what sets rulers apart. Men are puffed up when they hold office for a year. How can nobles not be proud, when they enjoy their honors for all time to come? But their arrogance is adorned by haughtiness, extravagance, wastefulness, a certain blending of vices, a kind

---

good; because of this, Caesar could seize the fatherland' (*Discourses on Livy* III, 24; Machiavelli 1996: 270).

[144] The full passage reads: 'A well-ordered city will then decree that this practice of warfare shall be used in times of peace for exercise and in times of war for necessity and glory, and will allow the public alone to practice it as a profession, as did Rome. Any citizen who in such an activity has another purpose is not a good citizen, and any city that conducts itself otherwise is not well governed' (Machiavelli 1958: 576). In *TP* VII, 22; *CWS* II, 554, Spinoza claims that 'the army's greatest reward is freedom' [*summum militiae praemium libertas est*]. Cf. also *TP* VIII, 9. Here is how Machiavelli puts it: 'One also considers, from the treatment written above, how much difference there is between *an army that is content and engages in combat for its own glory* and one that is ill disposed and engages in combat for the ambition of someone else. For whereas under the consuls Roman armies were always accustomed to be victorious, under the decemvirs they always lost. From this example one can know in part the causes of the uselessness of mercenary soldiers, which do not have cause to hold firm other than a little stipend that you give them. That cause is not and cannot be enough to make them faithful and so much your friends that they wish to die for you. *For in those armies in which there is no affection toward him for whom they engage in combat that makes them become his partisans, there can never be enough virtue to resist an enemy who is a little virtuous*. Because neither this love nor this rivalry arises except from your subjects, it is necessary to arm one's subjects for oneself, if one wishes to hold a state – if one wishes to maintain a republic or a kingdom – as one sees those have done who have made great profit with armies' (*Discourses on Livy* I, 43; Machiavelli 1996: 91, my emphasis).

of sophisticated folly [*docta insipientia*], and a refined shamelessness [*elegantia turpitudinis*]. Each of their vices, considered in itself, is disgusting and shameful, because then it's quite conspicuous. But [taken together], they seem honorable and becoming to the ignorant and naïve. Moreover [the reason] 'there's no moderation in the common people', [the reason] 'they're terrifying, unless they themselves are cowed by fear', is that freedom and slavery are not easily combined. To suspend judgment is a rare virtue. So it's sheer stupidity to want to do everything in secrecy, and then expect the citizens not to misjudge things, and not to interpret everything perversely. If the plebeians could restrain themselves, and suspend judgment on matters they know little about, or judge things correctly from scanty information, they would be more worthy to rule than to be ruled. But as we've said, nature is entirely the same for all. Everyone is proud when he's master; everyone terrorizes when he's not cowed by fear; and everywhere it's common for enemies and servile flatterers to bend the truth – especially when they're ruled despotically by one or a few men, who in their trials consider the size of the parties' wealth, not the right and the true.[145]

Reiterating a theme from the *TTP* about the difficulty for a majority to agree to something absurd,[146] Spinoza polemicises against Tacitus' claim regarding the common people: *terrere nisi paveant* (they are fearsome unless they are afraid).[147] Spinoza maintains instead that human nature is the same for all, nobles and common people alike. The echo of *Discourses on Livy* I, 58 resounds throughout Spinoza's polemic, a passage in which Machiavelli maintains, against *Titus Livy and all the other [ancient] historians*, that 'the multitude is wiser and more constant than a prince'.[148] According to Machiavelli, Livy's observation ('This is the nature of the multitude: either it serves humbly or it dominates proudly') concerns a people who are with-

---

[145] *TP* VII, 27; CWS II, 558–9. Translation modified.

[146] 'To this we may add that in a democratic state, absurdities are less to be feared. If the assembly is large, it's almost impossible that the majority of its members should agree on one absurd action' (*TTP* XVI, 30; CWS II, 288). In relation to this, cf. the following passage from the *Discourses on Livy*: 'For it is not the particular good but the common good that makes cities great. And without doubt this common good is not observed if not in republics, since all that is for that purpose is executed, and although it may turn out to harm this or that private individual, those for whom the aforesaid does good are so many that they can go ahead with it against the disposition of the few crushed by it' (*Discourses on Livy* II, 2; Machiavelli 1996: 130).

[147] The passage that Spinoza cites, as well as one by Livy that Machiavelli comments on, are collected together in de la Court's *Politieke Weegschaal* (van Hove 1662: 461).

[148] *Discourses on Livy* I, 58; Machiavelli 1996: 115.

out laws; in this case Machiavelli puts forward a statement that applies to all men, even princes, 'for everyone who is not regulated by laws would make the same errors as the unshackled multitude'.[149] In this way Machiavelli reverses the common opinion that finds peoples inconstant:

> I conclude, thus, against the common opinion that says that peoples, when they are princes, are varying, mutable, and ungrateful, as I affirm that these sins are not otherwise in them than in particular princes. Someone accusing peoples and princes together might be able to say the truth, but in excepting princes, he would be deceived; for a people that commands and is well ordered will be stable, prudent, grateful no other-wise than a prince, or better than a prince, even one esteemed wise. On the other side, a prince unshackled from the laws will be more ungrateful, varying, and imprudent than a people. The variation in their proceeding arises not from a diverse nature – because *it is in one mode in all*, and if there is an advantage of good, it is in the people – but from having more or less respect for the laws within which both live.[150]

Machiavelli therefore rejects the false dilemma of people vs. prince (in the same way that Spinoza rejects the dilemma of nobles vs. common people) by affirming the primacy of the law, which must define the roles and spheres of action for both. Machiavelli goes even further, declaring that the people are wiser than a prince not only where laws rule,[151] but also where there are no laws.[152]

---

[149] *Discourses on Livy* I, 58. Machiavelli 1996: 116.

[150] *Discourses on Livy* I, 58. Machiavelli 1996: 117. My emphasis.

[151] 'But as to prudence and stability I say that a people is more prudent, more stable, and of better judgment than a prince. Not without cause may the voice of a people be likened to that of God; for one sees a universal opinion produce marvelous effects in its forecasts, so that it appears to foresee its ill and its good by a hidden virtue. As to judging things, if a people hears two orators who incline to different sides, when they are of equal virtue, very few times does one see it not take up the better opinion, and not be persuaded of the truth that it hears. If it errs in mighty things or those that appear useful, as is said above, often a prince errs too in his own passions, which are much more than those of peoples. It is also seen in its choices of magistrates to make a better choice by far than a prince; nor will a people ever be persuaded that it is good to be put up for dignities an infamous man of corrupt customs – of which a prince is persuaded easily and by a thousand ways. [. . .] If princes are superior to peoples in ordering laws, forming civil lives, and ordering new statutes and orders, peoples are so much superior in maintaining things ordered that without doubt they attain the glory of those who order them' (*Discourses on Livy* I, 58; Machiavelli 1996: 117–18).

[152] 'If, thus, one is reasoning about a prince obligated to laws and about a people fettered by them, more virtue will always be seen in the people than in the prince; if one

If we listen carefully to Spinoza's words, we perhaps hear not only Machiavelli's rebuttal of the historians' prejudice against the people, but also his genealogy. For the famous passage in Machiavelli about the influence exercised by power over historians also reverberates through this page of Spinoza's. In *Discourses on Livy* I, 10, Machiavelli cautions the reader about the historians' tales of Caesar:

> Nor should anyone deceive himself because of the glory of Caesar, hearing him especially celebrated by the writers; for those who praise him are corrupted by his fortune and awed by the duration of the empire that, ruling under that name, did not permit writers to speak freely of him.[153]

The Return to Principles

In *TP* X Spinoza describes the causes of the dissolution of aristocratic states and possible remedies, that is, political interventions, that could be implemented in order to avoid such downfalls. As we noted earlier, he cites Machiavelli explicitly in the first paragraph of this chapter. However, it is the first three paragraphs overall that restore Spinoza's real confrontation with Machiavelli on this question:

> reasons about both as unshackled, fewer errors will be seen in the people than in the prince – and those lesser and having greater remedies. For a licentious and tumultuous people can be spoken to by a good man, and it can easily be returned to the good way; there is no one who can speak to a wicked prince, nor is there any remedy other than steel. From that can be made a conjecture of the importance of the illness of the one and the other: that if to cure the illness of the people words are enough, and for the prince's steel is needed, there will never be anyone who will not judge that where a greater cure is needed there are greater errors. When a people is quite unshackled, the craziness it does is not feared, nor is present evil feared, but what can arise from it, since in the midst of such confusion a tyrant can arise. But with wicked princes the contrary happens: the present evil is feared and the future is hoped for, since men persuade themselves that his wicked life can make freedom emerge. So you see the difference between the one and the other, which is as much between things that are and things that have to be. *The cruelties of the multitude are against whoever they fear will seize the common good; those of a prince are against whoever he fears will seize his own good'* (*Discourses on Livy* I, 58; Machiavelli 1996: 118–19, my emphasis).

[153] *Discourses on Livy* I, 10; Machiavelli 1996: 31–2. Cf. also this passage in the *Discourses*: 'Most writers obey the fortune of the victors' (*Discourses on Livy* II, Preface; Machiavelli 1996: 123), as well as the following from *The Art of War*: 'And even though in comparison with the Romans few others are named, that results from the malice of historians who follow Fortune; usually they are satisfied to honor the conquerors' (Machiavelli 1958: 622). This theme is also taken up by de la Court in the *Politieke Weegschaal* (van Hove 1662: 65).

The first remedy people thought of for this evil was that every few years they would appoint, for a few months, a supreme dictator who would have the authority to investigate, judge, and decide on any punishments for the deeds of senators and public officials, thereby restoring the state to its principles. [. . .] So since dictatorial power is absolute, it can't be anything but terrifying to everyone, especially if (as is required), the dictator is appointed at a fixed time. Then everyone eager to be esteemed would seek this honor most zealously. Certainly since excellence is not valued as highly in peace as wealth is, the grander a man is, the more easily he'll achieve honors. Perhaps this is why the Romans didn't usually appoint a dictator at a designated time, but only when some chance need forced them to. Even so, as Cicero says, 'talk of a dictator is unpleasant to good men'. Truly, since this dictatorial power is absolutely royal, the state can't be changed for a time into a monarchy without great danger to the republic, however short the time is. Moreover, if no definite time has been designated for appointing a dictator, there would be no reason to take account of the time between one dictator and another. But we said this ought to be preserved most carefully. Because the matter is also quite ill-defined, it may easily be neglected. So, unless this dictatorial power is permanent and stable – in which case it can't be entrusted to one man without changing the form of the state – it will be very uncertain. As a result, the well-being and preservation of the republic will also be uncertain.

On the other hand, we can't doubt that if it's possible to make the sword of the dictator perpetual, and a terror only to bad men, and at the same time to preserve the state's form, then the [state's] defects could never become so great that they can't be removed or corrected. To achieve all these conditions, we've said that the council of syndics ought to be subordinated to the supreme council, so that the dictatorial sword would be perpetual, not in the hands of some natural person, but in the hands of a civil person. [. . .]

But in Rome the Tribunes of the plebeians were permanent, yet they couldn't suppress the power of a Scipio. Moreover, they had to refer what they judged to be salutary to the Senate for decision. Often the Senate frustrated their efforts by ensuring that the tribune from whom the senators had less to fear would be the one most in favor with the plebeians. In addition, the authority of the tribunes against the patricians was defended by the support of the plebeians. Whenever they called upon the plebeians, they seemed to promote sedition rather than convene a council. These disadvantages have no place in the state we've described in the preceding two chapters.[154]

---

[154] *TP* X, 1–2; *CWS* II, 596–8. Translation modified.

In the first part of this passage, Spinoza explicitly references Machiavelli's theory of the return to principles, espoused in *Discourses on Livy* II, 1, a theory that Spinoza synthesises perfectly with the disjunction *aut virtus, aut fortuna*. The text that follows shows if not a debt, then at least a discussion of Machiavelli's examples. The two examples of the return to principles through institutions – dictatorship and the tribunes – are indeed both taken from Machiavelli and opposed to the institution that Spinoza advocates, the council of syndics [*Syndicorum Concilium*].

Regarding the institution of the dictatorship, the first possibility Spinoza invokes, a cyclical office, refers to an example taken from Machiavelli, the *balia*, an extraordinary government with full powers:

> Those who governed the state of Florence from 1434 up to 1494 used to say, to this purpose, that it was necessary to regain the state every five years; otherwise, it was difficult to maintain it. They called regaining the state putting that terror and that fear in men that had been put there in taking it, since at that time they had beaten down those who, according to that mode of life, had worked for ill. But as the memory of that beating is eliminated, men began to dare to try new things and to say evil; and so it is necessary to provide for it, drawing the state back toward its principles.[155]

But in terms of the institution of dictatorship properly speaking, Spinoza takes some distance from Machiavelli's opinion that 'the dictatorial authority did good, and not harm in the Roman republic'.[156] Machiavelli in fact holds, against the opinion of those who attribute to this institution the degeneration of the republic into tyranny, that actually the cause was 'the authority taken by the citizens because of the length of command'.[157] 'If the dictatorial name had been lacking in Rome', Machiavelli concludes, 'they would have taken another; for it is forces that easily acquire names, not names forces.'[158]

---

[155] *Discourses on Livy* III, 1; Machiavelli 1996: 211. Translation modified.

[156] *Discourses on Livy* I, 34; Machiavelli 1996: 73.

[157] 'If one considers well the proceeding of the Roman republic, one will see that two things were the cause of the dissolution of that republic: one was the contentions that arose from the Agrarian law; the other, the prolongation of commands. If these things had been known well from the beginning, and proper remedies produced for them, a free way of life would have been longer and perhaps quieter. Although, as to the prolongation of command, one does not see that any tumult ever arose in Rome, nonetheless one may see in fact how much the authority that citizens took through such decisions hurt the city' (*Discourses on Livy* III, 24. Machiavelli 1996: 269–70).

[158] *Discourses on Livy* I, 34; Machiavelli 1996: 74.

Regarding the tribunes, independently from the natural tumultuousness of this institution, which Machiavelli and Spinoza evaluate in opposing ways, one cannot help but notice that Spinoza's reference to the Senate practices designed to elect those from the plebs who are favourable to the Senate is directly indebted to Machiavelli:

> When the Senate feared that the tribunes with consular power would be made of plebian men, it held to one of two modes: either it had the position asked for by the most reputed men in Rome; or truly, through due degrees, it corrupted some vile and very ignoble plebian who, mixed with the plebeians of better quality who ordinarily asked for it, also asked them for it. This last mode made the plebs ashamed to give it; the first made it ashamed to take it.[159]

What can be learned from Machiavelli's historical examples thus comprises a basis on which to construct the model of a new institution capable of returning an aristocratic state to its principles, without the risk of sedition that is innate to the tribunes (and moreover deprived of any meaning in an aristocratic state, wherein only the patricians have the right to take up arms), or the risk of tyranny that looms over the institution of dictatorship.[160]

On the Continuity and Discontinuity of Spinoza's Use of Machiavelli

Machiavelli, the anti-Hobbes

This chapter has allowed us to highlight the place of Machiavellian thought within the argumentative structure of Spinoza's two political works, where at times it occupies a central position. However, we must interrogate some of the expressions we have used more closely, in order to identify their specific force. I have referred to Spinoza's debt towards (and symmetrically, loan

---

[159] *Discourses on Livy* I, 48; Machiavelli 1996: 99.

[160] 'This refusal of the sovereign dictator will be completed later by the refusal of the commissioning dictator: later, when Spinoza – in the footsteps of Machiavelli – will establish an organ capable of periodically reversing the changes introduced by time to the original institutional program, he does not think of an organ made up of a singular person, but a plurality of people. It is an organ with additional constitutional functions to revising such changes: the counsel of syndics. Its function would be the same as with Machiavelli, but in Spinoza the number, in this case as in others, brings along with itself the passage from quantity to quality' (Andújar 1989: 87, n. 1).

from) Machiavelli, to Machiavelli as a source for Spinoza, and to the translation of Machiavelli's arguments into Spinoza's philosophy. The implicit
risk with such metaphors lies in conceiving thought as a metaphysical object
susceptible to being transferred directly from one subject to another, as both
the images of money and water suggest. This risk is equally present in the
notion of meaning to which the image of translation refers, if we do not consider the various theories of translation in the twentieth century. Adopting
another metaphor, while not eliminating the risks intrinsic to this rhetorical
figure, will perhaps allow us to take distance from the implicit metaphysical
effect of these images and draw closer to the philosophical object. I refer to
the metaphor of war.

I will argue that Machiavelli's thought is inserted into a theoretical strategy elaborated in front of a new problematic, modern natural law theory,
and in particular the thought of Hobbes. Spinoza's reprisal of Machiavellian
arguments must be evaluated within the framework of this complex strategy
if we want to avoid the snares of a history of philosophy conceived as the
eternal return of the same. A second risk we must avoid is thinking this
strategy as timeless, as if Spinoza's political thought were offered to us as
an unchanging and in itself concluded object rather than as a process – as a
theoretical practice with its continuities and discontinuities. In this way, we
would be led to think Spinoza's deployment of Machiavelli as an invariant
given that, even if real, must emerge from the text.

Even taking into account the different objectives and moments that the
two works occupy in the development of Spinoza's thought, we must first
observe that there is continuity in Spinoza's strategic use of Machiavelli in
the *TTP* and *TP*.[161] The strictly anti-theological Machiavellian arguments
are absent from the *TP*. We do not find either a reference to Machiavelli's
theory of history as the conjunctural encounter of virtue and fortune, used
in order to deconstruct the Hebrew myth of election, or a reference to the
power instituted by Romulus through the intermediary of the nymph that
Numa encounters, which secularises the perspective on Moses' establishment of power and the legitimatisation of the table of laws as the divine
word. However, the basic aim of Spinoza's reference to Machiavelli, which
is in both texts, remains what we could perhaps call the double-inversion of
Hobbesian theory:[162]

---

[161] For an analysis of the difference between these two works, see Balibar 1998: 51–2.

[162] On the relation between Hobbes and Machiavelli from a historiographical point of
view, cf. the work attributed to Hobbes, 'A Discourse upon the Beginning of Tacitus',
in Hobbes 1995: 31–67. Also see Saxonhouse's commentary on this essay in the

1. The inversion of Hobbesian natural law (and, we could say, natural law *tout court*) through dissolving the eternal fiction established by the pact in the unstable and aleatory equilibrium of relations of force that constitute it in duration (certainly the term *pactum* is still found in the *TTP*, while in the *TP* only the complementary term *fides* is used).
2. The inversion of Hobbesian legal positivism[163] with the affirmation that determining the *salus populi* is not a simple emanation of the state, that is, a question between God and the conscience of the sovereign, but rather a question that concerns the relation between the sovereign and the people.

This all appears very strongly if, following Harrington,[164] Hobbes's political philosophy is read as a response to a theoretical challenge whose author is omitted.[165] In particular, Machiavelli's ghost is evoked in the *Leviathan* in two fundamental places, regarding the foundation and dissolution of the state. The first passage is a comment following the articulation of the third law of nature ('men must keep to the agreements they have made'), which the definition of justice as the fulfilment of the pact depends on:

The fool hath said in his heart: 'there is no such thing as justice'; and sometimes also with his tongue; seriously alleging: 'every man's conservation

same volume, which on the other hand has the tendency to exaggerate Machiavelli's importance in Hobbes's formation: 'Through his analysis of Tacitus, Hobbes offers a series of Machiavellian maxims as guides for the founders of political orders. In doing so, he also demonstrates his commitment to discovering the sources of political order' (Hobbes 1995: 128). On the relation between Hobbes and Machiavelli from a theoretical point of view, critics have avoided posing the question of Hobbes's silence about Machiavelli by taking two different approaches. On the one hand, with different undertones, there is a continuist hypothesis that regards Hobbes as integrating and completing Machiavelli (Meinecke 1976: 249–55; Horkheimer 1993; Habermas 1973: 41–81; Bovero 1992). On the other hand, there is the hypothesis that interprets the silence as a recognition of a radical alterity, making Hobbes the true founder of modern politics (Lazzeri 1990; Bobbio 1965).

163 Norberto Bobbio's observation is useful in clarifying the relationship between natural law theory and legal positivism [*positivismo giuridico*] in Hobbes's thought: 'We could say, in order to summarise Hobbesian thought in a synthetic formula on the respective validity of natural and civil law, that natural law puts all of its force in the service of positive right, and in this way dies in the very moment in which it brings its creature to light' (Bobbio 1963: 47).

164 Harrington 1977: 178.

165 There are no occurrences of Machiavelli's name in Molesworth's index, either in the Latin or English works.

and contentment being committed to his own care, there could be no reason why every man might not do what he thought conduced thereunto, and therefore also to make or not make, keep or not keep, covenants was not against reason, when it conduced to one's benefit'. He does not therein deny that there be covenants, and that they are sometimes broken, sometimes kept, and that such a breach of them may be called injustice, and the observance of them justice; but *he questioneth whether injustice*, taking away the fear of God (for the same fool hath said in his heart there is no God), *may not sometimes stand with that reason, which dictateth to every man his own good; and particularly then, when it conduceth to such a benefit as shall put a man in a condition, to neglect not only the dispraise, and revilings, but also the power of other men.* 'The kingdom of God is gotten by violence; but what if it could be gotten by unjust violence? were it against reason so to get it, when it is impossible to receive hurt by it? And if it be not against reason, it is not against justice; or else justice is not to be approved for good.' From such reasoning as this, successful wickedness hath obtained the name of virtue.[166]

The injustice that Hobbes refers to cannot be established in his philosophy in absolute terms,[167] because it can only exist once the pact is stipulated. Before this there is neither justice nor injustice. Here Hobbes cites the well-known passage in Machiavelli about respecting pacts (while rejecting its conclusions), although he is forced to admit that the laws of nature – particularly those that call for pacts to be respected, those that are nothing but the pure dictates of reason – actually have no efficacy unless a power is established that has sufficient force to make them respected, which itself will not be able to demand accountability for future violations. Justice and injustice find their ground in the establishment of the state, whose transcendence cannot but prove aporetic within a radically materialist ontology such as that of Hobbes.

The second passage on Machiavelli is found in *Leviathan* XXIX, which is dedicated to 'things that weaken or tend to the dissolution of a commonwealth'. According to Hobbes, such things can reside as much in the lack of absolute power required for the conservation of peace and the defence of the state as they can in the idea that 'every private man is judge of good and evil actions'. In addition, such things can reside in holding that the sovereign

---

[166] Hobbes 1994: 90. My emphasis. For a commentary on this passage and an analytic demonstration of Hobbes's polemic with Machiavelli, see Esposito 1984: 181–4.

[167] In *De homine*, Hobbes resolutely affirms the relativity of the concepts of good and evil.

is *subject to civil laws*, as well as within a conception of divisible sovereign power. In each of these cases, of which the most dangerous is the separation of civil and religious power, power loses its absolute status and, from the division that this creates, civil wars arise. Within this framework, the nature of Hobbes's opposition to Machiavelli's thesis of the political productivity of Roman social struggles is clear:

> As to the rebellion in particular against monarchy, one of the most fre-quent causes of it is the reading of the books of policy, and Histories of the ancient Greeks and Romans, from which young men (and all others that are unprovided of the antidote of solid reason), receiving a strong and delightful impression of the great exploits of war achieved by the conduc-tors of their armies, receive withal a pleasing idea, of all they have done besides, and imagine their great prosperity not to have proceeded from the *emulation of particular men*, but from the virtue of their popular form of government (*not considering the frequent seditions, and civil wars, produced by the imperfection of the policy*).[168]

Harrington unmasks Hobbes's reference to the fascination exercised by the classics, showing that it is an attack on Machiavelli. Harrington refutes Hobbes's judgement that the prosperity of ancient republics is founded on emulation rather than good political constitution, showing that it is contradictory:

> Where first, the blame he lays to the heathen authors is, in his sense, laid unto the Scripture; and whereas he holds them to be young men, or men of no antidote, that are of like opinions, it should seem that Machiavel, the sole retriever of this ancient prudence, is to his solid a beardless boy that hath newly read Livy. And how solid his reason is may appear where he grants the great prosperity of ancient commonwealths, which is to give up the controversy, for such an effect must have some adequate cause; which to evade, *he insinuates that it was nothing else but the emulation of particular men; as if so great an emulation could have been generated without as great virtue, so great virtue without the best education, the best education without the best laws, or the best laws any otherwise than by the excellency of their policy.*[169]

---

[168] Hobbes 1994: 214–15. My emphasis.
[169] Harrington 1977: 178. My emphasis.

Against Machiavelli, Hobbes first of all affirms the juridical value of pacts, and therefore the absolute value of justice, once a coercive power is established. Second, Hobbes maintains the indivisibility of state power (his critique of mixed states is also found in chapter twenty-nine), and its absolute character towards the society that generated it. These are precisely the two steps of Hobbes's argument that Spinoza overturns with his own political theory. Using an expression which Althusser is fond of, we could say that Spinoza takes a detour through Machiavelli in order to trace a line of demarcation between his philosophy and Hobbes's, in order to determine the differences that allow us to speak of a Spinozist philosophy of politics – that is, the differences that allow us to speak of Spinoza's philosophy of politics as such.

Roberto Esposito claims that modern political philosophy is 'structurally unable to think conflict because it is originally directed to questions which are entirely concentrated around order'. The order it deals with can neither combine with nor organise conflict, which it expels from the horizon of politics. According to Esposito, it is precisely in these terms that the relationship between order and conflict is thought by the founder of modern political philosophy, Hobbes:

> What else is his theory if not the strongest, most rigorous, and most unequivocal attempt to expel conflict from the sphere of politics and confine it within a natural setting that, precisely because it is incurably conflictual, is not susceptible to political definition? Indeed, it is the exact opposite. Against the solitary attempt by Machiavelli to keep order and conflict together, reading each inside of the other, Hobbes chooses the way of radical alternative: either politics, or conflict. When there is conflict – namely, in the state of nature – there is no politics. And when there is politics – in other words, after the formulation of the pact and the creation of the Leviathan-state – there is no conflict, and there can be no conflict.[170]

Spinoza's reprise of Machiavelli's attempt to think politics as order and conflict together is precisely the theoretical instrument that allows him to break with the Hobbesian partition between conflict, which characterises the state of nature, and order, which reigns in the civil state.[171] *Jus sive poten-*

---

[170] Esposito 1996: 2–3. On the theme of conflict in Machiavelli, cf. Dotti 1979; Sasso 1993; Bock 1990; Del Lucchese 2001.

[171] At a January 1997 conference at the Scuola Normale Superiore di Pisa, Étienne

tia sive virtus is the transposition into the framework of Spinoza's ontology of Machiavelli's centaur,[172] the half-beast, half-man that never transforms into a Leviathan – a mortal god – but rather lives in the space, at the same time aleatory and necessary, of encounters with fortune.

But this impossible metamorphosis allows us to take up another Machiavellian theme, 'the practice of simulation as the condition of legitimacy for the relation between power and knowledge',[173] as Esposito puts it, a theme excluded by Hobbes's identification of power and knowledge in the institution of the great Leviathan. It is precisely in refusing the *de jure* establishment of this identity that a possibility opens of formulating what we could anachronistically define as a theory of ideology. The dominant ideology of the time, religion, is at once an element of social cohesion and political domination. Confronting Hobbesian philosophy as a philosophy of the transparency of the mirroring pair reason and state, Spinozist philosophy presents itself as a philosophy of the opacity of the immediate, a philosophy of the necessary appearance, and all that departs from its elaboration, of several Machiavellian themes, whether those treated in the chapters devoted to Roman religions in the *Discourses on Livy*, or the affirmation of the necessity of appearing for the one who holds power in *The Prince* (this is without

Balibar underscored the absence of Spinoza from Esposito's sketch of the history of modern political philosophy.

[172] Regarding the metaphor of the centaur, Esposito writes: 'The double gives the image of modern subjectivity as form and scission and together as the triumph of scission over form. Nothing materialises this better than the concept-symbol of the Centaur, in the mythic-anthropomorphic depiction that Machiavelli gives to it. In it, all contraries are condensed into an emblem of exceptional explicit force. Divided, split between man and beast, law and force, order and power, the subject, in order to be able to "consist", in order to remain, defer, delay and/or negate the necessity of its own finitude, must "finish" being intact, dying insofar as it is a subject-man, to incorporate its own difference, its own other, its own in/humanity. The image of the man-beast, as is well known, is a long-lasting *topos* in the philosophical, theological and literary inventory of the medieval and humanistic world (and even the ancient world, if we think of Xenophon's *Cyropaedia*). From Origen to Gregory of Nyssa, Eusebius to Lactantius, Jerome to Ambrose, and then from Duns Scotus, through Peter Damian, Bernard of Clairvaux, Alain de Lille, up to Nicolas of Cusa, a whole legion of *pecora, jumenta, reptilia, bestiae, ferae, belluae* runs through [. . .] the progress of men and undermines its fragile nature. What is important to note, more than its diachronic endurance, is the overturning of the sense and direction that the myth of becoming a beast takes on with Machiavelli: it is no longer understood as a moment, the provisionally negative, low, telluric moment [. . .] of an itinerary whose height [. . .] inevitably goes up to God' (Esposito 1984: 34).

[173] Esposito 1984: 213. On the same theme, cf. also Duprat 1980.

doubt original to Spinoza, in whom there is a complex thematisation at more levels of the imaginary, where in Machiavelli this appearing is measured only in its immediate political effects).

The Different Evaluation of Roman History

A second element of continuity in the two political works lies in Spinoza's judgement about Roman history, where his greatest distance from Machiavelli is manifest:

1. The idea that war must only be defensive and therefore a negative evaluation of the Roman wars of expansion.[174]
2. A negative assessment of the institution of the tribune, which had generated numerous popular revolts.[175]

Machiavelli actually unites these two aspects of Roman history, which Spinoza disjoins and evaluates negatively, in his analysis of the Roman state model in *Discourses on Livy* I, 6, where he shows that without internal conflicts between the people and the Senate, not even external victories would have been possible. Indeed, in order to avoid hostilities and tumults, the Roman legislators had to 'either not employ the plebs in war, as the Venetians did, or not open the way to foreigners, as did the Spartans'; but actually they did both, 'which gave the plebs strength and increase and infinite occasions for tumult'.[176] Removing the cause of tumults here would have also meant taking away the cause of expansion, namely a strong and armed plebs. And here the typical Machiavellian procedure, ordered by the fact that 'nothing

---

[174] See Mugnier-Pollet 1976: 186.

[175] 'Perhaps someone [*aliquis*] will object that the example of the Romans shows that a people can easily remove a tyrant from their midst. I myself, however, think this example completely confirms our opinion. For though the Roman people were far more easily able to remove a tyrant from their midst and to change the form of government [*forma imperii*] – they themselves had the right to choose the king and his successor, and they had not yet been accustomed to obeying kings – rebellious and infamous men, they killed three of the six kings they had before – still all they accomplished was to elect a number of tyrants in place of one, tyrants who always had them torn apart wretchedly by both external and internal wars, until in the end the power [*imperium*] gave way again to a monarchy, changed only in name, as in England' (*TTP* XVIII, 35; CWS II, 330–1, translation modified). Gebhart notes in Vol. 5 that 'the *aliquis* who might raise the objection is Machiavelli' (Spinoza 1925: 103).

[176] *Discourses on Livy* I, 6; Machiavelli 1996: 21. Translation modified.

entirely clean and entirely without suspicion is ever found',[177] is put to work:

> If someone wished, therefore, to order a republic anew, he would have to examine whether he wished it to expand like Rome in dominion and in power or truly to remain within narrow limits. In the first case *it is necessary* to order it like Rome and make a place for tumults and universal dissensions, as best one can; for without a great number of men, and well armed, a republic can never grow, or, if it grows, maintain itself. In the second case, you can order it like Sparta and like Venice, but because expansion is poison for such republics, he who orders them should, in all the modes he can, prohibit them from acquiring, because such acquisitions, founded on a weak republic, are its ruin altogether.[178]

The fundamental disjunction at the base of the question of expansion does not allow an abstract response. It is in fact the social structure of each state that poses the possibility or impossibility of conquest: a powerful and armed plebs is in fact a danger inside and outside the state, and therefore the tumultuous republic of the Romans is precisely the effect of the structure of that type of society. In my view, Spinoza accepted the general framework of the disjunction ordered by the '*it is necessary*', which seems to be the Machiavellian name of Spinozist substance, choosing instead the second alternative in the dilemma, that is, the Venetian model.

The Dissolution of the State: From Individual Calculus to the Indignation of the People

In terms of the discontinuity between the *TTP* and *TP*, I think that the differences that appear in Spinoza's use of Machiavelli completely depend on the different problematic in which this use is inscribed. If we analyse Spinoza's language, it should be clear that while in the *TTP*, Spinoza gives an account of the genesis of the state in contractualist terms, in the *TP* such language is completely abandoned, corresponding to the emergence of a new theory of the social body. If Hobbes can indeed be classified among the utopians of *TP* I, 1, as Alexandre Matheron has suggested, he can perhaps also

---

[177] Machiavelli 1996: 22. This passage is cited as a proverb in the *Politieke Weegschaal* (van Hove 1662: 470). Francès notes that the Italian citations in this text often evoke Machiavelli's memory (de la Court and de la Court 1937).

[178] *Discourses on Livy* I, 6; Machiavelli 1996: 22. My emphasis.

be classified among those for whom society arises from a rational calculation of individuals in the form of a pact, to which Spinoza refers in *TTP* XVI. Not a utopia of the pact, because Spinoza already criticises natural law theory for thinking the pact as bound to the utility of the single individual, but a utopia of individual rationale which calculates the advantages and disadvantages of being in society. In the *TP*, we find instead 'a non-contractualist explication of the genesis of the state only through the play, anarchic and blind, of relations of force as they spontaneously operate in the state of nature according to the mechanism of affective imitation'.[179]

The difference in Spinoza's use of Machiavelli is perceptible not as it concerns the genesis of the state, but insofar as it regards its dissolution. In the *TTP* the dissolution of the state is implicitly thought on the basis of the model of the prince's utilitarian calculus, extended, however, to each individual. Here it is useful to reread the following passage from *The Prince* XVIII: 'A prudent lord, therefore, cannot observe faith, nor should he, when such observance turns against him, and the causes that made him promise have been eliminated.'[180] Prudence, which is wisdom in practice, is therefore at the basis of both the genesis, as well as the rupture of the pact, which conversely ceases to be a real pact because of the loss of its juridical character, in order to become simply the provisory result of a collective calculus, which has as its target goods that can be real as much as imaginary.

In the *TP* (in which, as we have noted, the term *pactum* has totally disappeared)[181] Spinoza approaches the question of the dissolution of the state by newly taking up Machiavellian arguments of an entirely different time. In fact, the dissolution of the state results from the indignation of citizens and revolts of this kind. In this passage from the *Florentine Histories*, Machiavelli strongly emphasises the dynamic of inescapable destruction in popular indignation:

> Thus did the citizens live full of *indignation* as they saw the majesty of their state ruined, the orders laid waste, the laws annulled, every decent being corrupted, all civil modesty eliminated [. . .]. Thus the *indignation* and *hatred* grew to such a degree that they would have inflamed not only the Florentines, who do not know how to maintain freedom and are unable to bear slavery, but any servile people to recover their freedom. Wherefore

---

[179] Matheron 1990: 258.
[180] *The Prince* XVIII; Machiavelli 1985: 69.
[181] Cf. CWS II, 666–712, which also provides the references for its occurrence in the *TTP*. On the use of *contractus* in *TP* IV, 6, cf. Cristofolini 1997: 24.

many citizens of every quality resolved to lose their lives or get back their freedom.[182]

The dissolution of the state is not the result of a calculus, but the effect produced by an affective dynamic; it is thus with this point that we take up Matheron's thesis that we just highlighted, namely that in the *TP* there is a non-contractualist explanation of the genesis of the state by means only of the anarchic and blind play of relations of force as they spontaneously operate in the state of nature according to the mechanism of affective imitation. I believe that this is confirmed by the definition of indignation that we find in the *Ethics*: 'Indignation is a hate toward someone who has done evil toward another.'[183] Indignation is therefore a passion that breaks the monadic closure of the individual and involves it, through the mechanism of affective imitation, in the inextricable weave of ideas and passions that constitute society. We can therefore conclude that the rupture with natural law theory is effected under the sign of Machiavelli, but carried out in two different phases, each of which leaves a different trace in the strategic use of his arguments.

---

[182] *Florentine Histories*, II, 36; Machiavelli 1988: 95. My emphasis.
[183] *Ethics* III, DA 20; CWS I, 535.

3

Causality and Temporality between
Machiavelli and Spinoza

Having established the role that Spinoza's repeated use of Machiavelli plays in his constructive philosophical-political project, we can now turn to the extensive changes that Spinoza's encounter with Machiavelli's theory of history and politics produced in his metaphysics. In this chapter, I will demonstrate that the passage from a conception of being organised serially, which Spinoza articulates in the *TdIE*, to a conception of being characterised as *connexio*, put forth in the *Ethics*, corresponds to Spinoza's elaboration of a theory of temporality that allows him, on the basis of several Machiavellian insights, to distance himself *ante litteram* from any philosophy of history. In chapter 4, I will traverse Lessing's and Vico's philosophies of history in order more precisely to carve out the stakes of this problem, which at first sight could seem purely terminological, through an analysis of the conceptual structures that they use in their readings of Spinoza.

Theory of Politics and Theory of History

In chapter 2, we analysed Spinoza's repetition of several essential touchstones in Machiavellian political theory. We can now take up the question of the meaning that this repetition assumes within Spinoza's overall architectonic. We have emphasised, first, Spinoza's reprisal of the conceptual pair virtue and fortune as part of a theory of history free from every projection of anthropomorphic categories on to its development.[1] Second,

---

[1] On this point, Moreau's observations about *TTP* Praef. being perfectly symmetrical with *Ethics* I, App. are very interesting. The former does for history what the latter does for nature: a critique of the 'spontaneous tendency to anthropomorphise' reality. 'For the same reason', Moreau concludes, 'that there is a teleology "in space", there is a teleology "in time"' (Moreau 1994: 471).

we emphasised the claim that every form of power rests on the power of the multitude and the passions that traverse it,[2] a claim that radically demarcates Spinoza's thought from both a theory of the legitimation of the political through the transcendence of the divine word, and the imposition of a moral model of humanity.[3] The common notions are in play at this level of reflection. The use of common notions characterises the second kind of knowledge, and they have the function of giving adequate knowledge of things by means of their common properties.[4] Regarding politics and history, Spinoza therefore draws from Machiavelli the common notions on the basis of which the common properties of the political body, that is, *mixed bodies* (to use Machiavelli's language), are able to be adequately thought.

It is precisely in light of the importance that this Machiavellian consideration has for Spinoza's idea of *ratio* that we can see an extremely important passage in Spinoza's corpus in a different light. I refer to a decisive step in the appendix to *Ethics* I. After deconstructing the traditional conception of God through the conceptual weave of the first thirty-six propositions, Spinoza analyses the necessary genesis of the teleological prejudice in which this conception is rooted. He shows how this prejudice is the spontaneous consequence of two elements, the opacity of the immediate and the tendency to seek one's own advantage. What follows from this combination is that man

---

[2] Here I follow Cristofolini's excellent suggestion that Spinoza's expression *passionibus obnoxius* can be translated, in a way inspired by Leopardi, with the phrase *attraversati dalle passioni* (traversed, crossed over, shot or crossed through by the passions) (Spinoza 1999: 242).

[3] In this sense, Walther maintains that recent studies on both Machiavelli and Spinoza have made possible a different reconstruction of the panorama of modern political thought: 'New research has clearly shown that, in addition to the traditional-normative tendency [. . .] and the positivist-authoritarian [*geltungspositivistisch-authoritären*] tendency established by Bodin and Hobbes, there is a third tendency [. . .], which should be signified as a Republican line, whose origin lies with thirteenth-century Italian city-states, having Machiavelli as its first culminating point [. . .] and Spinoza as its greatest representative in the seventeenth century' (Walther 1990: 248–9, my emphasis). While we can certainly agree with Walther regarding the extraneousness of Machiavelli and Spinoza to the two dominant currents of modern politics, it seems to me that there is little heuristic use in classifying them within a vague and indefinite Republican current. On the plurality of positions within the Republican constellation and the discontinuities between them, cf. Guena 1998.

[4] *Ethics* II, 40 Schol. 2; CWS I, 477–8. Regarding the concept of common properties, Gueroult rightly notes that they are common to all bodies, to *corpora simplicissima*, and common only to some bodies (the different *corpora composita*) on the basis of their own different levels of complexity in their composition (Gueroult 1974: 338–9).

imagines himself as the free centre of the world in a nature that, by analogy with the means he devises to reach his advantage, appears prepared for him by a benign divinity that he honours in order to receive favour. However, Spinoza writes:

> While they sought to show that nature does nothing in vain (i.e., nothing which is not of use to men), they seem to have shown only that nature and the Gods are as mad as men. [. . .] Among so many conveniences in nature they had to find many inconveniences: storms, earthquakes, diseases, etc. These, they maintain, happen because the Gods (whom they judge to be of the same nature as themselves) are angry on account of wrongs done to them by men, or on account of sins committed in their worship. And though their daily experience contradicted this, and though infinitely many examples showed that conveniences and inconveniences happen indiscriminately to the pious and the impious alike, they did not on that account give up their longstanding prejudice. It was easier for them to put this among the other unknown things, whose use they were ignorant of, and so remain in the state of ignorance in which they had been born, than to destroy that whole construction [*tota illa fabrica*], and think up a new one.
>
> So they maintained it as certain that the judgments of the Gods far surpass man's grasp. This alone, of course, would have caused the truth to be hidden from the human race to eternity, *if Mathematics, which is concerned not with ends, but only with the essences and properties of figures [figurarum essentiae et properietates], had not shown men another standard of truth. And besides Mathematics, we can assign other causes also [& praeter Mathesin aliae etiam adsignari possunt causae] (which it is unnecessary to enumerate here), which were able to bring it about [fieri potuit] that men would notice these common prejudices and be led to the true knowledge of things.*[5]

In order to withstand the test of experience, teleological prejudice must be transformed into the elaboration of a horizon of moral laws whose violation by men would be the cause of natural disasters: God the father becomes God the judge. But since conveniences [*commoda*] and inconveniences [*incommoda*] are driven by chance and indifferently strike both virtuous and evil men, teleological prejudice is forced to take shelter in the unintelligibility of projects of divine providence in order to be able to perpetuate itself. This horizon is simultaneously cognitive and emotive, which generates a justifi-

---

[5] *Ethics* I, App.; CWS I, 441–2. My emphasis.

cation of events as sentences pronounced from a divine will impenetrable to human intellect, which could turn out to be the one dynamic possible; but the factual existence of mathematics demonstrates, insofar as it is not concerned with goals, but only with the essences and properties of figures, the possibility of developing a different dynamic that does not at all derive from the first one. On the contrary, in breaking this force, mathematics poses a new standard of truth [norma veritatis] on the basis of which it is possible to produce *another* discourse on reality.

We must, however, guard against a positivist interpretation of this fragment. Indeed, it is neither true that the passage from superstition to science follows a necessary developmental law (a *loi des estades*), nor that mathematics attains hegemony as the way of thinking for all humankind, since it remains, as emphasised in the supplement of the *Nagelate Schriften*, a domain for few. Mathematics is therefore one singular event among others, while it is also the bearer of a universal *norma veritatis*. It was the fact of Euclid's material and 'spiritual' existence that made possible the opening of a new path leading to the true knowledge of things, a fact whose aleatory nature Spinoza emphasises with the expression *fieri potuit*, which indicates a necessity produced by the rupturing with a contingency ('was able to happen' and not 'had to happen', i.e., 'would have happened, sooner or later').

Many critics have underscored the importance of this passage: *Mathesis* as truth in contrast to prejudice, reason as opposed to imagination. What has gone (mostly) unobserved, and which Étienne Balibar was the first to underscore, is the phrase 'and besides Mathematics, we can assign other causes also' [*& praeter Mathesin aliae etiam adsignari possunt causae*]. According to Spinoza there are other causes constituting the second kind of knowledge, whose force contributes to breaking out of the dark woods of superstition. However, he believes them unnecessary to enumerate here [*quas hic enumerare supervacaneum est*]. We can hypothesise that these causes are, on the one hand, physics by way of Galileo's universal individuality, and on the other, political theory, once again despite Comte's law of stages, through Machiavelli's universal individuality. The field of reason opened by Euclid, Machiavelli and Galileo (to put them in chronological order) therefore divides into three domains, mathematics, political theory and physics. This division corresponds precisely to the partition of philosophy that Hobbes proposed in the epistle dedicatory of *De cive*.[6] While geometry and physics have legitimate fathers, however, Hobbes gives political theory a natural

---

[6] Hobbes 1998: 3–6.

father whose name cannot even be spoken, a name that in England as else-where evokes the presence of the Devil himself.[7]

However, the passage also suggests an additional direction: Spinoza says it is superfluous to enumerate these causes here [*hic*]. This implicitly signifies that Spinoza has spoken about or will speak about these causes in other places. And while it is not difficult to identify the place where he speaks about physics in the short treatise from *Ethics* II, for a political theory made possible by a new conception of history it is not easy to isolate a specific part in his theoretical project. Yet it seems that there are two specific pas-sages where, more strictly than elsewhere, Spinoza traces a line of demar-cation between the teleological knowledge of history and politics and the knowledge of the essence and characteristics of the political body – that is, between the imaginary sanctification of history and power, and the knowl-edge of their dynamics. I refer to *TTP* III, where Spinoza, clearly referring to Machiavelli, takes distance both from an ontology of history that we could define (with inevitable simplification) as Judeo-Christian,[8] and from every pagan conception of history. Second, in *TP* I he differentiates himself both from Thomistic politics and from the process of its decomposition put in place by theorists of reason of state, unequivocally emphasising the differ-ence between the latter and Machiavelli. It is nonetheless true that if these texts represent the clearest point of rupture with earlier tradition – the *pars construens* corresponding to Spinoza's three mature works taken as a whole (although they are not free of different nuances) – Machiavelli remains, in several respects, the point of departure.

On the basis of this interpretation of the second kind of knowledge, defined by common notions that are constituted by the adequate ideas of the common properties of figures, physical bodies and political bodies, it becomes necessary to view the third kind of knowledge – intuitive science – in a new light. In other words, once it is admitted that the second kind of knowledge has the common characteristics of these three objects as its exclusive field of inquiry, what follows for the third kind of knowledge? If the second kind of knowledge is knowledge of general laws, the third kind

---

[7] Raab mentions the fact that 'in a number of important respects', the English reaction against Machiavelli differs from the European reaction, above all because of the 'rig-idly national character of the English Reformation'. However, in spite of the differ-ences, the conclusions are the same: 'that Machiavelli's vision of the political world was fundamentally irreconcilable with the traditional theological view of the universe' (Raab 1965: 69).

[8] I follow André Tosel's use of this expression, while not ignoring its extremely general level (Tosel 1984).

of knowledge is knowledge of the essence of singular things: as Cristofolini writes, the third kind of knowledge is the capture of complexity.[9] But which complexity? It is clear that each theoretical field aims at a different complexity. We can first examine what Spinoza explicitly says, after defining the third kind of knowledge, by means of the famous example of the fourth proportional:

> In addition to these two kinds of knowledge, there is (as I shall show in what follows) another, third kind, which we shall call intuitive science. And this kind of knowing proceeds from an adequate idea of the formal essence of certain attributes of God to the adequate knowledge of the essence of things.
>
> I shall explain all these with one example. Suppose there are three numbers, and the problem is to find the fourth which is to the third as the second is to the first. Merchants do not hesitate to multiply the second by the third, and divide the product by the first, because they have not yet forgotten what they heard from their teacher without any demonstration, or because they have often found this in the simplest numbers, or from the force of the Demonstration of P7 in Bk. VII of Euclid, namely from the common property of proportionals. But in the simplest numbers none of this is necessary. Given the numbers 1, 2, and 3, no one fails to see that the fourth proportional number is 6 – and we see this much more clearly because we infer the fourth number from the ratio which, in one glance [*uno intuito*], we see the first number to have the second.[10]

Spinoza's example sets up a problematic knot that is difficult to untie. On the one hand, it follows from the definition of the third kind of knowledge, proposing a paradigmatic example for it, and yet, on the other hand, it does not explain it at all. Indeed, Spinoza writes that this knowledge '*procedit ab*

---

[9] Cristofolini notes that 'the concept of science therefore finds itself charged with a greater complexity than in Descartes, because (intuitive) science indicates the moment, immanent to reality differentiating itself, in which it is possible to grasp the necessity of causal concatenation' (Cristofolini 1987: 172).

[10] *Ethics* II, 40 Schol. 2; CWS I, 478. Translation modified. For commentaries on this scholium, cf. Robinson 1928: 350–5; Gueroult 1974: 381–6. For an analysis of the details of Spinoza's example, cf. Matheron 1986. For a precise reconstruction of the different kinds of knowledge in the *TdIE*, the *KV* and the *Ethics*, cf. Gueroult 1974: 593–608. On the difference between the *TdIE* and the *Ethics*, cf. Matheron 1988. On the possible confusion between the first and third kinds of knowledge introduced by Spinoza's example, cf. Macherey 1997: 322.

adaequata idea essentiae formalis quorundam Dei attributorum ad adaequatam':
how does the deduction of the fourth number from the first three put into
play the formal essence [*essentia formalis*] of an attribute and proceed from
this to the essence of singular things? This one glance [*unus intuitus*] seems
instead to be the effect of experience or praxis, that is, of the habit sedi-
mented in the glance by the memory of singular cases – by memory, and
therefore by a kind of inadequate knowledge.

Further, Spinoza's example causes a problem for two other essential reasons. First, the object that is shown according to the different cognitive
modalities is the number. But arithmetic, the science of the properties of
numbers, cannot come from the knowledge of an attribute of God, precisely
because numbers are the imaginary effect of the separation of the affections
of substance from substance itself, as Spinoza writes in his so-called 'letter on
the infinite' to Meyer:

> From the fact that we separate the affections of substance from substance
> itself and reduce them to classes [*ad classes redigimus*] so that as far as possi-
> ble we imagine them easily, arises number, by which we determine [these
> affections of substance].[11]

In the same way, geometry, or the science of the properties of shapes, does
not proceed from the totality of space (from the attribute extension) to the
essence of singular shapes. Instead, the figure derives from the negation of
the entire space of what it is not, according to the famous principle *deter-
minatio est negatio*, which the Romantic interpretation of Spinoza has transformed into the proof of his acosmism, illegitimately transposing it on to an
ontological level.[12] In Letter L to Jelles, Spinoza writes:

> As for shape being a negation, and not something positive, it's manifest
> that matter as a whole [*integra materia*], considered without limitation
> [*indefinite*], can have no shape, and that shape pertains only to finite and
> determinate bodies. For whoever says that he conceives a shape indicates
> nothing by this except that he conceives a determinate thing, and how
> it is determinate. So this determination does not pertain to the thing
> according to its being, but on the contrary, it is its non-being. Therefore,
> because the shape is nothing but a determination, and a determination is
> a negation, it can't be anything but a negation.[13]

---

[11] *Ep*. XII [to Lodewijk Meyer]; CWS I, 203.
[12] On the theoretical stakes of this interpretation, see Macherey 2011.
[13] *Ep*. L [to Jarig Jelles]; CWS II, 406–7.

Therefore, both the objects of arithmetic and the objects of geometry are only ever imperfect examples of intuitive science precisely because they are abstractions from the totality: they are the hypostases of the affections of substance, or in Spinoza's terms, *auxilia imaginationis* (aids of the imagination).[14]

The second reason why Spinoza's example causes a problem is that mathematical objects are universal objects, and therefore his argument finds itself at an impasse in the precise moment that it must demonstrate the difference between the second and third kinds of knowledge for the cognitive modality of such objects. Indeed, the essence and properties of the figure are the figure itself, and in this way it is difficult to understand how mathematical objects could be observed by the third kind of knowledge. There is in fact some difference between general laws and a singular object, as Matheron points out: 'Mathematical properties are precisely not real physical entities; they are common properties.'[15]

Although its effects are the object of *Ethics* V,[16] there is no other example of intuitive science in Spinoza's work. Here I will propose an interpretation which must take the risk of not being founded on the explicit content of Spinoza's text. Intuitive science is the adequate knowledge of two objects in their singularity: the knowledge of the human body derived from physics,[17]

---

[14] The strict distance that Spinoza takes from the idea of *mathesis universalis* such as that found in Descartes' *Rules for the Direction of the Mind*, or as the science of the order, or measure [*ordo vel mensura*] of things (AT X, 378; Descartes 1985: 19–20) is demonstrated both by the fact that in the letter on the infinite, Spinoza considers measure as an *auxilium imaginationis* (Ep. XII [to Lodewijk Meyer]; CWS I, 203), and by the fact that in the appendix to *Ethics* I he considers music, which is part of this universal science according to Descartes, to be one of the value-giving effects of teleological and anthropocentric prejudice (*Ethics* I, App.; CWS I, 445).

[15] Matheron 1986: 147.

[16] Cf. in particular *Ethics* V, 32 and its corollary.

[17] Already Descartes, in a letter added to the introduction of the French translation of *Principles of Philosophy*, had highlighted the link between medicine and physics through the famous metaphor of the tree: 'Thus the whole of philosophy is like a tree. The roots are metaphysics, the trunk is physics, and the branches emerging from the trunk are all the other sciences, which may be reduced to three principal ones, namely medicine, mechanics, and morals' (AT IX, 14; Descartes 1985: 186). Cf. also the following passage from Hobbes's epistle dedicatory to *De corpore*: 'I know that that part of philosophy wherein are considered lines and figures, has been delivered to us notably improved by the ancients; and withal a most perfect pattern of the logic by which they were able to find out and demonstrate such excellent theorems as they have done. I know also that the hypothesis of the earth's diurnal motion was the invention of the ancients; but that both it, and astronomy, that is, celestial physics, I think is not to be derived from farther time than from Nicolaus Copernicus; who in the age next

and the knowledge of the social body derived from a theory of history. Medicine and history thus make up the third kind of knowledge. Both in the case of medicine and in the case of history, the knowledge of general laws has the function of accounting for that form of individuality *par excellence* that is sickness, understood in its own sense and in a metaphorical sense, that is, in reference to the social body.

Taking up a long tradition whose origins lie with Thucydides and Aristotle, Machiavelli strongly emphasises the parallelism between medicine and politics, both in *Discourses on Livy* III, 1 (where we find the comparison between the sickness of the human body and the social body that Spinoza cites in *TP* X, 1) and in *The Prince*, where he writes:

> For the Romans did in these cases what all wise princes should do: they not only have to have regard for present troubles but also for future ones, and they have to avoid these with all their industry because, when one foresees from afar, one can easily find a remedy for them but when you wait until they come close to you, the medicine is not in time because the disease has become incurable. And it happens with this as the physicians say of consumption, that in the beginning of the illness it is easy to cure and difficult to recognize, but in the progress of time, when it has not been recognized and treated in the beginning, it becomes easy to recognize but difficult to cure.[18]

preceding the present revived the opinion of Pythagoras, Aristarchus and Philolaus. After him, the doctrine of the motion of the earth being now received, and a difficult question thereupon arising concerning the descent of heavy bodies, Galileus in our time striving with that difficulty, was the first that opened to us the gate of natural philosophy universal, which is the knowledge of the nature of *motion*. So that neither can the age of natural philosophy be reckoned higher then to him. Lastly, the science of *man's body*, the most profitable part of science, was first discovered with admirable sagacity by our countryman Doctor Harvey, principal Physician to King James and King Charles, in his Books of the *Motion of the Blood* and of the *Generation of Living Creatures*' (Hobbes 1839: vii–viii).

[18] *The Prince* III; Machiavelli 1985: 12. Cf. also the introduction to the *Leviathan*, where Hobbes compares the state to the human body and defines sedition as its sickness and civil war as its death (Hobbes 1994: 3). Gerbier claims that 'it is from medicine that Machiavelli borrows some of the lexical, syntactic and conceptual structures that allow him to think the historical crisis he is dealing with' (Gerbier 1999: 313). In this regard, the theory of humours is essential, which allows Machiavelli to construct a dynamic model of the division of the political body: 'medicine is the means for constructing a regulated description of troubles and divisions' (Gerbier 1999: 388).

Spinoza explicitly takes up this parallelism when he defines what it means for the state to violate the laws.

We have already noted that Spinoza never explicitly mentions the singular objects through which intuitive science forms an adequate idea in us. However, perhaps he has furnished an implicit model of this type of knowledge, which has remained invisible to the eyes of critics. Louis Althusser first advanced the hypothesis that *TTP* XVII and XVIII provide an example of the intuitive knowledge of the history of the Hebrew people insofar as it is a singular object.[19] In other words, given that nature does not produce peoples but individuals,[20] these chapters perhaps provide intuitive knowledge of the structure of society, institutions, laws and customs as the aleatory encounter of this structure with external happenings, that is, with fortune. It is an extraordinary analysis of the development of a clinical case, from birth to death, with particular attention to the sickness that provoked its death. Étienne Balibar's hypothesis that Spinoza would have written this history of the Hebrew people with the *Discourses on Livy* on his desk is not surprising.[21] I would add that this was, in Spinoza's eyes, the only example of the third kind of knowledge concerning the history of the Roman people.

However, such knowledge can never be the fruit of a direct narrative from history, but must be a 'second-order narrative'.[22] The first level, theological-political imagination, which organises facts according to a teleological design, imposes a moral significance on them, which is not the necessary foundation for the adequate knowledge of singular things. This knowledge cannot be achieved unless one starts from a critical re-elaboration of this foundation through the tools provided by the knowledge of the common properties of the social body, that is, through *ratio*. Both Machiavelli and Spinoza restore (or better, make us see adequately for the first time) two singular objects: the history of the Roman people and the

---

[19] Althusser writes: 'the famous "three kinds" appear very strange when you look at them close up, because the first is properly the lived world, and the last is specially suited to grasping the "singular essence" or what Hegel would in his language have called the "concrete universal" – of the Jewish people, which is heretically treated in the *Theological-Political Treatise*' (Althusser 1990: 224, translation modified).

[20] *TTP* XVII, 93; CWS II, 317.

[21] Balibar 1997b: 181.

[22] Balibar writes: 'That is why a science of history must be a second-order narrative – as Spinoza would say, a "critical history" (*TTP*, 141, 161). It will take as its object both the necessary sequence of events, in so far as it can be reconstructed, and the way in which historical agents, who are for the most part unaware of the causes influencing their actions, imagine the "meaning" of their history' (Balibar 1998: 37).

history of the Hebrew people.[23] They do this by reworking a story of Livy's,[24] on the one hand, and a biblical story, on the other, through the instruments of reason. Indeed, just as Machiavelli brings out the imaginary status of Plutarch's judgement regarding the fortune of the Romans, Spinoza demonstrates the imaginary status of the election of the Hebrews. Both produce the material causes and relations of force that are at the origin of the duration of the two states. Effectual truth does not therefore follow from a direct gaze at reality,[25] from the always youthful myth of being able to see, by means of a magical capacity of suspending judgement, *the things themselves*. Rather, effectual truth is the effect of a second-order reading that lets the facts and their relations emerge through the critical work of reason on the narrative passed down from these histories.

From the Concept of *series* to the Concept of *connexio*

In the previous section, I suggested that the causes that allow knowledge to open up a path within the dense forest of teleological prejudice are the mathematical sciences, physics and the theory of history and politics. The essential category of the second kind of knowledge is the category of cause; it constitutes the linchpin around which the general framework of the world is built, and is what allows for the formulation of necessary and universal laws that confer determinacy on it. To know in an adequate way means to

[23] Strauss affirms this explicitly: 'Livy's history is Machiavelli's Bible' (Strauss 1987: 307).

[24] Anselmi has emphasised the fact that in the *Discourses on Livy*, Machiavelli invents a new literary type and a new style: 'So it happens that in the *Discourses on Livy* the "comment", heavy with honours and glory in the medieval and Renaissance universities and in the academic philosophies and philologies of the ancient world, *we see a break in the rigid separateness that was canonical between text and gloss, such that it is constituted as a reflection, a continuous dialogue, a hermeneutic risk of great depth, in which the knowing series of Machiavelli-as-reader and Livy-as-text are no longer discrete, but, in a revolutionary way, contaminated*. So that the text that Machiavelli proposes to his readers is actually the result of an acrobatic combination of various levels of reading, whose constitutive point is precisely given by that particular "comment" of Machiavelli to Livy' (Machiavelli 1993: viii). Cf. also Dionisotti 1980: 258.

[25] This idea is at the root of Gallicet Calvetti's reading in *Spinoza lettore di Machiavelli* (1972). She suggests that there is an aporia between two methodologies in dealing with the political domain. On the one hand, there would be a deduction of politics from metaphysics, and on the other, a realistic consideration of human nature. In other words, Gallicet Calvetti constructs a methodological antinomy between *mos geometricus* and *verità effettuale*. In my view, instead, *mos geometricus* is precisely that which constructs the space of intelligibility for *verità effettuale*.

know through cause [*scire per causas*], as Aristotle claimed. What we must now interrogate is whether the category of cause remains the same in the different theoretical fields where the second kind of knowledge is applied according to the hypothesis we have formulated.

It is possible to find a response to this problem in the preface to *Ethics* III which, for its explosive power, has become the very symbol of Spinoza's theoretical endeavour:

> My reason is this: nothing happens in nature which can be attributed to any defect in it, for nature is always the same, and its virtue and power of acting are everywhere one and the same, i.e., the laws and rules of nature, according to which all things happen, and change from one form to another, are always and everywhere the same. So the way [*ratio*] of understanding the nature of anything, of whatever kind, must also be the same, viz. through the universal laws and rules of nature.
>
> The Affects, therefore, of hate, anger, envy, etc., considered in themselves, follow [*consequuntur*] from the same necessity and force of nature as the other singular things. And therefore they acknowledge certain causes, through which they are understood, and have certain properties, as worthy of our knowledge as the properties of any other thing, by the mere contemplation of which we are pleased. Therefore, I shall treat the nature and powers of the Affects, and the power of the Mind over them, by the same Method [*Methodus*] by which, in the preceding parts, I treated God and the Mind, and I shall consider human actions and appetites just as if it were a Question of lines, planes, and bodies [*ac si Quaestio de lineis, planis, aut de corporibus esset*].[26]

Spinoza's claim seems unequivocal: the theory of the passions makes use of the same category of causality utilised by mathematics and physics. An equivalence can be established between cause and premise, and between effect and consequence. Spinoza's expression *causa seu ratio* is therefore the tell-tale sign of an ontology dominated by a model of logical causality.

However, I will challenge this Spinozian claim by attempting to demonstrate that his confrontation with the historical-political field led him to produce a new conception of causality (which perhaps had a retroactive effect on his conception of physical causality).[27] For this we must turn

---

[26] *Ethics* III, Praef.; CWS II, 492.

[27] In this sense, Hans Jonas (1979) perfectly shows the originality of Spinozian physics within the theoretical horizon of his century. Cf. also Duchesnau 1978.

to Spinoza's earlier text, the *Treatise on the Emendation of the Intellect*, in order to analyse the theoretical constellation of the category of causality prior to Spinoza's encounter with the historical-political problematics of the *TTP*. The *TdIE* is known for being a methodological treatise, or better, to use Pierre Macherey's wonderful expression, the *TdIE* is a *discourse against method*.[28] This youthful sketch, left unfinished, contains several pages that are very important for outlining Spinoza's early ontology.[29] This ontology is the object of the fourth kind of knowledge, which has the characteristic of knowing a thing 'through its essence alone, or through knowledge of its proximate cause' [*per solam suam essentiam, vel per cognitionem suae proximae causae*].[30] In this way, if the thing is the cause of itself, it will be known through its own essence, and, if the thing requires a cause in order to exist, it must be known through its proximate cause. Therefore, in terms of real things, conclusions must not be drawn from abstract axioms, but rather from 'some particular affirmative essence, *or*, from a true and legitimate definition' [*ab essentia aliqua particulari affirmativa, sive a vera & legitima definitione*].[31] This entails the application of two rules for the relations of dependence of the properties on essence. The violation of either rule would undermine the concatenation [*concatenatio*][32] in the intellect that must refer [*referre debet*] to nature:

> If the thing is created, the definition, as we have said, will have to include the proximate cause. [. . .]
>
> We require a concept, or definition, of the thing such that when it is considered alone, without any others conjoined [*non cum aliis conjuncta*], all the thing's properties can be deduced from it.[33]

---

[28] Koyré magisterially interprets the spirit of the theoretical endeavour of this work: 'One does not begin from rules; one begins by thinking. One does not learn to swim on dry land, but is thrown into the water' (Spinoza 1984: xxi). For a bibliography on the *TdIE*, cf. Canone and Totaro 1991.

[29] Here I agree fully with Filippo Mignini, who has convincingly demonstrated that the *TdIE* is earlier than the *KV*. See Mignini 1979; Mignini 1983: 5–66; Mignini 1985; Mignini 1987; Mignini 1988. On the young writings of Spinoza, cf. *Studia Spinozana* 4 and *Revue des Sciences Philosophiques et Théologiques* 71.

[30] *TdIE* 19; *CWS* I, 13.

[31] *TdIE* 93; *CWS* I, 39.

[32] De Angelis translates *concatenatio* with *serie causale* (causal series), which respects if not the letter, then at least the theoretical context of the term. See his translation in Spinoza 1962: 81.

[33] *TdIE* 96; *CWS* I, 39–40.

At this point, it is possible to confront the long passage wherein Spinoza traces the fundamental framework of his ontology by starting from the problem of the order of deduction:

> As for order [ordo], to unite and order all our perceptions [ut omnes nostrae perceptiones ordinetur & uniatur], it is required, and reason demands, that we ask, as soon as possible, whether there is a certain being, and at the same time, what sort of being it is, which is the cause of all things [omnium rerum causa], so that its objective essence may also be the cause of all our ideas [causa omnium nostrarum idearum], and then our mind will (as we have said) reproduce Nature as much as possible. For it will have Nature's essence, order, and unity [essentia, ordo, & unio] objectively.
>
> From this we can see that above all it is necessary for us always to deduce all our ideas from Physical things, or from the real beings, proceeding, as far as possible, according to the series of causes [secundum seriem causarum], from one real being to another real being, in such a way that we do not pass over to abstractions and universals, neither inferring something real from them, nor inferring them from something real. For to do either interferes with the true progress [verus progressus] of the intellect.
>
> But note that by the series of causes and of real beings I do not here understand the series of singular, changeable things [series rerum singularium mutabilium], but only the series of fixed and eternal things [series rerum singularium fixarum aeternarumque]. For it would be impossible for human weakness to grasp the series of singular, changeable things, not only because there are innumerably many of them, but also because of the infinite circumstances [circumstantiae] in one and the same thing, any of which can be the cause of its existence or nonexistence. For their existence has no connection [connexio] with their essence, or (as we have already said) is not an eternal truth.
>
> But there is also no need for us to understand their series. The essences of singular, changeable things are not to be drawn from their series, or order of existing [ab earum serie sive ordine existendi], since it offers nothing but extrinsic denominations, relations, or at most, circumstances [denominationes extrinsecae, relationes, aut ad summum circumstantias], all of which are far from the inmost essence of things [intima essentia rerum]. That essence is to be sought only from fixed and eternal things, and at the same time from the laws inscribed in these things, as in their true codes [a legibus in iis rebus, tanquam in suis veris codicubus, inscriptis], according to which all singular things come to be, and are ordered. Indeed these singular, changeable things depend so intimately, and (so to speak) essentially,

on the fixed things that they can neither be nor be conceived without them. So although these fixed and eternal things are singular, nevertheless, because of their presence everywhere, and most extensive power, they will be to us like universals, *or* genera of the definitions [*universalia, sive genera definitionum*] of singular, changeable things, and the proximate causes of all things [*cauae proximae omnium rerum*].

But since this is so, there seems to be a considerable difficulty in our being able to arrive at knowledge of these singular things. For to conceive them all at once is a task far beyond the powers of the human intellect. But to understand one before the other, the order must be sought, as we have said, not from their series of existing, nor even from the eternal things. For there, by nature, all these things are at once [*simul natura*].[34]

This passage is very obscure,[35] and precisely for this reason it is difficult to resist the temptation to interpret it in light of the *Ethics*.[36] The identification of the level of *res fixae aeternaeque* in Spinoza's ontology causes a problem: these fixed things have been interpreted as attributes, as natural laws, as science's object, and as mathematical essences. None of these hypotheses are truly satisfactory, and perhaps we must recognise, as Piero Di Vona has argued, that 'asking what the *res fixae aeternaeque* and the laws and rules inscribed within them are does not have much significance, since Spinoza has not determined them in the *TdIE*, and there are good reasons to think that this is not simply due to the status of the text'. Indeed, he adds, 'Spinoza does not have an account or method of specifying what the unchangeable

---

[34] *TdIE* 99–102; CWS I, 41–2.

[35] As Joachim writes in his commentary on the *TdIE*: 'Of some passages in these last four pages of the text no interpretation can be more than conjectural. They bristle with difficulties and obscurities of detail, which the available evidence cannot enable the interpreter to elucidate completely or to solve' (Joachim 1940: 212).

[36] Mignini emphasises the difference between the *TdIE* and the works that follow it in terms that are decisive for the path I chart in this chapter: 'In the *TdIE*, the distinction between *Natura naturans* and *Natura naturata* is missing, but recurs in *Metaphysical Thoughts* and the *Ethics*. In at least six passages from the *TdIE*, one reads that the soul, in order to reproduce the exemplar of Nature, must deduce all of its ideas from the *ens perfectissimum* or God, considered as the cause of Nature. [. . .] It is a fact that in the *TdIE*, God is understood exclusively as first cause and that Nature is understood as his effect (a totality external to its effects, ruled by necessary and unchanging laws)' (Mignini 1987: 19–20). The difference that I stress, with respect to the finite, between the concept of *series* and the concept of *connexio* has its perfect correspondence, with respect to the infinite, with God understood as first cause and God understood as immanent cause.

and eternal realities are'; it is sufficient that they 'determine the kinds of reality which must lead to knowledge'.[37]

I will therefore try to isolate and emphasise the key elements of this lengthy passage in themselves, without forcing them into what would amount to an imaginary and atemporal Spinozian system. First, we can distinguish three ontological levels that Spinoza differentiates with precision:[38]

1. The level of the uncreated thing [res increata], the most perfect being [ens perfectissimum] or God.
2. The level of fixed and eternal things that are conceived as causal series of physical things or real beings [enti].
3. Finally, the level of singular things which undergo change, whose existence is due to circumstances.

Further, we can consider two elements of Spinoza's problematic in the TdIE as fundamental. First, the concept of definition, as an instrument of the knowledge of fixed and eternal things in their self-referential unity (which bars off any determination originating from external objects, and therefore is like an originary monad); and second, the concept of series, which relates these unities in causal terms as having the form of linear succession. In this way, to use Leibnizian terminology, the domain of fixed and eternal things is that of the truths of reason (which equally concerns the necessary thing, i.e., God, and impossible things, such as chimeras),[39] while the domain of singular things and things subject to change is that of the truths of fact. It is not an accident that in the TdIE, the fourth kind of knowledge is knowledge of eternal truths, which have as their object eternal things expressed in propositions whose contraries are impossible, whereas in the Ethics intuitive knowledge will be knowledge of the essence of singular things.[40] In this

---

[37] Di Vona 1960: 56. Cf. also Roland Callois's reflections in Spinoza 1954: 1403.

[38] See part two in Di Vona 1969.

[39] In note u of the TdIE, Spinoza writes: 'By an eternal truth I mean one which, if it is affirmative, will never be able to be negative. Thus it is a first and eternal truth that God is; but that Adam thinks is not an eternal truth. That there is no chimera is an eternal truth, but not that Adam does not think' (TdIE 54; CWS I, 24). The Ethics demonstrates a change in perspective with respect to this distinction, because the possible loses its ontological status and is only considered epistemologically: it is indeed nothing other than inadequate knowledge of the necessary connection of all things.

[40] Ethics V, 36; CWS I, 612–13. My interpretation thus stands in opposition to Joachim: 'The knowledge which is our aim – the knowledge of which Spinoza is setting forth the method – is not ratio, but scientia intuitiva' (Joachim 1940: 225). Joachim's error lies in a totally acritical superimposition of two distinct moments in the development of Spinoza's thought.

sense, the reason Spinoza gives in the *TdIE* for why singular things cannot be known is crucial:

> The essences of singular, changeable things are not to be drawn from their series, *or* order of existing, since it offers *nothing but extrinsic denominations, relations, or at most, circumstances,* all of which are far from the inmost essence of things. That essence is to be sought only from fixed and eternal things, and at the same time from the laws inscribed in these things, as in their true codes, according to which all singular things come to be, and are ordered.[41]

We are thus faced with a double-series: the series of singular things, subject to change, and the series of fixed and eternal things. The knowledge of singular things demands bracketing 'the order of existence, which is nothing but extrinsic denominations, relations, or at most, circumstances' (everything that is far removed from the inmost essence of things), in favour of the series of fixed and eternal things and the laws inscribed in them, which are genuine codes that regulate the becoming of things subject to change.[42] Spinoza therefore establishes a strict separation between the necessary, that is, the series of fixed and eternal things and their laws which comprise the inmost essence of singular things, and the contingent, which is the series of singular things subject to change, whose existential order is the effect of extrinsic relations and circumstances. The latter is not given by a science of the contingent, but only a science of the necessary.[43] Consequently, there can be no scientific knowledge of history and politics, because they are inclined to the sphere of relations and circumstances.

[41] *TdIE* 101; *CWS* I, 41. My emphasis. Translator's note: The entire passage is quoted in Latin in the original. It reads as follows: *Siquidem rerum singularium mutabilium essentiae non sunt depromendae ab earum serie, sive ordine existendi; cum hic nihil aliud nobis praebeat praeter denominationes extrinsecas, relationes, aut ad summum circumstantias; quae omnia longe absunt ab intima essentia rerum. Haec vero tantum est petenda a fixis, atque aeternis rebus, & simul a legibus in iis rebus, tanquam in suis veris codicibus, inscriptis, secundum quas omnia singularia, & fiunt, & ordinantur.*

[42] Bernard Rousset's reconstruction of the etymology of the term 'codex' is extremely interesting: 'In juridical Latin, the word *codex* means woodblock, then register, account book, and finally statute book. Afterwards, in religious language, it was traditionally used in order to designate the book in which the laws that are the divine word were written' (Spinoza 1992: 398).

[43] With this doctrine Spinoza, as Rousset notes, 'takes up and legitimates the Aristotelian thesis, contorted by the Scholastics, that "there is no general science" and prepares the Kantian thesis of the universality of the law in the necessity of causal relation: such is his philosophy of a "concrete universal", the foundation of all science' (Spinoza 1992: 401).

The conclusion we can draw from this hazy sketch of Spinoza's early ontology, independently of the interpretation provided of the nature of fixed and eternal things, is that what is decisive is the concept of series that Spinoza uses in order to represent the necessary order of the concatenation of the inmost essences of things. Although commentators have for the most part not focused on it,[44] the concept of series[45] is not epistemologically neutral: it is rather the symptom of a logical-mathematical contortion of ontology, namely, that things conceived as fixed and eternal monads possess the necessary relations that derive entirely from their inmost essence.[46] Reality thus finds its principle of order in the necessity that springs from the series of fixed and eternal things, the intelligible nucleus of singular things whose existence in turn offers nothing but aleatory and accidental relations unable to be the object of an adequate knowledge.

According to Mignini's quite convincing hypothesis, the drafting of the *TdIE* can be dated around the years 1658–59.[47] Proietti opts for an earlier date around 1656–57.[48] In any case, what is important for my claim is that the *TdIE* comes before the historical-political studies that Spinoza took up at the beginning of the 1660s and which flow into the project of the *TTP*. My hypothesis is as follows: Spinoza's encounter with the field of history and politics, and in particular with Machiavellian theory, compelled him to redefine, in the final draft of the *Ethics* between 1670 and 1675, his theory of knowledge, and more specifically the fundamental category in the second

[44] In his analysis of Spinoza interpretations in the German Enlightenment, Zac claims: 'With Spinoza the very notion of "series" is difficult' (Zac 1989: 62). As far as I am aware, the first strong emphasis on the inadequacy of the concept of series in light of Spinoza's *Ethics* (and, symmetrically, the concept of a set) is Diodato 1990a. Cf. also Diodato 1990b; Diodato 1994; Diodato 1997.

[45] The *TdIE*'s index points out another occurrence of the concept of series, much less relevant to the ontological level: 'Note that I here take the trouble only to enumerate the sciences necessary for our purpose, without attending to their series' [*seriem*] (*TdIE* 14; *CWS* I, 11). Translation modified.

[46] Joachim describes the logical-ontological horizon of the *TdIE* with precision: 'In the chain which constitutes our knowledge, every true idea (or link) will be a definition. It will define a singular member of "the series of causes and real things": i.e. it will state the inmost essence of a "created thing" – an effect of the First Cause. And every logical implication (or linkage) will reflect the bond really (i.e. essentially) uniting a singular "created thing" to its neighbour in the uniquely graded descent of a singular "created thing" or effects from the First Cause – in the eternal hierarchy or scale of their dependence as modes of Natura Naturata, upon the Absolute Individual' (Joachim 1940: 227).

[47] Mignini 1987: 19–20.

[48] Proietti 2001.

kind of knowledge, the category of cause. One fact, confirmed by the index of the *Ethics*, is that the term *series* completely disappears from the work, while the term *ordo* remains one of the central linchpins of Spinoza's ontology.[49] This is a first clue that the equivalence between order and series,[50] central to the description of the model of causality of the *TdIE* and therefore its fundamental ontological structure, cannot be imposed on the model of causality that Spinoza advances in the *Ethics*; the reason that this is impossible can be found in Spinoza's immersion in historical-political problematics at the time he was writing the *TTP*.

The potential objection that the mere absence of a word does not mean the absence of the concept seems corroborated by *Ethics* I, 28, which offers a model of transitive, and therefore serial, causality:

> Every singular thing, or any thing which is finite and has a determinate existence, can neither exist nor be determined to produce an effect unless it is determined to exist and produce an effect by another cause, which is also finite and has a determinate existence; and again, this cause also

---

[49] The only occurrence of *series* is found in *Ethics* I, 33 Schol. 2: 'Verum neque etiam dubito, si rem meditari vellent, nostrarumque demonstrationum seriem rectè perpendere' ['But I have no doubt that, if they are willing to reflect on the matter, and consider properly the series of our demonstrations . . .'] (*Ethics* I, 33 Schol. 2; *CWS* I, 437, translation modified). An analogous use of series can be found in Descartes' *Principles of Philosophy* (AT VIII, 328; Descartes 1985: 290). Cf. Meschini 1996: 251.

[50] The hendiadys *ordo et series* is found in Bacon's *The New Organon* in both paragraphs 39 and 59 of part one, and in both cases refers to the order of particular things of which the method must teach respect against the distortions produced by *idols*. Regarding the two ontological levels of the *TdIE*, recall this passage from Bacon on the distinction between physics and metaphysics: 'let the investigation of Forms, which are (in the eye of reason at least and in their essential law) eternal and immutable, constitute *Metaphysics*. And let the investigation of the Efficient Cause and of Matter, and of the Latent Process, and the Latent Configuration (all of which have reference to the common and ordinary cause of nature, not to her eternal and fundamental laws [*quae omnia cursum naturae communem et ordinarium, non leges fundamentales et aeternas respiciunt*]) constitute *Physics*' (Bacon 1999: 154). For other Baconian traces present in the *TdIE*, see Mignini 1997: 121–3. In Descartes, on the contrary, the hendiadys *ordo et series* is absent from both the *Rules for the Direction of the Mind* and the *Discourse on Method*. Cf. Armogather and Marion 1976; Cahné 1977. In the *Meditations*, Descartes speaks about the 'order and connection of my arguments' [*rationum mearum series et nexus*] (AT VII, 9; Descartes 1985: 8, translation modified), which refers to the analytic order of his philosophising, and to the 'continuous chain of events' [*continuata rerum series*] as a possible alternative to chance and fate which makes him 'the kind of creature that I am' [*ad id quod sum*] (AT VII, 21; Descartes 1985: 14). Cf. Marion 1996.

can neither exist nor be determined to produce an effect unless it is determined to exist and produce an effect by another, which is also finite and has a determinate existence, and so on, to infinity.[51]

The linear and horizontal series of finite causality thus seems juxtaposed with the vertical and immanent causality of God expressed in *Ethics* I, 18: 'God is the immanent, not the transitive [*non vero transiens*], cause of all things.'[52] However, to conceive immanent and transitive causality as two distinct causalities would be a very superficial way of reading *Ethics* I. Spinoza himself reminds us of the inseparability of the two planes of causality in *Ethics* I, 28 Schol.[53] Thinking immanent causality and transitive causality not as two orders of causality, but rather as the same order, means avoiding, on the one hand, immanence as the spiritual expression of the whole in the part, and on the other, transitivity as a mechanistic sequence of cause and effect.[54] The radical thought of immanent causality prohibits conceiving finite causality in a serial way, because the theoretical constellation that it necessarily brings with itself destroys the constitutive elements required for the functioning of transitive causality: the concept of the individual, a singular thing, loses the simplicity and unity that in the *TdIE* conferred on it its inmost essence. It yields to the complexity of a proportional relation in which essence does not differ from power, that is, its capacity to enter into relations with the outside (the more complex relations, the more the individual is powerful).[55] Cause therefore loses the simple relation of indictment with its effect in order to gain the structural plurality of complex relations with the outside.[56] All of these elements were excluded as inessential for the

---

[51] *Ethics* I, 28; CWS I, 432

[52] *Ethics* I, 18; CWS I, 428.

[53] *Ethics* I, 28 Schol.; CWS I, 432–3.

[54] Cf. Macherey 1992: 101; Balibar 1990: 69.

[55] See Zourabichvili 1994: 88–9.

[56] In a very interesting essay, Balibar uses Simondon's concepts in order to explain the Spinozist model of causality: 'the infinite connection does not take *the form of an independent linear series*, or genealogies of causes and effects (A "causes" B which "causes" C which etc.): it typically takes *the form of an infinite network of singular modi*, or existences, a dynamic unity of modulating/modulated activities (the action of B upon any A is itself modulated by some Cs, which is itself modulated by some Ds, etc.'. In this sense, a comparison with the Kantian schema of causality perfectly highlights the originality of the Spinozist model: 'Just as Kant, Spinoza has one and the same general scheme to explain the physical or causal order and the ethical or practical order. In Kant this is the *scheme of succession*, in Spinoza the *scheme of modulation* (using Simondon's terminology). But contrary to Kant, Spinoza's scheme is not intended to

adequate knowledge of singular things in the *TdIE*. It is barely an exaggeration to say that the essence–existence relation is inverted after the *TdIE*: the essence of things now resides in the accomplished fact of the relations and circumstances that produced this existence. In other words, the essence of a thing is only conceivable *post festum*, that is, uniquely on the basis of the fact of its existence, or more precisely, on the basis of its power of acting which reveals its true *interiority*. The barrier between interior (*essentia intima*) and exterior (*circumstantia*, or what surrounds it) is torn down; power is precisely the regulated relation of an exterior and an interior that is constituted in the relation itself.

At this point along our path it is necessary to highlight the emergence of a new term, which Spinoza employs for the first time in the *TTP* but which will only become fundamental in the *Ethics*:[57] *connexio*. The first occurrence of this term is in the famous proposition *Ethics* II, 7. Its absence from *Ethics* I is not at all by chance: Spinoza uses it in order to designate the relations between things after establishing the plane of immanence and the univocity of being.[58]

> *oppose* both orders, one being the inversion of the others (in Kant a causal order is a linear determination *ex post*; a final order is a linear determination *ex ante*, which operates by means of a representation of the goal or intention). It is intended to identify them, "practice" being a modulation in the same way as an individual causality (and therefore, ultimately, "freedom" being not the *reversal* of the natural order, but the necessary expression of its active side)' (Balibar 1997a: 14–15, my emphasis).

[57] Actually, there is an occurrence of this term in the *TdIE*, which is entirely different than the meaning it will take on in the *Ethics*. Spinoza uses it to negate the *connexio* of the existence and essence of singular things (*TdIE* 100; *CWS* I, 41). Cf. Canone and Totaro 1991: 46. In Descartes, the term is used as a synonym for the causal chain, which is not surprising given that, as Francesca Bonicalzi writes, causality takes on 'a semantic value very close to the notion of reason, and in this sense causality becomes equivalent to the deductive structure of geometry' (Bonicalzi 1997: 150). In particular, in the *Rules for the Direction of the Mind*, we find an equivalence between *connexio* and a long chain (*AT* X, 369–70, 389; Descartes 1985: 15, 26). In the same work Descartes refers to the *connexio* between the parts of a human body. In *Principles of Philosophy*, the term *connexio* is used only once as an equivalent to *necessaria conjunctio*, regarding the absence of such a link between the vessel and the body that it contains in the context of an argument attempting to deny the hypothesis of the void (*AT* VIII, 50; Descartes 1985: 230–1). Cf. Meschini 1996: 47. Gilead rightly notes that in Spinoza instead, 'the order and the connection of things are not constructed mathematically-deductively [. . .], and his "book of Nature" is not inscribed in geometrical characters' (Gilead 1985: 77).

[58] On the link between univocity and immanence as opposed to the neoplatonic tradition, see Deleuze's extraordinary 'Immanence and the Historical Components of Expression', in Deleuze 1992: 169–86.

The *order and connection* of ideas is the same as the *order and connection* of things [*Ordo, & connexio idearum idem est, ac ordo, & connexio rerum*].[59]

And in the corollary to the same proposition, Spinoza writes:

From this it follows that God's power of thinking is equal to his actual power of acting. I.e., whatever follows formally from God's infinite nature follows objectively in God from his idea in the same order and with the same connection [*eodem ordine, eademque connexione*].[60]

And again in the scholium:

Whether we conceive nature under the attribute of Extension, or under the attribute of Thought, or under any other attribute, we shall find one and the same order, or one and the same connection of causes [*reperiemus unum eudemque ordinem, sive unam, eandemque causarum connexionem*], i.e., that the same things follow one another.[61]

The index for the *Ethics* alerts us to nineteen other occurrences of the hendiadys *ordo et connexio*, which are not useful to cite here, since they are repetitions of *Ethics* II, 7.[62] An examination of the lexicon therefore clearly indicates that we have passed from the equation *ordo* = *series* in the *TdIE* to the equation *ordo* = *connexio* in the *Ethics*.[63] In both cases, the second

---

[59] *Ethics* II, 7; CWS I, 451. My emphasis. Balibar proposes translating 'the practically indecomposable expression "*ordo et connexio*" [. . .] with "order of connection" [*ordre de connexio*], thereby exploiting a classic figure of Latin grammar' (Balibar 1990: 71). In another article, Balibar proposes the translation of *ordo et connexio idearum* with 'syntax of ideas' [*syntaxe des idées*] (Balibar 1992b: 18). Balibar's proposal is very interesting, especially if we consider the fact that even Joseph Moreau, in a popularising work on Spinoza, interprets the proposition through the concept of a parallel series: 'The modes of thought and modes of extension are linked by the same order, forming two rigorously parallel series' (Moreau 1971: 41).

[60] *Ethics* II, 7 Cor.; CWS I, 451.

[61] Ibid.

[62] CWS I, 690. Cf. also Giancotti 1970: 216. The only occurrence of the term *connexio* beyond the hendiadys with *ordo* can be found in the definition of wonder [*admiratio*]: 'wonder is an imagination of a thing in which the Mind remains fixed because this singular imagination has no connection with the others' [*quia haec singularis imaginatio nullam cum reliquis habet connexionem*] (*Ethics* III, DA 4; CWS I, 532).

[63] Macherey proposes some interpretative nuances in the meaning of the *ordo* and *connexio*: 'As the text hardly provides the means of explaining the meaning of the

term is clearly determinant, while the first term only has the function of freeing itself from the semantic field of the Greek term *cosmos*,[64] that is, from allowing the thinking of an ontological order independent from a moral and aesthetic weave. We have earlier analysed the semantic memory of the term *series* and its reference to a logical-mathematical horizon. It is now necessary to account for the conceptual difference introduced by the term *connexio*. This term derives from the Latin *connectere*, composed of *cum* and *nectere*, which means interweaving [*intrecciare*].[65] Spinoza thus develops a conception of causality as a complex weave in the *Ethics*: the textile metaphor indeed evokes anything but the straight line of the cause–effect series. The knowledge of the essence of each individual thus passes through the knowledge of this complex weave. This knowledge could not be reached by excluding relations and circumstances from consideration, in the vain hope of achieving, through a correct definition, the inmost essence of things.

According to the hypothesis I have advanced, it is the encounter with politics and history that forced Spinoza to redefine the concept of causality. And, indeed, the first occurrence of *ordo et connexio* in Spinoza's work is precisely in relation to the biblical hermeneutic, at the outset of chapter nine in the *TTP*, when he tries to demonstrate that Ezra, author of the Pentateuch and the books Joshua, Judges, Ruth, Samuel, and 1 and 2 Kings, has done nothing but choose narratives, transmitting them to posterity without either examining them or putting them in order.[66] This is something that clearly follows from the few remaining fragments of ancient Hebrew narratives, according to Spinoza. Here is the passage:

juxtaposition of these two terms, we can propose, without reservation, the following interpretation: the former notion corresponds to the point of view of the infinite immediate modes, which is to say that it considers absolutely in its entirety, without going into detail, all that, at one stroke, follows from the nature of God considered as such or as his attribute; the latter corresponds to the point of view of the infinite mediate mode, which takes into consideration the totality of its particular internal concatenations as these were described once and for all by *Ethics* I, 28, and which confer on *connexio* the characteristics that belong to a *concatenatio*' (Macherey 1997: 75). Regarding Macherey's identification of *connexio* and *concatenatio*, I refer to my analysis that follows.

[64] For more on this context, cf. Morfino 2000.

[65] Glare 1982: 1166.

[66] 'Ezra [. . .] did not put the narratives contained in these books in final form, and did not do anything but collect the narratives from different writers, sometimes just copying them, and that he left them to posterity without having examined or ordered them' (*TTP* IX, 2; *CWS* II, 206).

There is no doubt that if we had these Historians, this conclusion would be established directly. But because, as I've said, we have been deprived of them, the only thing remaining for us is to examine the histories [which have survived]: their *order and connection*, the variations in their repetitions, and finally, the discrepancy in the computation of years [*nempe earum ordinem & connexionem, variam repetitionem, & denique in annorum computatione discrepantiam*].[67]

Not only is the Old Testament unthinkable as the effect of a first transcendent cause – of an author whose metaphysical unity is mirrored in the figure of Moses[68] – it is not even thinkable according to the linear sequence of the materiality of its writing, in which truth and time run parallel. The order and connection, that is, the order of the connection, the complex and incoherent weave of the narratives of the biblical books, demonstrates the imaginary status of this 'pretence' of linear sequence that imitates the flowing forth of the word of God from his mouth, the voice of God that makes scripture. It is thus on this field of study that the logical-mathematical ontology of the *TdIE* begins to vacillate.

However, saying that the encounter with the historical-political horizon pushed Spinoza to change his theory is insufficient. I would suggest that his encounter with Machiavelli's theory of history was the fundamental impulse for Spinoza to modify his theory of causality; I do not say, in other words, that Machiavelli transferred to Spinoza in a transitive way his theory of causality (which is moreover only found in its analytic effects), but rather that the encounter between Spinoza's earlier ontology, the study of Hebrew history and biblical criticism, and Machiavellian theory produced a new ontology.

In chapter 2 I emphasised that it was Machiavelli's theory of history as the encounter between virtue and fortune that enabled Spinoza to deconstruct the Hebrew illusion of election in *TTP* III. We can now bring out a fundamental concept of Machiavelli's thought, which I earlier left in the shadows: the concept of occasion [*occasione*]. According to Ludovico Ariosto, occasion covers the semantic field of happening [*avvenimento*] circumstance [*circostanza*] and situation [*situazione*],[69] and derives from the Latin *ob-cadere*,

---

[67] *TTP* IX, 7; CWS II, 207. My emphasis.

[68] After all, the fact that Moses was not the author of the Pentateuch had already been expressed by La Peyrère and by Hobbes, who probably frequented Paris. Cf. La Peyrère 1655. On the figure of La Peyrère, cf. Popkin 1979; on Hobbes's interpretation of scripture, cf. Pacchi 1998.

[69] Cortellazzo and Zolli 1985: 819.

that is, to fall forward, and from the supine *occasum*, or chance [*caso*] and happening [*avvenimento*]. In Machiavelli's political ontology, this concept precisely maintains the primacy of the relation of things over their inmost essence (to use the terminology of the *TdIE*), and the primacy of the aleatory over every theology or teleology of cause.[70] History is the field of occasions, of encounters that took hold or were missed, between virtue and fortune. It is in chapter six of *The Prince* that Machiavelli delivers his prodigious theory of history, thought as a complex and aleatory encounter:[71]

> To come to those who have become princes by their own virtue and not by fortune, I say that the most excellent are Moses, Cyrus, Romulus, Theseus, and the like. [. . .] As one examines their actions and lives, one does not see that they had anything else from fortune than the occasion, which gave them the matter enabling them to introduce any form they pleased. Without that occasion their virtue of spirit would have been eliminated, and without that virtue the occasion would have come in vain.[72]

A historical event such as the foundation of a state is therefore not the effect of a mythical first cause which is at the origin of a linear development of historical time (*ab urbe condita*), but instead the result of a complex and aleatory encounter between virtue and fortune in the form of an occasion, an

---

[70] 'The occasion is not the instant of a solitary becoming, but the instant complicated by a "polychronism", which is to say by the sporadicism and plurality of durations' (Jankélévitch 1980: 117).

[71] Esposito has very keenly emphasised Machiavelli's refusal of a model of 'linear and compact' reason: 'No reason is given, no project that does not discount in advance a productive relationship with its opposite: contingent, accidental circumstance.' Esposito sees the heart of this thesis expressed in the *Ghiribizzi* to Soderni (a letter from 1506), which historiography has understood as Machiavelli's lowest point of faith in the rationality of things and the possibility that humans can rule over them. It must be specified, according to Esposito, that 'the defeat of the humanistic project of dominating the world [. . .] results precisely with the incapacity of substituting a "simple reason", a "blocked expectation", pinned to the unilinear relation of "means" to "ends", or "cause" to "effect", with another that is more pliable and attentive to the complexity of the world and its infinite chances [*casi*]. [. . .] Between cause and effect is written a temporal variable that does not allow the direct passage from means to ends. On the contrary, this is a theoretical breakthrough [*conquista*] that Machiavelli will take care not to abandon or blur.' He concludes: 'Only when it puts down any pretext of integral visibility, and recognised spaces of opacity – the discontinuity that enriches experience – will modern reason be capable of extending its own project to the highest power' (Esposito 1984: 204–5).

[72] *The Prince* VI; Machiavelli 1985: 22–3. Translation modified.

encounter that can either give birth to a world or bring one to an end (as in the atomists,[73] beloved by both Machiavelli and Spinoza). We can see here the deconstruction of the imaginary first cause[74] in favour of a putting into relation of virtue and fortune, a complex weave of which virtue constitutes one part. This part must not be understood as a *pars totalis*, but rather as an intervention in a conjuncture, that is, an intervention into a given field of forces, which it neither fatalistically rejects nor teleologically succumbs to. The conjuncture is not the untranscendable horizon of virtue, but the effect of a conjugation between virtue and fortune, and thus something that can be modified thanks to new conjunctions:

> I indeed affirm it anew to be very true, according to what is seen through all the histories, that men can second fortune but not oppose it, that they can *weave its warp* but not break it. They should indeed never give up for, since they do not know its end and it proceeds by oblique and unknown ways, they have always to hope and, since they hope, not to give up in whatever fortune and in whatever travail they may find themselves.[75]

Machiavelli's metaphor, according to which human virtue can only 'weave the warp of fortune', cannot fail to return us to Spinoza's *connexio rerum* – to fortune as a complex, non-transitive causality,[76] which acts on different

---

[73] Here cf. Althusser 2006: 163–207.

[74] Regarding this claim, we can note that the expression 'first cause' [*causa prima*] in Machiavelli refers not to an *Ursache*, or an origin [*ursprungliche Sache*], but to a relation of forces – in Hegelian terms, a *Wechselwirkung*. Cf. the following passage from the *Discourses on Livy*: 'I say that to me it appears that those who damn the tumults between the nobles and the plebs blame those things that were the *first cause* of keeping Rome free, and that they consider the noises and the cries that would arise in such tumults more than the good effects that they engendered. They do not consider that in every republic are two diverse humors, that of the people and that of the great, and that all the laws that are made in favor of freedom arise from their disunion, as can easily be seen to have occurred in Rome' (*Discourses on Livy*, I, 4; Machiavelli 1996: 16, my emphasis). On the distinction between *Wechselwirkung* and *causa sui*, cf. Morfino 2014: 18–45.

[75] *Discourses on Livy* II, 29; Machiavelli 1996: 199.

[76] The concept of *fortuna* represented by the metaphor of the weave and the warp is opposed to the concept of fate, which is instead linked to the metaphor of the chain and the series. To give only a few examples, Cicero speaks of fate [*fatum*] as an 'eternal causal series' [*sempiterna causarum series*] in *On Fate*, and Campanella speaks of a 'long causal series' [*longa causarum series*] in a chapter on fate in his *Metaphysicorum dogmatum*, elsewhere defining it as '*causarum ordo a prima sapientia institutus*' (Campanella 1967: 329–33). The concept of *series* is also found in the definition of *fortuna* by the

levels, and to virtue understood as individual action, but also as a political institution or military organisation, which encounter each other through the occasion on the *Kampfplatz* of history. The latter is the only judge, not as in Hegel for whom 'world history is world judgment',[77] but in the sense of a radical negation of every consolation and every teleological legitimation of the past, opening on to the hope of the future without eschatological illusions. And this Machiavellian context allows us to better understand Spinoza's claim that 'necessity does not take away but gives freedom' [*necessitas non tollit sed ponit libertatem*], which must be interpreted not in the Hegelian-Marxist sense of the knowledge of necessity, but rather as the degree of power in the open and aleatory space of the conjuncture.

Time and Eternity between Nihilism and the Philosophy of Progress

As we know, after Kant the concept of causality is strictly linked to the concept of time.[78] In this section, I want to bring out the transformations of a Spinozist conception of temporality underlying the passage from a model of causality ordered by *series* to one ordered by *connexio*, a passage to all of the decisive effects in order to understand the action that reading Machiavelli has for Spinoza's theory.

In order to confront this controversial point, I believe it is necessary to pass through the interpretations of Spinoza in the German Spinoza Renaissance at end of the eighteenth century.[79] During the pantheism quarrel there indeed appeared some interpretative positions that make up veritable paradigms clarifying how the question of time and eternity comes to be read. In one of the most important passages of the account of his conversations with Lessing, Jacobi observes that in Spinoza, 'what we call consequence or duration is mere illusion' [*was wir Folge oder Dauer nennen, [ist] bloßer Wahn*]:

> For since a real effect is contemporary with the totality of its real cause, and is distinguished from it only in representation, consequence and duration must in truth only be a certain way of intuiting the manifold in the infinite.[80]

historian Saavedra: 'The series and eternal disposition of divine providence in human affairs is called fortune' (Saavedra 1681: 46).

[77] Hegel 2008: 316. Translation modified.

[78] Kant 1998: 271–7.

[79] For a bibliography of texts related to this argument, see Morfino 1998: 39–48.

[80] Jacobi 1994: 188. Translation modified.

Jacobi maintains that Spinoza developed two models of temporality: a logical temporality that supposes the contemporaneity [*Zugleichsein*] of parts in the infinite totality (the logic of immanent causality), and a mechanistic temporality that supposes the succession of cause and effect according to a serial order (the logic of transitive causality). Because of the pre-eminence of the principle of sufficient reason in Spinoza's system (characterised as a logical principle founded on the categories of ground [*Grund*] and consequent [*Folge*])[81] over the principle of causality (founded on the categories of cause [*Ursache*] and effect [*Wirkung*]), eternity would compress the entire past, present and future into an atemporal instant. Here is Jacobi's account:

> Hence the finite is in the infinite, so that the sum of all finite things, equally containing within itself the whole of eternity [*die ganze Ewigkeit*] at every moment [*in jedem Momente*], past, present, and future, is one and the same as the infinite thing itself.[82]

Thus, for Jacobi the series of causes that constitutes the rhythm of mechanistic temporality exists only as a human representation. What is actually there is a series of consequences [*Folgen*] that derive logically, and not temporally, from the first principle [*Grund*], because they are simultaneous (in order to understand the theoretical importance of such an interpretation, it is sufficient to remember that an entirely analogous position was maintained by Einstein in his meetings with Popper at Princeton in 1950, which earned him the nickname of Parmenides).[83]

---

[81] Schopenhauer claims that Spinoza had no clear concept of the difference between the conceptual pairs 'premise' and 'consequence' and 'cause' and 'effect' (Schopenhauer 2012: 17).

[82] Jacobi 1994: 217.

[83] Here is Popper's description of a conversation that he had with Einstein during which he tried to disprove Einstein's 'metaphysical determinism': 'I first tried to describe his own metaphysical determinism, and he agreed with my account of it. I called him "Parmenides", since he believed in a four-dimensional block-universe, unchanging like the three dimensional block-universe of Parmenides (the fourth dimension was time, of course). He completely agreed with my account of his views, and with the motion picture analogy: in the eyes of God, the film was just there, and the future was there as much as the past: nothing ever happened in this world, and change was a human illusion, as was also the difference between the future and the past' (Popper 1982: 90) Among the objections Popper raises to this kind of reason, this one stands out: 'If we were experiencing successive shots of an unchanging world, then one thing, at least, was genuinely changing in this world: our conscious experience. A motion picture film, although existing now, and predetermined, has to *pass*, to *move*, through the projector

The great defender of the Enlightenment, Moses Mendelssohn, while opposed to Jacobi's interpretation in its entirety, accepted this reading of temporality, proposing one slight correction: the substitution of the term illusion [*Wahn*], which to him seemed to suggest a too subjectivist character, with the term appearance [*Erscheinung*] (an objection that essentially corresponds with the position taken by Popper in his confrontation with Einstein). We find the following in an appendix to the 1 August 1784 letter from Mendelssohn to Jacobi:

> What you say about 'consequence' and 'duration' in this connection has my full assent, except that I would not say that they are mere 'illusion'. They are necessary determinations of restricted thought, and hence 'appearances' that must nonetheless be distinguished from mere 'illusion' [*also Erscheinungen, die man doch von bloßem Wahn unterscheiden muß*].[84]

A far more powerful defence of Spinoza's conception of temporality can be found in Herder's interpretation. Herder first emphasises the strict separation of intellect and imagination in Spinoza, and connects this separation to the difference between time and eternity:

> PHILOLAUS: It has cheered me up much more that he, deliberately ignoring the usual tedious discourses which have nothing philosophical about them, has correctly distinguished between time and eternity, the endless indeterminate [*Endlos-Unbestimmte*] and the infinite for itself [*das durch sich selbst Unendliche*]. The eternity of God cannot be explained through any duration or time [*Dauer oder Zeit*], even if they are supposed without end (indefinite). Duration is an indefinite continuation of existence [*eine unbestimmte Fortsetzung des Daseyns*] which, however, at each point brings along with itself the measure of transitoriness. It cannot be in any ways attributed to that which is not transitory or changeable.

(that is, relative to ourselves), in order to produce the experience, or the illusion, of temporal change. Similarly, we should have to move, relatively to the four-dimensional block-universe; for the conversion of our future into our past means a change for us. And since we are part of the world, there would thus be change in the world – which contradicts Parmenides' view' (Popper 1982: 91–2). Rensi uses precisely the metaphor of the film (together with the sentence of a novel) in order to explain the relationship between time and eternity in Spinoza which he outlines on a purely conceptual level: 'For Spinoza time does not appear in Being [. . .] In Being and concerning Being there does not exist a transversal section of a moment of the eternal presence, in which everything, all that there is (was, and will be) is concentrated' (Rensi 1993).

[84] Jacobi 2000: 185.

THEOPHRON: Is the world therefore not eternal, like God?

PHILOLAUS: It cannot be, because it is the world, which is a system of the duration of things, ordered among them by communion and through succession [*ein System der Dauer zu- und nach einander geordneter Dinge ist*], to none of which concerns absolute existence or unchangeable eternity without measure and temporal duration [*ohne Maas und Zeitendauer*].[85]

God therefore cannot be represented by the *idols* [*idola*] of space and time. God is pure force of which nothing else can be said than that it acts:

> The substances of the world are all supported by divine force [*von göttliche Kraft*], in such a way that they received their existence only through the divine force; they constitute, if you like, phenomena modified by divine forces, each according to the place, time and organs [*nach der Stelle, nach der Zeit, nach der Organen*] in which and with which they appear [*erscheinen*].[86]

According to Herder's interpretation of Spinoza, God, by virtue of his omnipotence, created all that is possible and this is found 'connected through space and time [*durch Raum und Zeit*], [. . .] according to that firmly established eternal order [*ewige Ordnung*], which is the very property and action of the infinite reality, and therefore rests on nothing less than its indivisible and eternal infinity'.[87]

Herder's interpretation of temporality in Spinoza radically rejects Jacobi's attempt to reduce succession to vain illusion. The order of all possible contemporaneities and all possible successions is God himself, who, as the spatio-temporal order of the real, cannot be measured either in terms of simultaneity (eternity understood as *tota simul* or as *nunc stans*), or in terms of succession (eternity understood as duration without beginning or end, i.e., as *sempiternitas*).

However, we must note that Herder's reading presumes a conception of time that is not Spinozist, but rather Leibnizian. This is not difficult to ascertain if we examine a passage from Leibniz's polemic with the Newtonian Clarke, which precisely hinged on the concepts of space and time. Leibniz writes the following in his third response to Clark:

---

[85] Herder 1967–68: 445.
[86] Herder 1967–68: 441.
[87] Herder 1967–68: 489.

As for my own opinion, I have said more than once that I hold space to be merely something relative, as time is, that I hold it to be an order of coexistences, as time is an order of successions.[88]

Herder introduces a relational theory of time as the order of successive things into Spinoza's thought, eliminating Leibniz's problematic of the mystery of incompossibility, and, with it, the mystery of divine transcendence. Such a theoretical move is not without significant consequences, however. Leibniz's theory of time implies the monadicity of the elements that enter into relation and the unicity of the spatio-temporal order of the world, which is nothing other than the order of nature and history, guaranteed by the divine intellect.[89]

* * *

This detour through the pantheism controversy clarifies the two extremes between which interpretations of temporality in Spinoza's thought oscillate. On the one hand, we have the annihilation of time in an eternal logical instant; on the other, the superimposing of the specificity of Spinoza's conception of temporality with a philosophy of progress rooted in the relational conception of Leibnizian time: logical determinism against historical determinism. Our analysis of the conceptual differences introduced by the term *connexio* as opposed to *series* allows us to demarcate Spinoza's theory of temporality from both of these interpretations, which far from being simple exercises of academic erudition, actually form two of the major lines of philosophical modernity. It is clear that in both cases the concept of series is fundamental for the coherence of the interpretation. For Jacobi, it allows him to inscribe Spinozian dyads into a perfect isomorphism between the pairs *Grund–Folge* and *Ursache–Wirkung*:[90] the logical *sequitur* and the

---

[88] Leibniz 1989: 324.

[89] 'The monads must be obedient in their development and life to an immanent law, to an internal principle that constitutes the concept of history. A history [. . .] which subsists in a general agreement with all of the various individual histories among them' (Mugnai 1976: 177).

[90] More recently, this position has been put forward by Bennett: 'Spinoza did not distinguish what is absolutely or logically necessary from what is merely causally necessary. In his way of thinking, there is a single relation of necessary connection, which links causes with effects in real causal chains and premises with conclusions in valid arguments' (Bennett 1996: 61). Macherey provides an implicit critique of this type of interpretation through several reflections on Spinoza's *mos geometricus*: 'This form of exposition, *which is more of a network* than a chain of reasons, *is consequently irreducible to a linear concatenation* which, starting from a cause given by the absolute, would

physical *sequitur* are one and the same, the sequence does not exist except in human representation, being always-already there from a logical point of view. The world is nothing other than the series of logical passages effected by an infinite deduction that in human knowledge takes the form of the illusion of temporal succession. In Herder, this concept allows him to establish a theory of temporality as the relation between worldly elements that develop according to a unique serial law [*lex seriei*] – the divine order – which constitutes the continuous and progressive order of history.

It is necessary to reconsider the fundamental elements of Spinoza's theory of temporality – time [*tempus*], duration [*duratio*] and eternity [*aeternitas*] – in order to analyse the links that bind them and the contexts in which they are used. In other words, we must, while building our interpretation, open up these elements in light of the difference between *series* and *connexio* by means of the weave of the materiality of Spinoza's text itself.

For this, an inescapable point of departure is Spinoza's 20 April 1663 letter to Meyer on the question of the infinite:

> Let me briefly explain these four concepts: Substance, Mode, Eternity, and Duration. The points I want you to consider about substance are: (i) that existence pertains to its essence, i.e., that from its essence and definition alone it follows that it exists (if my memory does not deceive me, I have previously demonstrated this to you in conversation, without the aid of any other Propositions); (ii), which follows from (i), that Substance is not multiple, but that there exists only one of the same nature; and finally, (iii) that every Substance can be understood only as infinite.
>
> I call the Affections of Substance Modes. Their definition, insofar as it is not the very definition of Substance, cannot involve any existence. So even though they exist, we can conceive them as not existing. From

univocally deduce all effects that are connected to it; such a knowledge, Spinoza knows perfectly well, is impossible, and its representation, which is a product of the imagination, is deeply irrational; all that it enables is giving a correct idea of the order of things conceived in its infinity, an infinity which precisely forbids containing the content in the limits of a finite rational construction designed to exhaust one of its particular determinations.' And we can read these comments in connection to his further remarks on the function of demonstration: 'In this consists [. . .] the genuine function of demonstration, which goes far beyond the ritual exercise of proof: by reverting to propositions already established in different contexts or where they had been led to join with other propositions, demonstration, by tying together these matters of thought, gradually *spins* [*tisse*] the *weave* [*trame*] of intelligibility' (Macherey 1998: 21–2, my emphasis). Macherey's use of the textile metaphor agrees with my interpretation of causality in the *Ethics*.

this it follows that when we attend to the essence of modes, and not to the order of the whole of Nature [*ordos totius Naturae*], we cannot infer from the fact that they exist now that they will or will not exist later, or that they have or have not existed earlier. From this it is clear that we conceive the existence of Substance to be entirely different from the existence of modes.

The difference between Eternity and Duration arises from this. For it is only of Modes that we can explain the existence by Duration. But we can explain the existence of Substance by Eternity, i.e., the infinite enjoyment of existing, or (in bad Latin) of being [*infinita existendi, sive, invita latinitate, essendi fruitio*].[91]

This text allows us to highlight a first level of the strategic apparatus that Spinoza's argument employs: Spinoza posits an equivalence between *substantia*, *aeternitas* and *necessitas* (in the sense of one thing whose essence implies its existence), and symmetrically, between *modus*, *duratio* and *contingentia* (in the sense of a thing whose essence does not imply its existence). The fundamental elements of Spinoza's ontology, substance and modes, are therefore integrally translatable into the pair eternity and duration, as well as into the modal categories necessity and contingency. However, modes or durations are contingent in themselves, but not if put into relation with the order of the whole of nature: modes or durations are therefore necessary insofar as they have causes.

Once he establishes the symmetrical definitions of eternity and duration, Spinoza must determine the place and role of the concept of time for this conceptual pair, which he does a few lines later:

From the fact that when we conceive Quantity abstracted from Substance [*hanc a Substantia abstractam concipimus*] and separate Duration from the way it flows from eternal things [*a rebus aeternis fluit*], we can determine them as we please, there arise Time and Measure [*Tempus, & Mensura*] – Time to determine Duration and Measure to determine Quantity in such a way that, so far as possible, we imagine them adequately. Again, from the fact that we separate the Affections of Substance from Substance itself and reduce them to classes [*ad classes redigimus*] so that as far as possible we imagine them easily, arises Number, by which we determine these affections of substance.

You can see clearly from what I have said that Measure, Time, and

---

[91] *Ep.* XII [to Lodewijk Meyer]; CWS I, 201–2. Translation modified.

Number are nothing but Modes of thinking, or rather, of imagining. [. . .] There are many things which we cannot at all grasp by the imagination, but only by the intellect (such as Substance, Eternity, etc.), if someone strives to explain things by Notions of this kind, which are only aids of the Imagination, he will accomplish nothing more than if he takes pains to go mad with his imagination. And if the Modes of Substance themselves are confused with Beings of reason of this kind, *or aids of the* imagination [*auxilia imaginationis*], they too can never be understood.[92]

Time and measure are thus ways of imagining duration and quantity. They have the same epistemological status as number, which is the effect of dividing the affections of substance into classes: they are aids of the imagination and must not be confused with the things themselves.[93] Not only substance but also modes are irreducible to these abstract beings of reason, and they cannot be understood through these aids except inadequately, that is, by separating them from substance and depriving them of their links with the eternity from which they flow (we will see below what eternity means).

If time and duration are confused with one another, then paradoxes similar to Zeno's follow:

When someone has conceived Duration abstractly [*abstracte*], and by confusing it with Time begun to divide it into parts, he will never be able to understand, for example, how an hour can pass. For if an hour is to pass, it will be necessary for half of it to pass first, and then half of the remainder, and then half of the remainder of this. So if you subtract half from the remainder in this way, to infinity, you will never reach the end of the hour. Hence many, who have not been accustomed to distinguish Beings of reason from real beings [*entia rationis a realibus*], have dared to hold that Duration is composed of moments. In their desire to avoid Charybdis, they have run into Scylla. For composing duration of moments is the same as composing Number merely by adding noughts.[94]

Spinoza works on two distinct levels in the letter to Meyer. On the one hand, he proceeds to a distinct definition of the notions of eternity, duration and time. On the other, he specifies the relationships established between these different concepts. The effect of this argumentative strategy consists

---

[92] *Ep.* XII [to Lodewijk Meyer]; *CWS* I, 203.
[93] On this point, see Breton 1982–83.
[94] *Ep.* XII [to Lodewijk Meyer]; *CWS* I, 203–4.

in taking distance from the traditional scholastic articulation of time and duration. Duration no longer belongs to a kind of time with the *aevum* and eternity,[95] but instead becomes the temporal fabric of being, which time measures extrinsically, imagining the complex weave of events arranged along the successive points of a straight line.

The *Ethics* provides other elements of Spinoza's theory of temporality. First, we have the definition of eternity, which is the final definition in part one:

> By eternity I understand existence itself, insofar as it is conceived to follow necessarily from the definition alone of the eternal thing [*Per aeternitatem intelligo ipsam quatenus ex sola rei aeternae definitione necessario sequi concipitur*].[96]

Spinoza claims that eternity is the existence that follows from the definition of an eternal thing.[97] The importance of the definition lies much more in what it excludes than in what it affirms. Indeed, in the explanation that follows it, Spinoza takes distance from the philosophical tradition that has preceded him:

> For such existence, like the essence of a thing, is conceived as an eternal truth, and on that account cannot be explained by duration or time, even if the duration is conceived to be without beginning or end.[98]

Eternity cannot be explained by either time or duration.[99] What Spinoza rejects is the double-form through which the Western tradition has thought the concept of eternity: simultaneity and sempiternity, which are made up of the absolutisation of two forms of finite temporality, the contemporaneous and the successive. In both cases we have a *human, all too human* conception of eternity, which not only derives from an application of finite temporality to the infinite, but also constitutes a transcendent model with respect to finite temporality.[100] While the application of a model of indefinite succes-

---

[95] Cf. sections 3–8 of disputation L in Suarez's *Disputationes Metaphysicae* (Suarez 1965: 922–48).

[96] *Ethics* I, Def. 8; CWS I, 409.

[97] Cf. Gueroult 1968: 78.

[98] *Ethics* I, Def. 8; CWS I, 409.

[99] For an analysis of the interpretative problems that arise in confronting Spinoza's concept of eternity, see Moreau 1994: 503–16.

[100] Cf. Kneale's schematic reconstruction of the two lines that cross Western thought

sion to eternity is explicitly rejected in several passages of Spinoza's text, the model of absolute simultaneity[101] is implicitly rejected by means of the care that Spinoza takes to avoid using the adverb *simul* for the temporality of substance.[102] If he wanted to think eternity as absolute simultaneity, it is likely that he would have explicitly proposed an equation such as *aeternitas* = *tota simul* or *aeternitas* = *nunc stans*, but such an equation is completely absent from his work.

We can now consider the definition of duration in *Ethics* II:

regarding the conception of eternity: 'In the western philosophical tradition we have found two strongly opposing views. According to the one (held by Plato, Augustine, Boethius, and St. Thomas in his Platonic moods) eternity and sempiternity are incompatible, while according to the other (held by Aristotle, Epicurus, and St. Thomas in his Aristotelian moods) eternity, whether as timelessness or necessity is identical with sempiternity or related to it by mutual entailment' (Kneale 1973: 236). For an accurate reconstruction of the Greek, Arabic, Hebrew and Latin sources of Spinoza's theory of temporality, Wolfson's classic text remains fundamental, although his attempt to explain Spinoza's through his sources is overall contestable. See Wolfson 1932: 331–69.

[101] It was Boethius who formulated this concept in paradigmatic terms: 'Eternity, then, is the total and perfect possession of life without end [. . .] So what does rightly claim the title of eternal is that which possesses simultaneously the fullness of life without end; no part of the future is lacking to it, and no part of the past has escaped it. It must always appear to itself as in the present, and as governing itself; the unending course of fleeting time it must possess as the here and now' (Boethius 1990: 110–11). Cf. the problematisation of this definition in article one of question ten in Aquinas's *Summa theologiae* (Aquinas 2006: 92–5).

[102] The index shows that Spinoza uses the adverb *simul* at three different levels of his argument: 1) a level for indicating the simultaneity of conclusions to premises, the identity of essence and existence in God and the true idea and its knowledge; 2) a level of modal existence to indicate the concurrence of several causes at the same time in producing an effect, the simultaneous perception of two or more modes and the co-presence of two passions; 3) at the level of totality in order to indicate the simultaneity of attributes and, in particular, thought and extension. We must observe that Spinoza considers this third sense inaccurate, as the following passage demonstrates: 'All these things, indeed, show clearly that both the decision of the Mind and the appetite and the determination of the Body are contemporaneous with nature [*simul esse natura*], or rather [*vel potius*] are one and the same thing, which we call a decision when it is considered under, and explained through, the attribute of Thought, and which we call a determination when it is considered under the attribute of Extension and deduced from the laws of motion and rest' (*Ethics* III, 2; CWS I, 497, translation modified). If the expression *simul natura* already differs from *simul tempore*, as Christian Wolff rightly notes (Wolff 1984: 179), with the *vel potius* Spinoza indicates that he considers the term inadequate in order to explain the identity of the two orders.

Duration is an indefinite continuation of existing [*Duratio est indefinita existendi continuatio*].[103]

And here is Spinoza's explanation of the definition:

I say indefinite because it cannot be determined at all through the very nature of the existing thing, nor even by the efficient cause, which necessarily posits the existence of the thing, and does not take it away [*Dico indefinitam, quia per ipsam rei existentis naturam determinari nequaquam potest, neque etiam a causa efficiente, quae scilicet rei existentiam necessario ponit, non autem tollit*].[104]

For Spinoza, duration is an indefinite continuation of existence. An origin constitutes duration, it has an efficient cause, and yet once it begins to exist, it is subject to aleatory encounters with other durations that can strengthen or destroy it.[105] In other words, origin does not here function as the harbinger of a destiny, but as the simple, factual determination of one existence among others.

Spinoza defines the concept of *conatus* in the same way in *Ethics* III, 7:

The striving by which each thing strives to persevere in its being is nothing but the actual essence of the thing [*Conatus, quo unaquaeque res in suo esse perseverare conatur, nullum tempus*[106] *finitum, sed indefinitum involvit*].[107]

---

[103] *Ethics* II, Def. 5; CWS I 447.

[104] Ibid.

[105] In this sense, the following passage from Gabriel Albiac is extremely interesting: 'We are in front of the final key of the *Ethics* and all of Spinozism, of that irreversible philosophical revolution which, after having emptied beings of all of their underlying essence, places us within the materialist horizon of a modernity that is ours: we are in front of a logic of essences – which until now has been that of metaphysics – *a logic of powers in conflict, which is a logic of war*' (Albiac 1987: 360, my emphasis). Laurent Bove provides an extremely interesting clarification of Albiac's position. He claims that Spinoza's ontology approaches the logic of Machiavellian politics much more than the logic effective in the Hobbesian state of nature (the war of all against all, *bellum omnium contra omnes*), precisely because of the fact that Machiavelli's conflict presupposes a web of alliances: if there is in each case a logic of war, it is not a war of all against all. Cf. Bove 1999: 53.

[106] It is clear that Spinoza does not use the term *tempus* in a technical way here.

[107] *Ethics* III, 7; CWS I, 499. On this point, Bove finds a harmony between Machiavelli and Spinoza: 'For Machiavelli as for Spinoza, the necessity of the real is therefore, at

In the *conatus*, which is the actual essence of the singular thing[108] whose passions are nothing but the continuous variation of its degree of power,[109] nothing is determined by the origin except the regulated[110] and selective[111] structure of encounters with the outside. This structure, however, is not an *entelechia*, a teleologically organised reality. It does not last or have duration because it is well regulated in advance, but the opposite: it proves to be well regulated in the event that it lasts.[112] In order to reject it, Aristotle set forth a similar theory with great efficaciousness in the *Physics*:

> Why should not nature work, not for the sake of something, nor because it is better so, but just as the sky rains, not in order to make the corn grow, but of necessity? [. . .] Wherever then all the parts came about just what they would have been if they had come to be for an end, such things survived, being organised spontaneously in a fitting way; whereas those which grew otherwise perished and continued to perish, as Empedocles says his 'man-faced oxprogeny' did.[113]

Rejecting, in Letter XII, the conception of duration as composed of successive moments, Spinoza once more excludes the application of the

---

the same time, that of the dynamic of the individuation of affirmation/conservation (of the *conatus*), and that of the relations of force that these plural affirmations of power necessarily engender' (Bove 1999: 51).

[108] *Ethics* III, 7; CWS I, 499.

[109] *Ethics* III, Def. 3; CWS I, 493.

[110] On this point, Balibar writes: 'Any individual's conservation [. . .] must be compatible with a "continuous regeneration" of its constituent parts, i.e., what in modern terms we would call a regulated inward outward flow, or material exchange with other individuals. [. . .] The conservation is nothing but this regulated process of "continuous regeneration." [. . .] Finally we can say that the complete concept of an individual is that of an equilibrium which is not fixed, but dynamic, a *metastable* equilibrium which must be destroyed if it is not continuously recreated' (Balibar 1997a: 18, 22).

[111] Filippi's comment is very clear on this point: 'The body is in this way introduced physically as an open structure founded on a continuous but given interaction of a selective and not disordered interchange. It can absorb a certain gradient of negative interchange, in relation to the functional internal complexity of its apparatus; however, when it is overcome by such a gradient, the kinetic relation that individuates the body breaks, but a state of chaotic disorder of freely rendered parts does not take over, but rather a new proportion immediately emerges: new bodies rise from the dissolution of the pre-existing structure' (Filippi 1985: 33–4).

[112] For a useful summary of this thesis as it relates to Spinoza's concept of organism, see Sportelli 1995: 156–8.

[113] Aristotle 1984a: 339.

geometrical metaphor of the straight line to the theory of temporality. This metaphor indeed implies an image of time as the serial succession of instants by means of the binaries of a metaphysically given point (for example, the Leibnizian monad in Herder's interpretation). The concept of duration, instead, requires an even more radical theoretical effort: Spinozist duration is certainly a relative concept, as time is for Leibniz, because both concepts refer to the order of the simultaneity and succession of things. However, the relation that Spinozist duration expresses is not founded on the metaphysical unity of a subject, but on the unstable and aleatory relation with other durations. In other words, it is a relation that is founded on other relations, and so on, to infinity.[114]

Consequently, a conception such as Baumgarten's in his *Metaphysics* could not be applied to Spinoza. Here are paragraphs 238–9 of that manual so dear to Kant:

> When posited next to one another, conjoined beings are SIMULTANEOUS; when they are posited after each other, they are SUCCESSIVE. A whole composed of simultaneous beings is a SIMULTANEOUS BEING, and that of successive beings, is a SUCCESSIVE BEING.
> The order of simultaneous beings that are posited mutually outside of each other is SPACE, and that of successive beings is TIME.[115]

Space and time, arranged according to the Cartesian axes of simultaneity and succession, postulate a model of serial causality that survived until Kant's Copernican revolution (although certainly, he would prohibit the totalisation of the world). The infinite multiplicity of durations in Spinoza, instead, is not susceptible to totalisation, because eternity is not the result of the sum of durations: the totality of durations escapes the Cartesian axes

---

[114] In this sense, the definition of *individuum* is decisive when it is understood, against the very etymology that is the Latin mould of the Greek term *atomon*, as a complex and composed structure: cf. *Ethics* II, 11 Def.; CWS I, 460. Regarding this definition, Cristofolini rightly emphasises the dynamic meaning of the Latin verb *componi*: 'nothing can be understood if it is taken in the static sense, such as when it is said that a wall is made up of bricks, or, in geometry, when a line is made by placing one point after another. These must be understood dynamically: a wall is composed, or built, by the series of acts that make up the labour of the bricklayer; a line is composed, or made, by sliding a point along a surface; a solid figure is composed, or produced, by the rotation of a level figure around an axis, etc.' (Cristofolini 1993: 30). Cristofolini's analysis of *corpora simplicissima*, whereby he establishes the primacy of the dynamic relation over form-*entelechia* in Spinoza, is equally interesting.

[115] Baumgarten 2013: 144.

of simultaneity and succession. The concept of *connexio* forces us to a more radical thought, conceiving durations as the effects of the encounters among rhythms *ad infinitum*.[116] This means that by departing from the knowledge of an existing duration, we can access those durations that exist in relation to it (and those linked with them), both under the abstract and inadequate form of time, which absolutises a particular rhythm by making it the measure of all the others, and *sub specie aeternitatis*,[117] adequately conceiving the relational constitution of time as a complex connection of durations and taking distance from any attempt to metaphysically anchor time to totality (by understanding it on the model of the General Scholium of Newton's *Principles*, according to which time is God's omnipresence in such a way that every indivisible moment of duration lasts everywhere). Therefore, simultaneity and absolute succession cannot be given. There are no successions and simultaneities except in relations, and because of the individual encounters of rhythms, in relations of particular speed and slowness.[118]

Thus, if the essence of duration is relation, eternity is nothing other than the principle of objectivity of this relation, which consists more in its necessity (in its intelligibility) than in the ban on projecting modal temporality on to the totality by means of an ontologisation of the aids of the imagination, that is, time, measure and number. Knowledge *sub specie aeternitatis* is nothing other than the knowledge of relations of speed and slowness, knowledge of finite relations between rhythms, knowledge that derives from

---

[116] The following summary that Bachelard makes of the most important theoretical results of contemporary physics is interesting in terms of Spinoza's position: 'Matter is not spread out in space and indifferent to time; it does not remain totally constant and totally inert in a uniform duration. Nor indeed does it live there like something that wears away and is dispersed. It is not just sensitive to rhythms but it *exists*, in the fullest sense of the term, on the level of rhythm. The time in which matter develops some of its fragile manifestations is a time that undulates like a wave, that has but one uniform way of being: the regularity of its frequency. As soon as the different substantial powers of matter are studied in their detail, these powers present themselves as frequencies' (Bachelard 2000: 137).

[117] For an astute analysis of all of the occurrences of *sub specie aeternitatis* in Spinoza, see Di Vona 1995. In addition to the analysis itself, Di Vona's summary and discussion of earlier interpretations is very useful (Di Vona 1995: 99–112).

[118] What resonates here, in my view, is the Lucretian motif of time understood in a plural way as 'events [. . .] of bodies and locations' [*eventa (. . .) corporis atque loci*]: 'Time also exists not of itself, but from things themselves is derived the sense of what has been done in the past, then what thing is present with us, further what is to follow after. Nor may we admit that anyone has a sense of time by itself separated from the movement of things and their quiet calm' (Lucretius 1992: 39, translation modified).

the knowledge of the totality as immanent cause, but it is never knowledge of eternity in itself, because substance does not fall under the infinite intellect as one object among others, but as a complex relation of objects (that is, as a *connexio*). In other words, the eternity of substance, being the immanent structure of encounters of modes that last, is never given to be seen as presence, as in the absolute knowledge of the *Phenomenology of Spirit*,[119] but only in the finite weave of a fragment of eternity (which is eternal precisely because it is free from every hypostasisation of time, that is, from every anthropomorphic image of eternity).

If we now return to the example Spinoza proposes in the *TTP* – the history of the Hebrew people – we discover that it is precisely through the deconstruction of the absolute temporality of the myth of foundation (by Moses) and divine election – which established an origin and gave a measure to the multiplicity and interweaving of worldly temporalities (organising the different rhythms of social life through the divine calendar of rituals) – that it is possible to highlight the complex relation of durations, their singular *connexio*. In other words, it is possible to know real history *sub specie aeternitatis*, beyond every attempt at the totalisation of a singular history. Eternity is therefore at the same time the principle of intelligibility of the *weave* of durations and what prohibits the projection of the human chronological imaginary over the totality. As such, eternity forbids the conception of history as both a straight line and a cycle, in order to open on to an antihumanistic conception of eternity as the aleatory interweaving of necessity, an eternity that does not impose any binary as obligatory for history.

At this point we must return to the concept of time in order to try and understand why history is in fact represented by the geometrical metaphors of the straight line or the circle (the same recursive history seems to be a synthesis of the two conceptions). What we find is not the interweaving of real durations, but the imaginary representations of these durations. In other words, we must now confront the power and limits of the imagination. In the scholium of the first corollary to *Ethics* II, 44, Spinoza tries to explain the reason that leads the imagination to represent things as contingent. Beyond this explanation of the contingency-effect, what is particularly interesting in this passage is the reification of time (i.e., the transformation of the measure of one relation between durations into a thing subsistent in itself). For

---

[119] The interpretation of Spinozist temporality requires a distance to be taken from the final section of Hegel's *Phenomenology of Spirit*, and the allure that it employs in conceiving the memory of absolute spirit as the presence in the concept of all of the finite spirits that it succeeded in time (Hegel 1997: 589–91).

representation, time becomes one imagined object among others, making it possible to establish a relation between the abstract instant of perception and its content (almost as if the instant could exist for itself outside of the encounter that constitutes it):

> No one doubts but what we also imagine time [*quin etiam tempus imaginemur*], viz. from the fact that we imagine some bodies to move more slowly, or more quickly, or with the same speed. Let us suppose, then, a child, who saw Peter for the first time yesterday, in the morning, but saw Paul at noon, and Simon in the evening, and today again saw Peter in the morning. It is clear from P18 that as soon as he sees the morning light, he will immediately imagine the sun taking the same course through the sky as he saw on the preceding day, or he will imagine the whole day, and Peter together with the morning, Paul with noon, and Simon with the evening [*& simul cum tempore matutino Petrum, cum meridiano autem Paulum, & cum vespertino Simeonem imaginabitur*]. That is, he will imagine the existence of Paul and of Simon with a relation to future time. On the other hand, if he sees Simon in the evening, he will relate Paul and Peter to the time past, by imagining them together with past time. And he will do this more uniformly, the more often he has seen them in this same order [*ordo*].[120]

The time reified in the form of the imaginary line traced by the path of the sun, and therefore, in an abstract way, of the straight line or the circle of the three moments of the day (*tempus matutinum*, *tempus meridianum* and *tempus vespertinum*), acquires the content of the successive aleatory encounters, transforming it into a normative model for both the future and the past:

---

[120] *Ethics* II, 44 Schol.; CWS I, 480–1. In the note to *Ethics* IV, Def. 6, Spinoza declares another necessary rule that structures the imaginary representation of durations (*id est* time): 'But here it should be noted in addition that just as we can distinctly imagine distance of place only up to a certain limit, so also we can distinctly imagine distance of time only up to a certain limit. I.e., we usually imagine all those objects which are more than 200 feet away from us, or whose distance from the place where we are surpasses what we can distinctly imagine, to be equally far from us; we therefore usually imagine them as if they were in the same plane; in the same way, we imagine to be equally far from the present all those objects whose time of existing we imagine to be separated from the present by an interval longer than that we are used to imagining distinctly; so we relate them, as it were, to one moment of time' (*Ethics* IV, Def. 6; CWS I, 546–7). The imagination arranges events along a segment of a line and represents those too far in the future and the past as the limit-points of the segment (the origin and the end).

time is therefore nothing but the arrangement of events according to a serial order, which memory inscribes in habit, producing the transformation of this order into laws.[121] While real durations in fact are irreducible to the serial succession of events that run on the tracks of a temporal substratum, the imaginary representation of this order *necessarily* produces an inadequate image of temporality in the form of a succession of empty instants which are filled by the content of the perceptive effect of an encounter of the body with the surrounding environment.

Spinoza claims that the imagination necessarily represents temporality in this way. We can explain this necessity even further. It is the way imagination and memory[122] function that produces the chain-effect, or to use Spinoza's word, the *concatenatio*. Indeed, if we take up the text of the *Ethics* and observe it by following this perspective (with the help of the index), an almost[123] rigorous division of the terms *connexio* and *concatenatio* can be

---

[121] This is the common order of nature [*ordo communis naturae*], which is precisely differentiated from the order of understanding [*ordo ad intellectum*]: 'I say expressly that the Mind has, not an adequate, but only a confused knowledge of itself, and of external bodies, so long as it perceives things from the common order of nature, i.e., so long as it is determined externally, from fortuitous encounters with things, to regard this or that' [*quoties ex communi naturae ordine res percipit, hoc est, quoties externe, ex rerum nempe fortuito occursu, determinatur ad hoc, vel illud contemplandum*] (*Ethics* II, 29 Schol.; CWS I, 471).

[122] In commenting on the corollary of *Ethics* II, 17, De Deugd correctly writes: 'In this Corollary and in the subsequent Proof Spinoza without at all using the word presents his own account of the particular phenomenon called memory, but he does it in a way which reveals that to a certain extent he sees memory and imagination as identical concepts, though he does not say so verbatim' (De Deugd 1966: 202). On Spinoza's concept of memory, see Bordoli 1994 (especially 93–7, where the evolution of Spinoza's conception of memory is adumbrated between the *TdIE*, which is affected by both Aristotelian-Scholastic and Cartesian themes, and the *Ethics*). On the imagination, cf. Semerari 1970: 747–64, which emphasises the plurivocity of the term; Bertrand 1983, whose interpretation is traversed by a Freudian thread; Mignini 1981, which brings Spinozist aesthetics to light; Cristofolini 1988, in which the active and socialising function of the imagination is emphasised; and Laux 1994, which analyses the political-theological aspect. For a history of the discovery of the positive aspects of the imagination in twentieth-century Spinoza criticism from Appuhn to Bodei, see Bostrenghi 1992a. Finally, with great attention to the interpretative nuances of the materiality of the text, see Bostrenghi 1997.

[123] Two exceptions to this division can be observed, where Spinoza does not use the term *concatenatio* in the precise sense that it acquires in his theory in *Ethics* II, 18 Schol. The first time he uses it is in the appendix to part one, speaking about the concatenation of things [*rerum concatenatio*] (*Ethics* I, App.; CWS I, 439); here the use seems even closer to that of the *TTP*, when, in defining the *directio Dei*, Spinoza speaks of a

found. While the use of the term *connexio* is required at the ontological level of the argument, the use of the term *concatenatio* is required at the epistemological level (and, concerning this, the identity in Spinoza's epistemology between the cognitive and emotive aspects must not be forgotten).[124]

If we take the rigour of Spinoza's terminology seriously, this means that the complexity of the relation between things – their *connexio*, their order – is perceived as a *concatenatio* of ideas according to the order of the affections of the body, as the serial order of events, which reproduces, in the form of a mnemonic chain, the succession of the moments of an individual experience. All the effort of reason and the intellect consists precisely in trying to break this simple and linear order with the aim of establishing on the level of ideas, with a new *concatenatio*,[125] the complexity of the relations between

fixus & immutabilis naturae ordo, sive rerum naturalium concatenatio (*TTP* III, 7; CWS II, 112). Cf. also *TTP* IV, 4; CWS II, 126, where Spinoza refers to a *rerum coordinatio et concatenatio*. The second use appears in the scholium to *Ethics* III, 2: 'These things are more clearly understood from what is said in IIP7S, viz. that the Mind and the Body are one and the same thing, which is conceived now under the attribute of Thought, now under the attribute of extension. The result is that the order, *or* connection, of things is one' [*Unde fit, ut ordo, sive rerum concatenatio una sit*] (*Ethics* III, 2 Schol.; CWS I, 494). We should emphasise that the scholium to which this passage refers, in II, 7, uses the formula *ordo sive connexio causarum* (*Ethics* II, 7 Schol.: CWS I, 452).

[124] On this point, De Deugd writes: 'Spinoza sees two *series* of associations of ideas. This view cannot be anything but an implicit reference to his well-known theories, in fact one of the most basic doctrines of his system: "*Ordo & connexio idearum idem est ac ordo & connexio rerum*". What he proposes here comes down, of course, to saying that the order and connection of the ideas of "memory" is the same as the order and connexion of the modification of man's body. This order is not the *ordo intellectus*, the logical order of the mind. The mind can order and connect its ideas in a way which is the same in all men. But in the case of the association of ideas set into motion by something from the realm of imagination it is usually a matter of haphazard connexions; only occasionally do they turn out to be in accordance with the mind's order' (De Deugd 1966: 216). De Deugd overlooks the fact that it is not two serial orders, but one serial order (*concatenatio*), memory, and one structural order (*connexio*), intellect, which derive from the same structural order of things as products of an immanent causality: it is not by chance that when referring to the order of understanding (*ordo intellectus*), Spinoza never uses the word *concatenatio* except in the *TdIE*, of which I have already emphasised the differences in the fundamental structures of ontology.

[125] It is precisely in the possibility of ordering the ideas of the affections of the body in a different way that the effort of liberation in Spinoza's philosophy consists. In this sense, it is not an accident that the verb *concatenare* is used above all in part five (a total of nine times), particularly around V, 10, which constitutes the Archimedean point from which Spinoza shifts his theory of necessity into a theory of freedom: 'So long as we are not torn by affects contrary to our nature, we have the power of

things. For this reason, Spinoza never defines the order of the intellect as order by concatenation, but rather reserves for it, as knowledge of reality departing from God (that is, from the concept of immanent causality), the definition of order by connection.

On this question, Christian Wolff's interpretation of Spinoza's so-called parallelism is essential: 'Spinoza claims that the series of perceptions and the series of movements are by nature simultaneous; according to Leibniz, they are simultaneous only in time.'[126] This fundamental interpretative error, which had extraordinary force in the effective history [*Wirkungsgeschichte*] of Spinozism, lies in postulating a parallelism between the series of perceptions and the series of movements, that is, in a mirroring [*Wiederspiegelung*] of movements through perceptions, in a point-by-point correspondence.[127] This kind of interpretation inscribes Spinoza's philosophy into the history of modern metaphysics as it was described in Heidegger's epochalisation, as a philosophy of subjectivity representative of a mechanistic objectivity.

The distinction in Spinoza's text between *connexio* and the term *concatenatio* leads to an interpretation that causes problems for the framework of Heidegger's reading. Six of the nine occurrences[128] of the term *concatenatio* appear in the scholium of *Ethics* II, 18, which analyses the functioning of memory:

> Memory [. . .] is nothing other than a certain concatenation of ideas [*concatenatio idearum*] involving [*involventium*] the nature of things which are

ordering and connecting the affections of the Body according to the order of the intellect' [*potestatem habemus ordinandi, & concatenandi Corporis affectiones secundum ordinem ad intellectum*] (*Ethics* V, 10; CWS I, 601). Ideas and passions are concatenated in a different way than the concatenation of memory, following the structural order of ideas in the intellect (or better, the structural order that the intellect is). See the commentary on this proposition in Macherey 1994: 78–80.

[126] Wolff 1984: 64. I note in passing that Leibniz, in notes that were only published in 1948, had translated Spinoza's concept of order into serial terms in commenting on *Ethics* III, 1–2: 'Actually the series of ideas is distinct from the series of bodies, and they only mutually correspond' (Bouveresse 1992: 293).

[127] For example, this is Lukács's interpretation when he poses the problem of the incorrect use of *Ethics* II, 7 by Hegel and Schelling in their Jena collaboration: 'The statement has a somewhat different meaning for Hegel and Schelling. In Spinoza it had been an expression of his materialist tendencies. Schelling and Hegel aim to transform it into a constituent of objective idealism. From the materialist standpoint the strength of the statement had been its anticipation of the materialist theory of reflection, but this becomes a defect in the context of idealism' (Lukács 1966: 273).

[128] Cf. CWS I, 669.

outside the human Body – a concatenation that is in the Mind according to the order and concatenation of the affections of a human Body [*ordo & concatenatio affectionum Corporis humani*]. I say, first, that the concatenation is only of those ideas that involve [*involvunt*] the nature of things which are outside the human Body, but not of the ideas that explain [*explicant*] the nature of the same things. For they are really (by P16) ideas of the affections of the human body which involve both its nature and that of external bodies. I say, second, that this concatenation happens according to the order and concatenation of ideas of the affections of the human Body in order to distinguish it from the concatenation of ideas which happens according to the order of the intellect [*Dico secundo hanc concatenationem fieri secundum ordinem, & concatenationem affectionum Corporis humani, ut ipsm distinguerem a concatenatione idearum, quae fit secundum ordinem intellectus*], by which the Mind perceives things through their first causes, and which is the same in all men.[129]

Memory is nothing other than a certain concatenation of ideas involving the nature of things external to the human body, and this concatenation has a place in the mind according to the order and concatenation of the affections of the body. Thus, history as tradition, as the collective memory of a people, derives from a chronology of the affections of the social body: these are ideas that involve the social body and external bodies (the *auxilium Dei internum* and *auxilium Dei externum* of the *TTP*) at the same time, but not ideas that explain nature. Consequently, history as inadequate knowledge, produced by the concatenation of memory, arises as the simple linear succession of events, while history of the second kind, which we have evoked in the first section of this chapter, is precisely the deconstruction of this simple order on the basis of the concept of immanent causality, which does not grasp things as effects on the transitive model of serial causality, but rather on the model of *connexio*, or as structural causality.[130] For Spinoza, the linear conception of historical time therefore results from a function of memory

---

[129] *Ethics* II, 18 Schol.; CWS I, 465–6. Translation modified.

[130] Peña Garcia rejects, rightly in my view, the identification of the concept of order as *ordo et connexio* with *ordo geometricus*, even though this identification seems to be confirmed at several points by Spinoza and is held by the majority of critics: 'Spinoza clearly established that all order is causal order. In my view, the specific character of *ordo et connexio* is that it establishes a concept of *causality* that governs, as an ontological rule, every aspect of ontologically-considered reality: a causality that we could call *structural*' (Peña Garcia 1974: 179). On the concept of *ordo geometricus* in Spinoza, see Hubbeling 1967.

that proceeds by the serial concatenations of ideas and affections of the body while ignoring the complex connection of causes that subtends and produces this apparent simplicity.

4

Machiavelli and Spinoza: Theory of the Individual as Anti-philosophy of History

A Philosophy of the History of Humanity: From Spinoza to Lessing

In the final section of chapter 3, we focused on the different uses of the terms *concatenatio* and *connexio* in the *Ethics*. The latter refers to the complex weave of singular modes, and therefore to the weave of durations, whose measuring point is immanent to the process. The former indicates the linear series of the ideas of the affections of the body (to the idea of the succession of geometric points, the metaphor of the chain adds the idea of a necessary link between the elements), and therefore the arrangement of events along a straight line or circle that represents the flux of the absolute temporality of the imagination. Its unit of measure is constituted by the massive, regular movements of nature.[1] In light of this distinction, we must now analyse the passages of the *TTP* which have been interpreted as the sketches of a philosophy of the history of humanity by Lessing as well as Herder (a type of philosophy whose posterity was immense if we bring to mind Hegelianism, Marxism and that *Jünger Spinoza* himself, Moses Hess).[2] In other words, we can ask whether Spinoza participated in the philosophical dream of modernity – or, to use Fulvio Papi's adept expression, the philosophical dream of history.

The first passage that seems to legitimate an interpretation of the *TTP* in the sense of a philosophy of history (understood as an attempt to give a

---

[1] 'To determine [. . .] duration, we compare it with the duration of other things which have a certain and determinate motion. *This comparison is called time*' (CM IV; CWS I, 310).

[2] 'Adam, the natural human, is the prototype of antiquity; Christ, the God-man, is prototype of the middle ages, and Spinoza, the absolute human [*der Mensch schlechtin*], is the prototype of the modern age' (Hess 1961: 90). Cf. also Hess 1961: 1–74.

meaning, direction or end goal to the set of historical facts) appears at the beginning of chapter three. Concerning the election of the Hebrew people, Spinoza distinguishes true happiness or blessedness as enjoying a good from the enjoyment of a good at the exclusion of all others. Election, as declared in Scripture, is the evidence of the Hebrews' incapacity to apprehend and know true blessedness, an incapacity that in this context is the consequence of a childish mentality:

> Though we say that in the passages of the Pentateuch just cited Moses was speaking according to the Hebrews' power of understanding [. . .] we mean only that Moses wanted to warn the Hebrews in this way [. . .] so that he might bind them more to the worship of God, in accordance with their childish power of understanding [ut eos ex ipsorum puerili captu ad Dei cultum magis devinceret].[3]

The content of the Pentateuch, the Torah, is therefore nothing other than a message conformed to the still infantile state [ex ipsorum puerili captu] in which Moses found the Hebrew people. The parallel between the people's capacity to understand and the child refers to a form (the mature human; the people who arrive at an understanding of the nature of the true good), to an entelechy, which guides the progression of becoming in a goal-oriented way.

In *TTP* IV, Spinoza describes the next stage of historical evolution and analyses the differences between the Hebrew and Christian conception of the law. While Moses imposed the divine law on the Hebrew people as the law of a monarch God (and therefore as a coercive law), Jesus communicates as eternal truth, which cannot be imposed from the outside, but which rather each one finds in themselves. Spinoza writes:

> The Decalogue was a law only in relation to the Hebrews, because of a defect in their knowledge [ob defectum cognitionis]. For since they did not know God's existence as an eternal truth, they had to perceive [percipere debuerunt] as a law what was revealed to them in the Decalogue: that God exists and that he alone is to be worshipped. If God has spoken to them immediately, without using any corporeal means, they would have perceived this, not as a law, but as an eternal truth.
>
> What we say about the Israelites and Adam must also be said about all the Prophets who wrote laws in the name of God: they did not perceive God's decrees adequately, as eternal truths. [. . .] I say this only about the

---

[3] *TTP* III, 6; CWS II, 112.

Prophets, who wrote laws in the name of God, but not about Christ. For however much Christ too may seem to have written laws in the name of God, nevertheless we must think that he perceived things truly and adequately. Christ was not so much a Prophet as the mouth of God. [. . .] Christ [. . .] perceived the things revealed truly and adequately. If he ever prescribed them as laws, he did this because of the people's ignorance and stubbornness. [. . .] But doubtless when he was speaking to those to whom it was given to know the mysteries of the heavens, he taught things as eternal truths and did not prescribe them as laws. In this way he freed them from bondage to the law. Nevertheless, he confirmed and established [the law] more firmly, and wrote it thoroughly in their hearts.[4]

We can summarise the historical evolution that Spinoza designates through the figures that symbolise the different epochs. Moses, who has an imaginary knowledge of God's nature, symbolises an epoch wherein the law is particular and coercive, and thus, adapted to an infantile stage of humankind. Jesus, on the contrary, communicates immediately with God (*Deus enim per mentem Christi quaedam humano generi revelavit*), and although he sometimes transmitted this revelation through laws, it was only because of the ignorance of the people and the necessity of adapting it to their way of thinking [*forma mentis*]. We can read a movement of history from the particularity of the imagination to the universality of reason, and from the law as coercion to law as internalisation: a movement that was not accomplished with Christ, but that must still be completed.

TTP V points in the same direction, when Spinoza distinguishes between Old Testament content with a particular value, concerning the temporal prosperity [*temporanea fœlicitas*] of the Hebrew state, and eternal truth. There is thus within the first phase of the development of the history of humankind a rational kernel and mystical, or irrational, shell, which has no value for divine law, the source of blessedness and teacher of true life. This shell is made up of ceremonies:

Scripture itself also establishes that ceremonies contribute nothing to blessedness, but only concern the temporal prosperity of the state [*imperii temporanea fœlicitas*]. For it promises nothing in return for ceremonies except the advantages and pleasures of the body, and promises blessedness only in return for following the universal divine law. [. . .] And although those five books contain, in addition to ceremonies, many precepts related

----

[4] *TTP* IV, 28–34; CWS II, 132–4.

to morals, nevertheless they do not contain those precepts as moral teachings, universal to all men, but as commands especially accommodated to the grasp and mentality of the Hebrew nation [*mandata ad captum, & ingenium solius Hebrae nationis maxime accomodata*], and so as commands which concern only the advantage of the state.[5]

History, according to a movement well-known to readers of Hegel, therefore seems to be a univocal flowing of time from the contingent particular to the necessary universal. Next to the contingency of ceremonies that comprise temporal prosperity there is the necessity of moral precepts. However, the rationality of these precepts is still shrouded in the haze of the imaginary representation of a monarch God, who coercively imposes them through his earthly image. Moses' commands against killing, stealing and committing adultery possess a rationality *in nuce*, not yet transparent to itself, still a contingency among contingencies, even though it will demonstrate itself as necessity, as eternal truth, when Christ condemns 'not only the external action, but also the consent of the mind itself' [*animi consensus*].[6] The way that Moses prohibits a certain immoral action is therefore contingent and concerned only with the singular structure of the Hebrew people's way of thinking [*forma mentis*], while the content of the law is universal and necessary. This is a history constructed in the future anterior, like every philosophy of history, because Judaism is read in light of the developments it will have in Christianity, and its rational content – its unconscious, as it were – can only be measured in relation to its development.

This plan of historical flowing, of time as an oriented arrow, also emerges in *TTP* XII, where Spinoza claims that the divine law is written in human hearts rather than in a book whose text is fragmentary, defective, mixed and contradictory:

> Both reason itself and the statements of the Prophets and Apostles clearly proclaim that God's eternal word and covenant are inscribed by divine agency in men's hearts, i.e., in the human mind, and that this is the true original text of God [*Dei syngraphum*], which he himself has stamped with his seal, i.e., with the idea of him, as an image of his divinity. To the first Jews Religion was imparted as a law, handed down in writing, because then they were considered as like infants [*nimirum quia tum temporis veluti infantes habebantur*].[7]

---

[5] *TTP* V, 6–7; CWS II, 139–40

[6] Ibid.

[7] *TTP* XII, 2–3; CWS II, 248. Blumenberg shows that Spinoza, 'having freed the place

And the very division of the Bible into Old and New Testaments demarcates, according to Spinoza, two successive historical phases. Before the
birth of Christ, the prophets preached religion as the law of Israel by renewing the pact between Moses and the people, while after the birth of Christ
the apostles preached a catholic, or universal, religion, whose validity had
no borders and united all men.[8]

At this point we can trace the outlines of the philosophy of history
sketched in Spinoza's pages. It would seem to be a history divided into three
stages, represented symbolically by three fundamental figures and texts:
Moses (and the prophets) and the Torah, Jesus (and the apostles) and the
Gospels, and Spinoza and the *Ethics*. Human history would develop along a
straight line, whose divisions would correspond to the stages of growth for
the human being. First, Moses imposes the divine law as one coercive rule
among others, establishing cultural ceremonies with the purpose of rendering docile a people who had become wild during the years of slavery in
Egypt. Second, Jesus imparts the divine law as eternal and universal truth,
even though it must sometimes be presented in the form of a law due to the
ignorance of the people. The third stage, which to tell the truth Spinoza
never described and which, however, orders the entire historical unfolding
from within, corresponds to reason, within which the book that contains
it (the *Ethics*) appears as the eternal truth, in complete clarity, without the
support of any coercive power.[9]

At the root of interpretations of the *TTP* as a philosophy of the history
of humanity lies Spinoza's concept of true religion [*vera religio*], which he
distinguishes from superstition. On this question, if Leo Strauss's method of

---

for this writing, prepared the way for its re-employment': 'with the writing returned to
its original plurality, it gains a new unity. This unity is historically unconditioned and
historiographically unassailable: not the unity of the presumed missive from heaven,
but the unity of the lost original document [*syngraphum*] of the contract in which God
had established with the Hebrews the legal order of an earthly kingdom. This gives
the metaphor: what God has written in the human mind is the *real* original document,
which he directly marked with his own seal – the idea of himself – almost an image of
his divinity' (Blumenberg 1984: 104–5).

[8] *TTP* XII, 24; CWS II, 253.

[9] For an interpretation of the *TTP* in this sense, cf. Forni 1990. The same interpretation,
but with explicit reference to Lessing, appears in Hammacher: 'An exact observation
of that which the Jewish religion understood as obedience showed him that the fulfill-
ment of the Law was a form of education for initiation in the divine order of nature – a
thought which Lessing would later take up and expound in his *The Education of the
Human Race*' (Hammacher 1978: 187). In this respect, Chamla's critique is important.
Cf. Chamla 1996: 58–9.

reading is adopted (reading Spinoza as Spinoza proposes to read Scripture),[10] Spinoza's argument about true religion becomes nothing more than a tactical concession for the apprehension of common people [*captu vulgi*], and the differences in kind within the religious sphere disappear, with the sole surviving distinction being one between philosophy (which aims at the truth) and religion (which instead aims at obedience).

However, the materiality of Spinoza's text resists such an interpretation. In a very important passage in *TTP* XV, which in fact concludes the entire theological section of the *TTP*, Spinoza writes:

> Before I proceed to other things, I want to remind you – even though I've said this already – that I judge the utility and necessity [*utilitas, & necessitas*] of Sacred Scripture, or revelation, to be very great. We can't perceive by the natural light that simple obedience is a path to salvation [*quod simplex obedientia via ad salutem sit*]. Only revelation teaches that this happens, by a special grace of God, which we cannot grasp by reason. It follows that Scripture has brought great comfort to mortals. Everyone, without exception, can obey. But only a very few (compared with the whole human race [*totum humanum genus*]) acquire a habit of virtue from the guidance of reason alone. So, if we didn't have this testimony, we would doubt nearly everyone's salvation [*de omnium fere salute dubitaremus*].[11]

Spinoza affirms on the one hand the social utility of Scripture, and on the other the necessity of the moral teaching that it provides for the salvation of the ignorant. It is therefore possible to outline a philosophy of history that leads humankind from the obscurity of superstition to the light of reason through the instrument of minimal credos of faith,[12] wherein lies the only possibility of salvation for anyone incapable of understanding divine law [*lex divina*] as eternal truth [*aeterna veritas*]. There would thus be a sort of cunning of reason within the horizon designated by superstition that guides humankind towards salvation. Both the diachronic and synchronic phases of history (i.e., what is co-present, at different levels, in each society)[13] out-

---

[10] Strauss 1948.

[11] *TTP* XV, 44–5; CWS II, 281–2. Translation modified.

[12] For the essential points of this minimal doctrine, see *TTP* XIV, 24–34; CWS II, 268–70. On these themes, see Matheron 1971.

[13] For example, Spinoza's reflections on the necessity, for anyone wanting to teach a doctrine to a people or directly to all of humankind, of adapting it to the intelligence of the common people [*ad captum plebis*] 'who form the greatest part of the human race' [*quae maximam humani generis partem componit*] (*TTP* V, 37; CWS II, 148).

line a path from particular to universal religion, and indeed to the universal teachings of reason, a path along which the coercive force of law is inversely proportional to the persuasive force of reason.

It would not be difficult to raise general objections against this inter-pretation of the *TTP*, which is the object of a systematic incoherence, namely the contradictions between such a philosophy of history and the anti-teleology pervading all of Spinoza's texts.[14] However, I think it is more interesting to push this type of reading to its extreme consequences in order to assess all of its theoretical implications. Although, as we have shown, it has grounds in the materiality of the text, the interpretation of the *TTP* as a philosophy of history wherein reason emerges gradually, but surely, from the abyss of superstition cannot but call to mind Lessing's *The Education of the Human Race* for the contemporary reader. A detour through this philosophical masterpiece and symbol of the *Aufklärung* will allow us to understand more precisely the stakes of the interpretation of the *TTP* as a philosophy of history.

In the preface, Lessing lays out the meaning of the challenge presented: responding to the question of the significance of positive religions. His answer brings out all of the difference separating the *Aufklärung* from the *Lumières*. The phenomenon of positive religions must not be mocked or denounced; instead, what must be understood is the function each had for the development of human intelligence along the path that 'was the only one possible'. Lessing's fundamental theoretical move, taught to German culture by Leibniz, consists in giving reason to a negative by making it the function of a positive, of the best of all possible worlds. In other words, errors taken by themselves are errors, but they acquire a meaning when seen as necessary moments along the path of truth. One must comprehend the spe-cific function, the meaning, which religions had for the path of the intellect, and grasp the necessity of them as stages for this path.

The first two paragraphs contain the new response to the fundamental question about the meaning of the religions:

What education [*Erziehung*] is to the individual human being, revelation [*Offenbarung*] is to the whole human race.

Education is revelation imparted to the individual; and revelation is education which has been, and still is, imparted to the human race.[15]

---

[14] For example, this is Timm's objection to Lessing's alleged Spinozism. Cf. Timm 1964.
[15] Lessing 2005: 218.

The main idea, which will have enormous efficacy for the philosophical tradition that follows, consists in establishing a parallel between the growth of an individual and the history of humankind as a whole (*Menschengeschlecht* literally translates the *totum humanum genus*), subject of the historical progress sketched in the *TTP*. It is clear that speaking of individual growth is equivalent to speaking of successive stages represented by age difference, both chronologically and axiologically: the flow of time is increasing and brings the individual from infancy, through youth, up to maturity. Religions therefore do not arise by chance in the historical order, but rather according to a precise divine strategy for the education of humanity:

> And just as education is not indifferent to the order [*Ordnung*] in which it develops the human faculties, and just as it cannot impart everything to an individual at once, so also has God had to observe a certain order, a certain measure [*eine gewisse Ordnung, ein gewisses Maaß*], in his revelation.[16]

The order of education is thus the order of God's revelation. History is simply this gradual revelation of God to humankind, a revelation proportional to the capacity of the people to understand it.

Lessing's first level is the people of Israel, to whom God revealed himself by adapting to their unrefined character [*ingenium rude*] (to use an expression typical of the *TTP*, which Lessing certainly had in mind).[17] Although God communicated the concept of his indivisibility to each man, human religion, when left to itself, did not have the force to support this concept and began to divide the incommensurable, hence the origin of polytheism [*Vielgötterey*] and idolatry [*Abgötterey*]. However, in order to make humankind escape from the labyrinths into which reason had wandered, God gave a new push to historical progress:

> But as he no longer could or would reveal himself to each individual human being, he chose an individual people [*ein einzelnes Volk*] for his special education [*zu seiner besondern Erziehung*]; and he chose precisely the most uncultivated and barbarous [*das ungeschliffenste, das verwildertste*] people, in order to start with it from the very beginning.[18]

The Hebrews were a people of slavery, who were even prohibited from participating in the cult of the Egyptians, and whose years of brutalisation not

---

[16] Lessing 2005: 218–19.
[17] Cf., for example, *TTP* III, 12–14; *CWS* II, 113–14; *TTP* V, 27; *CWS* II, 145.
[18] Lessing 2005: 219.

only made them forget the God of their fathers, but also convinced them that they did not have the right to a God, because 'to have a god or gods was the exclusive right of the superior Egyptians'. And truly a people of slaves, who had lost the very idea of God in their subjugation, was the most fitting to be educated by the concept of the One [*Begriff des Einigen*]. Now the condition of this people, and here once again a direct echo of the *TTP* emerges, shows itself as coarse[19] but immature at the same time; immaturity adds the prospect of a path for the coarseness to follow, showing it as a transitory phase. God thus undertakes the moral education of the Hebrew people through a revelation suitable for infancy, first giving himself to be seen simply as the God of their fathers, to convince them that they had a right to God. Then, through the miracles that freed them from Egyptian slavery and placed them in Canaan, he convinced them he was the most powerful God, and with this, being the single most powerful, they were 'gradually habituated to the concept of the One'. However, this concept was very far from the true concept of religion. It was present in an infantile form, and the moral education that God imparted to the people was childish:

> But what kind of moral education was so uncouth a people capable of, a people ill equipped for abstract thoughts and still so completely immersed in its childhood? – Of none other than that which is appropriate to the age of childhood [*als die dem Alter der Kindheit entspricht*], namely an education through immediate punishments and rewards of a sensuous kind.[20]

The stage of the Hebrew people thus explains the absence of the doctrine of the immortality of the soul [*die Lehre der Unsterblichkeit der Seele*] in the Old Testament texts, as well as, strictly linked to it, the ideas of suffering and compensation in a future life. As a good pedagogue, God avoided burdening his child with concepts too soon: it was necessary that the law be respected as a result of entirely worldly hope and fear, because the sensory-driven gaze of the Hebrews 'did not yet extend beyond the horizon of this life'.[21]

---

[19] The theme of a coarse or rough people is repeated in paragraphs 11, 16, 18 and 27 (Lessing 2005: 220–1, 224).

[20] Lessing 2005: 221.

[21] 'Once again: the lack of those doctrines in the Old Testament writings does nothing to disprove their divinity. Moses was indeed sent by God, although the sanction of his law extended only to this life. For why should it extend further? He was sent only to the people of Israel, to the Israelites of that time; and his assignment was perfectly appropriate to the knowledge, capacities, and inclinations, of the Israelites of that time, as well as to their future destiny. And that is sufficient' (Lessing 2005: 223).

However, in the same way that a good book for children can conceal important points in the argument because the pedagogue deems them unsuitable for the age of the readers, but must not contain any doctrine that results in an obstacle to understanding the concealed points, so also can revelation pass over fundamental truths in silence, on the condition that nothing is contrary to the spiritual path of the people following the revelation, or anything susceptible to slowing their development. In paragraph 27, Lessing writes:

> Thus, the doctrine of the soul's immortality and future retribution could also perfectly well be omitted from the writings of the Old Testament, those primers for the uncouth people of Israel who had so little practice in thinking [in diesen Elementarbüchern für das rohe und im Denken ungeübte Israelitische Volk]; but they could on no account contain anything which might even delay the people for whom they were written on their way to this great truth [auf dem Wege zu dieser großen Wahrheit].[22]

Therefore, according to Lessing, the Old Testament was a good book 'for children and a childlike people'.[23] But no good elementary book must be left with the child for longer than necessary, because otherwise it would become dangerous. Once the propaedeutic function of the Old Testament had exhausted itself, it was necessary that a new pedagogue appear on stage to snatch it out of the child's hands: 'Christ came'.[24] Christ's practical teaching of the immortality of the soul marks a new fundamental stage in the education of humankind. This lesson does not derive from philosophical speculation on the immortality of the soul, which would not have any originality, but consists in the transmission of rules for internal and external conduct in relation to the hope of another life. The great merit of his disciples was precisely in propagating this doctrine beyond the confines of Judaism, for which Christ only seemed to have transmitted a new message. And it is only the disciples who can be considered 'the supporters and benefactors of the human race' [Pfleger und Wohlthäter des Menschengeschlechts].[25]

The Gospel is therefore the second elementary book for the education of humankind. These two books teach rational truths in the form of divine revelation: the doctrine of the indivisibility of God is taught by the Old

[22] Lessing 2005: 224.
[23] Lessing 2005: 230.
[24] Lessing 2005: 231.
[25] Lessing 2005: 232.

Testament to the child-like people, and the doctrine of the immortality of the soul is taught by the New Testament to humankind in its adolescence. The course of history, determined 'by a singular level of divine education', moves in the direction of transforming revealed truths into truths of reason (as Lessing himself affirms in paragraph 73 on the doctrine of the trinity, a paragraph that Jacobi would declare incomprehensible except on the basis of Lessing's adherence to Spinozism):

> The development of revealed truths [geoffenbarte Wahrheiten] into truths of reason [Vernunftwahrheiten] is absolutely necessary if they are to be of any help to the human race. When they were revealed, of course, they were not yet truths of reason; but they were revealed in order to become such truths.[26]

For this reason, not only are the revelations of revealed truth positive for society (in their rational elaboration), they are actually 'the most fitting exercises for all the human understanding' [die schicklichsten Übungen des menschlichen Verstandes],[27] because understanding 'must at all costs be exercised on spiritual objects if it is to *attain complete enlightenment* and generate the *purity of heart* which enables us *to love virtue for its own sake*' [*Er will schlechterdings an geistigen Gegenständen geübt seyn, wenn er zu seiner völligen Aufklärung gelangen, und diejenige Reinigkeit des Herzens hervorbringen soll, die uns, die Tugend um ihrer selbst willen zu lieben, fähig macht*].[28]

The stages of history that correspond to the levels of humankind's education are thus represented by three essential books: the Old Testament, the New Testament and the eternal Gospel, announced in John's Revelation and taken up by Joachim of Fiore and Dutch and German mystics in the fourteenth century. The first two books anticipate and prepare the kingdom of reason through revelation, which, if we believe Jacobi's account,[29] also finds its symbol in one book, the *Ethics*, whose essential teaching consists precisely in claiming that 'blessedness is not virtue's reward, but virtue itself' [*beatitudo non est virtutis praemium, sed ipsa virtus*]. This kingdom has not yet reached fulfilment, and yet it is not even possible to think that humankind has foreclosed 'the supreme level of self-illumination and purity'.

We can thus read Lessing's *The Education of the Human Race* as a radical

---

[26] Lessing 2005: 236.
[27] Ibid.
[28] Lessing 2005: 237. My emphasis.
[29] Jacobi 2000: 19–36.

interpretation of the passages in the *TTP* that I have treated extensively. Indeed, we can perhaps say that for the contemporary reader, who for the most part is immersed under the current of the most diverse common historicisms, this is a very persuasive model of reading. It is precisely this radicality, in any case, that allows us to grasp the theoretical stakes, that is, to disembowel the fundamental categories that constitute the conditions of possibility for this interpretation (or to use a mechanistic metaphor, the gears that make the machine work). Indeed, it is clear that such a reading relies on a conception of temporality for which time is articulated with eternity according to the model of a floating image. The educative stages of revelation are nothing other than the temporal platform entirely present as reason both in the eternity of the divine intellect and in the final stage, the *Aufklärung*, wherein reason in fact becomes transparent to itself. Between divine eternity and the eternity of human reason, between the Origin and the End of history, there is a path crossing over obscurity, which is such only if taken in itself, but can instead become rational if thought as part of the scope of an educative project of humankind. The path of history therefore traces a temporal line,[30] which is at the same time a spatial line. The geographical areas of the history of humankind are only those of the Near East and Europe, and moreover, this is thought in hierarchical terms. Clearly, claiming that the religion of the Israelites is a religion for a child-like people means proposing its survival within Christianity as on an inferior level, considering it like a child who does not want to grow up. The people, therefore, who do not belong to these areas or who have fallen within them before revelation gave them the elementary books are regarded as children without a teacher, more or less intelligent, more or less mature, but not part of the unique level of history.[31]

In one of Lessing's texts from the 1750s, *The Christianity of Reason* (which he would repudiate later in his career as baseless metaphysical prejudice),

---

[30] The relation between time and eternity, thought in terms of the adequacy of the former to the latter, is true only over a long duration, rather than as a path definable by a straight line; 'it is not true that the shortest line is always the straight one' (Lessing 2005: 239).

[31] Mendelssohn's criticism of Lessing's philosophy of history is precisely along these lines: 'I, for my part, cannot conceive of the education of the human race as my late friend Lessing imagined it under the influence of I-don't-know-which historian of mankind. One pictures the collective entity of the human race as an individual person and believes that Providence sent it to school here on earth, in order to raise it from childhood to manhood. In reality, the human race is – if the metaphor is appropriate – in almost every century, child, adult, and old man at the same time, though in different places and regions of the world' (Mendelssohn 1983: 95–6).

we can see the categorical elements that anchor his theory of temporality. Lessing sketches his theory of eternity in the opening four paragraphs:

> The one most perfect being cannot have been occupied from eternity [*von Ewigkeit*] with anything other than the contemplation of that which is most perfect.
>
> That which is most perfect is himself; thus God can have thought from eternity only of himself.
>
> To represent, to will, and to create [*vorstellen, wollen, und shaffen*] are one and the same for God. One can therefore say that everything which God represents to himself, he also creates.
>
> God can think of himself in only two ways: either he thinks of all of his perfections at once [*alle seine Vollkommenheiten auf einmal*], and himself as the embodiment of them all [*Inbegriff*]; or he thinks of his perfections discretely, one separated from the other, and each divided by different degrees [*nach Graden*] within itself.[32]

The two fundamental dimensions of temporality, time and eternity, unfold as a function of the way God thinks himself: if he thinks everything at once [*auf einmal*] as a concurrence [*Inbegriff*] of perfections, then this lies in the dimension of eternity. If he instead thinks according to the degrees of his particular perfections, which are distinct and organised hierarchically, then this lies in the dimension of time.

In paragraphs 13–14 and 17–18, Lessing specifies the way this second dimension of temporality functions, thanks to the mediation of a concept that he will call, in a way clearly linked to his reading of Spinoza, the concept of series:[33]

> God thought of his perfections discretely, that is, he created beings each of which has something of his perfections; for – to repeat it once more – every thought is for God a creation [*jeder Gedanke ist bei Gott eine Schöpfung*].

---

[32] Lessing 2005: 25.

[33] It is interesting to note that Merker identifies the fundamental bond between this young writing of Lessing's and Spinoza's metaphysics precisely in the concept of series: 'The *Christianity of Reason* remains interesting as a document of Spinozian suggestions which are already present in the young Lessing. This is expressed in his insisting on the concept of God as One (what Spinoza called "Substance") *from which follows by immanent necessity a series of infinite things* [*enti*] *that are, in Spinoza's terminology, the "modes" of the One*' (Lessing 1991: 13, my emphasis). Lessing's model of Spinozist causality clearly corresponds much more to the *TdIE* than the *Ethics*.

All these beings together are called the world [Welt]. [. . .]

The beings in this world must therefore be ordered by such degrees [nach solchen Graden]. They must form a series [Reihe] in which each member [Glied] contains everything which the lower members contain, plus something more; but this additional something never reaches the final limit.

Such a series must be an infinite series [unendliche Reihe], and in this sense, the infinity of the world is incontrovertible.[34]

The necessary complement to the introduction of the concept of series is the simplicity of the beings that make up this world, a simplicity Lessing introduces in the next paragraph, claiming that 'God creates nothing but simple beings, and the complex is merely a [secondary] consequence of his creation.'[35] In spite of the differences between the two works, what remains clear is the continuity of the fundamental theoretical elements, namely the concept of a set of worldly perfections in the eternity of the divine intellect and the concept of the series of worldly perfections arranged in time by a hierarchical order. In *The Education of the Human Race*, this hierarchical order, which is made up of the serial succession of simple elements, takes on the empirical content of the three stages of history as Judaism, Christianity and the religion of Reason (the latter is not the end of the series, because the series is infinite, but rather the infinite work of reason over revelation, i.e., the attempt, never fully realised, of time to make itself into eternity).

However, this theoretical schema is much more Leibnizian than Spinozist. Both a metaphysics founded on ultimate simple elements arranged in a perpetual series with a hierarchical order, and a conception of time as the indefinite progress towards a perfection already contained in the eternity of the divine intellect, are characteristically Leibnizian. The following passage from Leibniz cannot but convince us of this fact:

We must also recognise a certain constant and unbounded progress in the whole universe, so that it always proceeds to greater development, just as a large portion of our world is now cultivation and will become more and more so. And while certain things regress to their original wild state and others are destroyed and buried, we must, however, understand this in the same way that we interpreted affliction a bit earlier. Indeed, this very destruction and burying leads us to the attainment of something better, so that we make a profit from the very loss, in a sense.

And there is a ready answer to the objection that if this were so,

[34] Lessing 2005: 27–8.
[35] Lessing 2005: 28.

then the world should have become Paradise long ago. Many substances have already attained great perfection. However, because of the infinite divisibility of the continuum, there are always parts asleep in the abyss of things, yet to be roused and yet to be advanced to greater and better things, advanced, in a word, to greater cultivation. Thus, progress never comes to an end.[36]

The concepts of eternity understood as a set of perfections thought at once [*auf einmal*], and time understood as a progressive series of perfections, therefore comprise the inheritance of the concept of the law of development that 'had made a splash in German thought with the publication of Leibniz's *New Essays*'.[37] Contrary to Victor Delbos's claim, namely that 'a broader and more precise idea of the development of humanity was a matter reducible to the form of synthesis that had produced Spinozism',[38] the transplantation of such a conceptual constellation produces, on the basis of the passages in the *TTP* we examined earlier, a philosophy of the history of the progress of humanity. In other words, it establishes a hierarchical order within the modal plurality arranged along a simple temporal line (along with, obviously, deviations and relapses, as Leibniz himself affirms in the *Theodicy*), whose content is the gradual revelation of God-Reason. Such a construction, which transforms the material scene of a fragment of history into its destiny and its totality, is rendered unthinkable both by the substitution of *connexio* for *series*, and by Spinoza's specific articulation of the concepts of duration, time and eternity: the problematic that arises precisely prohibits the, in the last analysis, Platonic way of thinking 'time as the moving image of eternity',[39] as its double. In short, the Spinozist problematic prohibits reducing the complex weave of historicity to the simple tale of a history.

The Cycles of History: From Machiavelli to Vico

In chapter 3 I suggested that Spinoza's encounter with Machiavelli is at the origin of a new ontology, no longer grounded in the idea of a series of fixed and eternal things that make up the model for changeable things, but rather in the idea of a *connexio rerum*, or complex weave of things. With such a

---

[36] Leibniz 1989: 154–5.
[37] Delbos 1990: 239. For some criticisms of Delbos's interpretation, cf. Dujovne 1945: 151.
[38] Delbos 1990: 242.
[39] Plato 1997: 1241.

change in theoretical terrain, the concept of essence finds itself completely modified. Indeed, essence can no longer be conceived as the atemporal model of the real object, nor as the form immanent to it,[40] nor even, as in Leibniz, as the non-contradictory idea in the divine intellect. Essence no longer logically or chronologically precedes existence, but, as Carlo Sini has clearly shown,[41] the essence of a mode paradoxically falls after its existence. In other words, the essence of a mode is determined by the space between the maximum and minimum power of acting that unfolds in all of the relations in which it is *de facto* capable (a space that is precisely not given in advance, but is constituted only in the relation). The knowledge of the essence of an object presupposes the knowledge of all of the historical *occasions* through which it was constituted as such. The essence of things is given in their singular *connexio*, in their history, and is the result, as it were, of their very interweaving.

We have seen how such a conception of modal relations linked to a prodigious theory of temporality forbids us from considering Spinoza's theory of history as a philosophy of progress à la Lessing. Before analysing the specificity of this theory, it is necessary to traverse *Discourses on Livy* I, 2, where Machiavelli outlines a philosophy of history, in order to evaluate the stakes and theoretical results that will find their most radical expression in Vico's *New Science*.

Machiavelli dedicates this chapter to the question of the different forms of republics, and specifically, to the form that the Roman Republic had.[42] Concerning his argument on the forms that political power has taken historically, he excludes before anything else those cities that were already subject to a foreign power, in order to turn his attention to those cities that govern with their own laws, either as republics or principalities. Machiavelli tells us that these cities have had diverse origins and consequently different laws and institutions. At the origin of several of these we find a legislator who immediately and *in one stroke* established the orders and laws of the city, such as the case of Sparta, while others received orders and laws 'by chance

---

[40] Moreau summarises the status of the concept of form in Spinoza's thought well: 'The term form has [. . .], under Spinoza's pen, a variety of uses: a rejection of substantial forms, a technical term for designating the essential, and, above all, an element of the general view of the world, where things are ordered by fixed and eternal laws, where their transformations are regulated, where their knowledge is first of all knowledge of their production' (Moreau 1989: 18).

[41] Sini 1992. On essence in Spinoza's philosophy, cf. Rivaud 1906; Di Vona 1977: 39–52; Turlot 1988: 11–18.

[42] *Discourses on Livy* I, 2; Machiavelli 1996: 10.

and at many different times, and according to accidents', as was the case of Rome.

Before moving on to the singular case of the Roman form of power, Machiavelli finds it necessary to recall Polybius' classification of forms of power:

> Wishing thus to discourse of what were the orders of the city of Rome and what accidents led it to its perfection, I say that some who have written on republics say that in them is one of the three states – called by them principality, aristocrats, and popular – and that those who order a city should turn to one of these according as it appears to them more to the purpose. Some others, wiser according to the opinion of many, have the opinion that there are six types of government, of which three are the worst; that three others are good in themselves but so easily corrupted that they too come to be pernicious. Those that are good are the three written above; those that are bad are three others that depend on these three; and each one of them is similar to the next to it so that they easily leap from one to the other. For the principality easily becomes tyrannical; the aristocrats with ease become a state of the few; the popular is without difficulty converted into the licentious. So if an orderer of a republic orders one of those three states in a city, he orders it there for a short time; for no remedy can be applied there to prevent it from slipping into its contrary because of the likeness that the virtue and the vice have in this case.[43]

Until this point, we have the traditional classification of forms of power, based on the Platonic model in book eight of the *Republic* and the Aristotelian model in book three of the *Politics*.[44] Machiavelli's interest lies in taking up

---

[43] *Discourses on Livy* I, 2; Machiavelli 1996: 11.

[44] Actually, as far as the names of the forms of power, there is no exact correspondence with any of Plato, Aristotle or Polybius. In book eight of the *Republic*, Plato speaks of five forms of the state corresponding to five forms of the individual soul: aristocracy (the only form considered positively), timocracy or timarchy, oligarchy, democracy and tyranny (Plato 1997: 1155–7). In book three of the *Politics*, Aristotle proposes a classification that is based on the number of those who govern and their end: when there is one, few or many governing for the common good, they have a correct constitution (monarchy, aristocracy, polity); when instead they are based on their own interest, they are deviations (tyranny, oligarchy, democracy). Cf. Aristotle 1984b: 2058–60. Larivaille provides a comparative table of terms used by Machiavelli and those in the Latin translations of Aristotle and Polybius, and the terms in the treatises of Savonarola and Aquinas, thereby clarifying that no series of terms used by these authors corresponds exactly with those used by Machiavelli (Larivaille 1982: 174).

the Polybian theme of anacyclosis, that is, a cyclical movement that links together the different forms of ruling in one single process of historical development.

Machiavelli describes the passage from the natural state to the civil state as a continuous process: humans, initially dispersed like wild beasts, spontaneously constitute the first form of power by multiplying and gathering themselves together, appointing the strongest and most courageous among them as the leader. The first civil form is thus still imbued with animality – it is the kingdom of the strongest, namely whoever possesses the physical and moral qualities of a leader. But the establishment of civil life and the emergence of the idea of justice ('the knowledge of honest and good things, different from dangerous and guilty') that comes from it, brings with itself a change in the essential properties required for a monarch. Monarchs are no longer chosen insofar as they are *strong and healthy* [*gagliardi*], but rather insofar as they are *prudent and just*. The degeneration of monarchy into tyranny is due, according to Machiavelli, to the passage from an elective to a hereditary form of choosing the king. The dynamic that produces this degeneration is the heirs of 'just and prudent' kings considering the king's prerogatives not as 'virtuous works', but rather the exceeding of 'their own lavishness, lechery, and every other kind of license'. This triggers a destructive, heated dialectic between the king and the people, because the people hate the king, and the king, fearing the people, oppresses them tyrannically:

> From this arose next the beginnings of ruin and of plots and conspiracies against princes, done not by those who were either timid or weak but by those who were in advance of others in generosity, greatness of spirit, riches, and nobility; who were unable to endure the dishonest life of that prince. The multitude, thus following the authority of the powerful, armed itself against the prince and obeyed them as its liberators when he was eliminated.[45]

The passionate circle between hate and fear brings monarchy to its point of no return: tyranny. Once it has become tyranny, monarchy produces conspiracies within itself, whose leaders gain the favour of the multitude and therefore become, once they have defeated the tyrannical power, the new rulers of the state. In this way the aristocratic form of power arises, and initially it owes its fortune to the memory of vanquished tyranny and the values it represented. Aristocracy brings new rulers who govern themselves

---

[45] *Discourses on Livy* I, 2; Machiavelli 1996: 12.

'according to the laws ordered by them, placing the common utility before their own advantage'.[46] However, just as it was for monarchy, generational change is decisive for aristocracy, because the children, not knowing the horrors of tyranny, abandon themselves 'to avarice, to ambition, to usurpation of women', and transform the form of power into an oligarchy. From this arises the same passionate circle between fear and hatred that brought tyranny to ruin: 'disgusted by their government, the multitude made for itself a minister of whoever might plan in any mode to offend those governors; and so someone quickly rose up who, with the aid of the multitude, eliminated them'.[47] The conspirators who bring oligarchic power to an end thus have the same logic of passions as those who wiped out the monarchy. This logic arises from hatred and indignation against power. If tyranny gives rise to aristocracy, oligarchy gives rise to democracy:

> Since the memory of the prince and of the injuries received from him was still fresh, and since they had unmade the state of the few and did not wish to remake that of the prince, they turned to the popular state. They ordered it so that neither the powerful few nor the one prince might have any authority in it.[48]

Even for democracy, generational change brings corruption, just as it does for the other forms of power. Once the generation who established democratic power becomes the minority, according to Machiavelli, a state of anarchy [licenzia] spreads in which neither the public nor the private is respected, and injustice becomes daily, such that 'constrained by necessity, or by the suggestion of some good man, or to escape such license, they returned anew to the principality; and from that, degree by degree, they came back toward license, in the modes and for the causes said'.[49]

This is thus the cycle through which all republics pass. Machiavelli apparently proposes a cyclical theory of history: six classical conceptions of power are arranged in a straight line and chained together with a dialectic of passions (virtue → vice → hate → fear → indignation → virtue), and the line folds back upon itself to dialectically link the last form of government with the first.

Before analysing how Machiavelli distances himself from this conception

[46] Ibid.
[47] Ibid.
[48] Ibid.
[49] *Discourses on Livy* I, 2; Machiavelli 1996: 13.

of history, it is necessary to show its ultimate consequences by looking at an early eighteenth-century thinker who presents himself as simultaneously anti-Spinozist and anti-Machiavellian, even though on a specific point he builds a creative synthesis between them: Giambattista Vico.[50] According to Horkheimer,[51] in the *New Science* Vico takes up Machiavelli's idea of the historical cycle and develops it in a new way. For the great Neapolitan thinker, new science – that is, history – is capable of describing an 'ideal eternal history traversed in time by every nation in its rise, development, maturity, decline, and fall'.[52] Each society must therefore follow the inevitable tracks of this ideal eternal history, starting with savage and ferocious times, and crossing through three epochs: gods, heroes and men. To use Spinoza's language in the *TTP*, these are the codes in which the eternal laws of changeable things are inscribed.

What is striking, however, is that Vico uses a part of Spinoza's *Ethics* where, *a priori*, we would least expect it. Indeed, in order to account for the necessity of the path leading from barbarism to civilisation (a path that is never secured from new collapses into barbarism), Vico takes up *Ethics* II, 7 in a very original form. The interpretation of this proposition, as we noted in chapter 3, is determinant for understanding the whole of Spinoza's mature work.

> The order and connection of ideas is the same as the order and connection of things [*Ordo et connexio idearum idem est ac ordo et connexio rerum*].

Vico rewrites this proposition by situating it among his axioms (64), in particular between the fundamental axioms that he posits at the base of his historical science:

> The order of ideas must develop according to the order of things [*L'ordine delle idee dee procedere secondo l'ordine delle cose*].[53]

---

[50] Cristofolini claims that Vico represents Spinoza through five fundamental concepts: 'utilitarian, deist, fatalist, atheist, and devastator of republics' (Cristofolini 2001: 53–63). The first two also apply to Machiavelli.

[51] Horkheimer 1993: 313–88.

[52] Vico 1948: 71.

[53] Vico 1948: 70. Cristofolini underscores that 'the powerful and iconic Spinozist claim enters at the strategic point in Vico's *New Science* where he offers an unparalleled example of his methodology which is based on etymologies. Most importantly, there is not a doubling (between ideas and things), but a tripling – between things, ideas and words – and the idea of a philology, already pronounced in *De constantia*, as a science of words, which is the science of ideas and therefore of things' (Cristofolini 1995: 81).

At first glance, a simple consideration of the materiality of the text clearly shows two elements. On the one hand, Vico eliminates the term *connexio*, which as we have seen, explains the meaning of the term *ordo* in Spinoza's formula (order understood not as a succession of elements, but as conjuncture, as the effect of a conjunction). On the other hand, Vico uses the verb must [*dee*], which suggests conformity to a model, while Spinoza's *idem est* simply affirms the identity of the two orders (this seems to be the same difference as that between *sollen* and *müssen* in Kant, i.e., between necessity as tension with respect to a law and necessity as a natural law).

If we look closer, however, independently of a comparison with Spinoza's proposition, whose meaning is misleading for a correct understanding of Vico's statement, then we see that the latter can be read as the expression of a sociology of knowledge. In fact, what Vico understands by the order of things is precisely the eternal ideal history, which forms the model for the development of 'the course of nations' from the 'dregs of Romulus to Plato's *Republic*', an order that is the manifestation of the divine project residing there. According to Vico, the history of things has an anthropological foundation: each stage of historical development corresponds to the blooming of a particular human faculty; the new science is thus also 'a history of human ideas, on which it seems the metaphysics of the human mind must proceed'.[54]

The history of things, the three stages that comprise it, is thus also a history of ideas, a history of different conceptions of the world. In his most famous axiom, Vico claims that 'men at first feel without observing, then they observe with a troubled and agitated spirit, finally they reflect with a clear mind'.[55] These three stages of feeling, imagination and reason correspond to the age of gods, heroes and men respectively. The first two epochs are those of poetry, which is the art of the child's world:

> The most sublime labor of poetry is to give sense and passion to insensate things; and it is characteristic of children to take inanimate things in their hands and talk to them in play as if they were living persons.
>
> This philological-philosophical axiom proves to us that in the world's childhood men were by nature sublime poets.[56]

What is interesting here is the parallel Vico establishes between phylogenesis and ontogenesis, equally present in Lessing's *The Education of the Human*

[54] Vico 1948: 92.
[55] Vico 1948: 67.
[56] Vico 1948: 64.

Race, which also appears to be a reprise and radicalisation of some passages in the *TTP*. The imagination is conceived as the capacity of children and immature peoples, while reason is conceived as the capacity of adults and mature peoples. Maxim 36 shows the influence of a famous passage from the *TTP*:

> Imagination is more robust in proportion as reasoning power is weak.[57]

This is almost a literal transcription of a passage in *TTP* II, where Spinoza analyses the fundamental anthropological characteristic of prophets, imaginative power:

> For those who have the most powerful imaginations are less able to grasp things by pure intellect [*qui maxime imaginatione pollent, minus apti sunt ad res pure intelligendum*]. On the other hand, those who have the more powerful intellects, and who cultivate them most, have a more moderate power of imagining, and have it more under their power. They rein in their imagination, as it were, lest it be confused with the intellect.[58]

Vico takes up this idea and inscribes it into a division of the different modalities of the knowledge of humankind according to the successive stages of the ideal eternal history. At the heart of this development, religion played a fundamental role in the constitution of society:

> The world of peoples began everywhere with religion. [. . .]
> Wherever a people has grown savage in arms so that human laws have no longer any place among it, the only powerful means of reducing it is religion.
> This axiom establishes the fact that divine providence initiated the process by which the fierce and violent were brought from their outlaw state to humanity and entered upon national life. It did so by awakening in them a confused idea of divinity, which they in their ignorance attributed to that to which it did not belong. Thus through the terror of this imagined divinity, they began to put themselves in some order.[59]

---

[57] Vico 1948: 63.
[58] *TTP* II, 1; CWS II, 94.
[59] Vico 1948: 62–3. Here Machiavelli's reference to Numa and Spinoza's to Moses are very evident.

We thus find in Vico the same schema that we earlier identified in Lessing: a progression of the history of humanity in three stages, wherein religion carries out a pedagogical function that both call Providence. It is clear that some general objections against applying this schema to Spinoza's theory could be made, and yet it is precisely in the turning of the theoretical gears of this reading that we will measure the full distance between Vico and Spinoza. I have already indicated the theoretical importance of Vico's rewriting of *Ethics* II, 7. The axiom that follows this rewriting contains an essential element for understanding this distance:

> This was the order of human things: first the forests, after that the huts, thence the villages, next the cities, and finally the academies.
>
> This axiom is a great principle of etymology, for this *series* of human things sets the pattern for the histories of words in the various native languages.[60]

The expression *series of human things*[61] finally clarifies the meaning of the term *order*. Vico's translation of Spinoza's *ordo et connexio* with *ordo sive series* conforms to his conception of the 'course that nations follow', which is presented as a linear succession of stages that radiate around an expressive centre (which Vico calls *nature*), a uniform present.[62] With this, Vico wards

---

[60] Vico 1948: 70. My emphasis. Translation modified.

[61] For the other occurrences of the term series [*serie*] in the *New Science*, cf. the index compiled in Vico 1977: 723.

[62] 'We shall now [. . .] in this fourth book discuss the course nations take, proceeding in all their various and diverse customs with constant uniformity upon the division of the three ages which the Egyptians said had elapsed before them in their world, namely, the successive ages of gods, heroes and men. For the nations will be seen to develop in conformity with this division by a constant and uninterrupted order of causes and effects present in every nation, through three kinds of natures. From these natures arise three kinds of customs; and in virtue of these customs three kinds of natural laws of nations are observed; and in consequence of these laws three kinds of civil states or commonwealths are established. And in order that men, having reached the stage of human society, may on the one hand communicate to each other the aforesaid three most important matters [customs, laws, commonwealths], three kinds of languages and as many characters are formed; and in order that they may on the other hand justify them, three kinds of jurisprudence assisted by three kinds of authority and three kinds of reason in as many of judgments. The three kinds of jurisprudence prevail in three sects of times, which the nations profess in the course of their history. These [groups of] three special unities, with many others that derive from them and will also be enumerated in this book, all lead to one general unity. This is the unity of the religion of a provident divinity, which is the unity of the spirit informing and giving life to this

off a conception of history understood as the aleatory encounter of necessity – as conjunctions of a differential temporality that result in conjunctures that are not subject to an essential section – and instead re-establishes, albeit in accordance with a perspective typical of modernity, the Platonic conception of time as the moving image of eternity.

The Aleatory of History as Connection of Necessities

In the first two sections of this chapter, we focused on the elements in both Spinoza's and Machiavelli's texts that were used as footholds for interpreting their thought as a philosophy of history, an interpretation that entails the possibility of reading the totality of historical development according to the logic of a unitary and continuous Sense [Senso] that human knowledge, through the mnemonic faculty (anamnesis), retraces to its origins (a model that is more applicable to Lessing than Vico). This conception constitutes the most powerful theoretical line running through the Western philosophical tradition under the name of idealism.[63] It is Plato who inaugurates this powerful form of philosophy with the thought of truth [ἀλήθεια] as the absence of forgetting [λήθη] – in other words, remembrance – and it is Hegel who carries it into the very heart of the infinite totality, identifying remembrance [Erinnerung] and absolute knowledge [absolutes Wissen]. 'Science is but an image of the truth' [Omnis scientia nihil aliud est, quam reminiscientia]: breaking the ancient alliance between memory and truth that sets up the originality and primacy of Sense, this is

---

world of nations. Having discussed these matters above in a fragmentary fashion, we shall here exhibit the order of their development' (Vico 1948: 301).

[63] In his analysis of the mythic conceptions of memory in ancient Greece, Vernant finds that, in a first sense, Mnemosyne, the sister of Chronos, presides over the poetic function: 'Memory transports the poet into the midst of ancient events, back into their own time' and 'the organisation of time in [the poet's] account simply reproduces the sequences of events at which he is somehow present, in the order in which they occurred, from the beginning' (Vernant 2006: 117). In particular, Hesiod's Theogony established the alliance between memory and truth, which allows one to tap into 'the primeval reality from which the cosmos arose, and which makes it possible to understand the process of becoming as a whole' (Vernant 2006: 120). However, in a second sense, within the doctrine of the reincarnation of souls, memory is no longer that which furnishes mortals with the secret of origins, but the means for reaching the end of time, putting an end to the cycle of generations. The soul, by means of anamnesis, has understood how to connect the end with the beginning and close its cycle, not in order to start over again, but 'to escape definitively from it and leave time forever' (Vernant 2006: 132).

the challenge, always brought in a new way, of the tradition that runs from the Greek atomists up to Spinoza.

I will now demonstrate the elements within Machiavelli's work that allow us to outline the crucial aspects of this challenge. From this perspective, it is necessary to reread the pages of *Discourses on Livy* I, 2, where Machiavelli describes the cyclical movement that regulates the historical development of every form of power. Remember that the chapter is an interrogation of the particular form of the Roman Republic in relation to the Platonic-Aristotelian typology of power. After describing the six forms of government and the generational dialectic of passions (the first generation is always virtuous and the second is always corrupt), which provokes the passage from one form of power to another, Machiavelli emphasises the abstract character of this serial conception of forms once it is in relation with the concrete level of historical relations. In other words, to use Spinozist terminology, the simple logic of *ordo sive series* is shattered by the complex logic of *ordo sive connexio*:

> It is while revolving in this cycle that all republics are governed and govern themselves. But rarely do they return to the same governments, for almost no republic can have so long a life as to be able to pass many times through these changes and remain on its feet. *But indeed it happens that in its travails, a republic always lacking in counsel and forces becomes subject to a neighboring state that is ordered better than it*; assuming that this were not so, however, a republic would be capable of revolving for an infinite time in these governments.[64]

The serial temporality of the succession of forms of power appears as an abstraction of the imagination before the reality of complex historical-political relations. No laws of development for the forms of power of a society exist independently from the relations of force with other societies. Consequently, the intersection of different cyclical linearities produces a temporality that is by no means linear, but rather traversed by ruptures and discontinuities.

But the distance taken from the theory of pre-fixed cycles is even more radical: Machiavelli does not in fact limit himself to rendering Polybius' framework more complex.[65] At the moment that he confronts his object –

---

[64] *Discourses on Livy* I, 2; Machiavelli 1996: 13. My emphasis.

[65] On the differences between Polybius' naturalism and Machiavelli's, cf. Sasso 1987; Garin 1993.

the specific form of the Roman Republic – he discards all of the conceptual instruments of the theory of pre-fixed cycles in order to study it in its singular and enduring complexity. It is precisely the question of the duration of republics that allows Machiavelli to take distance from a cyclical theory of history.[66]

> I say thus that all the said modes are pestiferous because of the brevity of life in the three good ones and because of the malignity in the three bad. So those who prudently order laws having recognized this defect, avoiding each of these modes by itself, chose one that shared in all, judging it firmer and more stable; for the one guards the other, since in one and the same city there are the principality, the aristocrats, and the popular government.[67]

When beginning to analyse the singular objects of history, namely enduring states, the philosophy of history must be abandoned for the sake of a study of the institutions and laws (*ordini e leggi*, to use Machiavelli's language) that allow a state to regulate and stabilise the relations of force among the parts that make up society. Machiavelli here recalls the example of Lycurgus, who gave Sparta a constitution, securing its political stability for eight centuries, and the counter-example of Solon, whose laws established a form of precarious power, soon transformed into tyranny:

> Among those who have deserved most praise for such constitutions is Lycurgus, who in Sparta ordered his laws so as to give their roles to the kings, the aristocrats, and the people and made a state that lasted more than eight hundred years, achieving the highest praise for himself and quiet in that city. The contrary happened to Solon, who ordered the laws

[66] 'If we revert to the third thesis – the cyclical theory of history – we discover that Machiavelli proposes it solely in order to demarcate himself from it while he is relying on it. Just as the thesis of continual change contradicted the thesis of the immutable order of things, so too *Machiavelli's position on the duration of the state contradicts the thesis of the endless cycle of revolutions in forms of government.* In fact, what Machiavelli wants is not a government that passes away, but a state that endures. And in order to impart and guarantee duration to it, he assigns it to a "composite" form of government that does not feature in the typology of governments in continual transition – hence an utterly *original* form of government, unlike all the forms inventoried in the typology in so far as it is *durable* [. . .] whereas the recorded states are of such brief duration that the law of the historical cycle, according to which governments are not durable, cannot even be verified in their case' (Althusser 1999: 40).

[67] *Discourses on Livy* I, 2; Machiavelli 1996: 13.

in Athens: by ordering only the popular state there, he made it of such short life that before he died he saw the tyranny of Pisistratus born there. His heirs were expelled after forty years and Athens returned to freedom, yet because it took up the popular state again, according to the orders of Solon, it lasted no more than a hundred years. To maintain it, [Athens] made many constitutions that had not been considered by Solon, by which the insolence of the great and the license of the collectivity were repressed. Nonetheless, because it did not mix them with the power of the principality and with that of the aristocrats, Athens lived a very short time in respect to Sparta.[68]

Regarding Machiavelli's examples, two implicit theoretical consequences must be highlighted. First, the mythical nature of Lycurgus' character, which has the function of exemplifying a legislator *at one stroke* in Machiavelli's text (as opposed to legislation as the result of chance), suggests that every form of first causality would actually be nothing but a form of the mythology of origins (and his irony towards Moses as a lawgiver seems to reinforce this hypothesis). Second, Athenian history invalidates the theory of fixed cyclical history: it actually passes from a democracy to a tyranny, then again to a democracy and finally to an oligarchy after its defeat at the hands of Sparta in 404 BCE.

Similarly, the history of Rome must be analysed independently from the belief in the omnipotence of a legislator as well as a predetermined historical development. History is the place of aleatory encounters of forces internal and external to the state, and it is precisely the continuous regulation of these forces that renders the duration of a state possible. The broad description of the singular object of the theory of history in the *Discourses on Livy* (the history of the Roman people) therefore appears as a distance taken from two fundamental ideas of classical philosophy: the myth of the legislator, and the cyclical time of the eternal return of the same. Here is the passage that closes the chapter:

> But let us come to Rome. Notwithstanding that it did not have a Lycurgus to order it at the beginning in a mode that would enable it to live free a long time, nonetheless so many accidents arose in it through the disunion between the plebs and the Senate that what an orderer had not done, chance did. For if the first fortune did not fall to Rome, the second fell to it; for if its first orders were defective, nonetheless they did not deviate

---

[68] Ibid.

from the right way that could lead them to perfection. For Romulus and all the other kings made many and good laws conforming also to a free way of life; but because their end was to found a kingdom and not a republic, when that city was left free, many things that were necessary to order in favor of freedom were lacking, not having been ordered by those kings. Even though its kings lost their empire by the causes and modes discoursed of, nonetheless those who expelled them expelled from Rome the name and not the kingly power, having at once ordered two consuls there who stood in the place of the kings; so, since there were the consuls and the Senate in that republic, it came to be mixed only of two quali-ties out of the three written of above – that is, the principality and the aristocrats. It remained only to give a place to the popular government; hence, when the Roman nobility became insolent for the causes that will be told below, the people rose up against it; so as not to lose the whole, it was constrained to yield to the people its part, and on the other side the Senate and the consuls remained with so much authority that they could keep their rank in that republic. Thus arose the creation of the tribune of the plebs, after which the state of that republic came to be more stabilised, since all three kinds of government there had their part.[69]

In the same theoretical move, the negation of the first cause embodied in the legislator-founder, who occupies the place of the God of Christian cosmology in the space of politics, brings about the negation of the series of transitive causes that derive from it. What is affirmed here is the reality of the power of the occasion – understood as what occurs in the sense of the emergence, on the basis of a given mesh of forces, of new possibilities for political action (which for Machiavelli means the creation of new institutions). It is there-fore fortune in its plural encounters with the established political forms of ancient virtue (petrified virtue, so to speak, or fixed habits) that constitutes the field of action, the occasion, for new interventions of virtue. And this claim of an unceasing labour of virtue present in the established institutions and laws of the past – the continued and reiterated attempt to stabilise what, by nature, remains in any case unstable, namely the constitutive relations of a society – this claim breaks both on the ontological terrain and on the more immediate terrain of politics with every thought of the origin. At the same time, this claim breaks with a linear temporality in which events are serially inscribed according to a teleological level, in order to open on to a conception of reality as the aleatory space of the conjuncture, a space

[69] *Discourses on Livy* I, 2; Machiavelli 1996: 14

of struggle, whose result is never pre-established, but depends on the risks virtue takes, without guarantee, in the complex and unpredictable weave of fortune.[70]

The essence of the Roman state thus does not reside in a form of power (the mixed form,[71] which Polybius had already evoked for Rome), but in the relations of force between the fundamental elements of the people (the king, nobles and plebs), whose aleatory encounter established the occasion (only the occasion, which as a concept is perhaps the implicit deconstruction of every form of teleology) of creating new institutions and new laws, for a continuous regulation without which the state could not last. In this way, the study of the specific logic of the specific object, to use the expression of the young Marx, leads Machiavelli to discard both the myth of the legislator who establishes the order for the whole people *at one stroke* (a form of creation that recalls the way Lessing's God conceives the totality of the development of the world: *auf einmal*), and also the philosophy of history based on a cyclical movement of forms of power. As such, in the *Discourses on Livy* Machiavelli elaborates a theory of the individual (of the inchoate [*in fieri*] individuality of the Roman people) as an anti-philosophy of history, that is, as a rejection of the inscription of Roman society into a totalising narrative.

Is a general theory of history completely absent from Machiavelli's text, in that case? The answer is no. Machiavelli actually puts forth his conception of history in *Discourses on Livy* II, 5 in the form of a reflection on the memory of humankind: 'That the Variation of Sects and Languages, Together with the

[70] As Esposito writes: 'Every specific time needs a specific "foundation". This is because the act of "founding" does not exhaust itself in a *primum* logical guarantor of the entire subsequent development. [. . .] To the founding act of (self)-conservation, Machiavelli therefore opposes an innovative process of expansion. But does this mean the full secularisation of politics, an absolute eradication of every presupposition, a linear projection to the future? A reading in this sense – while present in the critical literature – is completely misleading. This is so not only because it reduces the complexity that is generally at work in the double-sided concept of secularisation (the politicisation of theological categories and the continuity of the theological nucleus in the new political language). But, more specifically, this is misleading because the subtraction of visibility of the fact that the elision of (once and for all) decisive [*risolutivo*] foundation means exactly the opposite of the linearisation of history: and that lies in taking on the contradiction (not understood in the dialectical sense, but as contrasting oppositions) as the constitutive principle of political action' (Esposito 1984: 199).

[71] Berns convincingly demonstrates the difference between the mixed constitution in Polybius and Machiavelli. In the former, it represents the perfect constitution capable of neutralising conflict, while in the latter it is what allows conflict to persist as the 'motor' of politics (Berns 2000: 71–129).

Accident of Floods or Plague, Eliminates the Memories of Things'. Already chapter fifteen of *The Prince* proposes a theory of history as the encounter of virtue and fortune. Its object is the history of military-political relations, whose paradigm is the account of the adventures of Cesare Borgia, the Duke of Valentinois. Machiavelli's theory of history in *Discourses on Livy* II, 5 has a completely different object. It could appear as a fully fledged philosophy of the history of humanity, if it were not precisely the open refusal of the totalisation of the record of memory.

The opening lines of the chapter are clear, even if seemingly difficult to interpret:

> To those philosophers who would have it that the world is eternal, I believe that one could reply that if so much antiquity were true it would be reasonable that there be memory of more than five thousand years – if it were not seen how the memories of times are eliminated by diverse causes, of which part come from men, part from heaven.[72]

Here Machiavelli affirms, despite a very complex syntactical construction, two very simple philosophical theses:

1. The world is eternal.
2. Some causes exist that erase the memory of things.

The philosophical power of the first thesis is clear: Machiavelli emphatically takes up the Averroesian thesis, which, starting from the Arabic Enlightenment, ran through the late Middle Ages and Christian humanism like an underground river, everywhere resisting the dominant philosophy. It

---

[72] *Discourses on Livy* II, 5; Machiavelli 1996: 138–9. Anselmi's note (in the Italian edition) seems useful for correcting some misunderstandings of this text: "How [. . .] they are eliminated" is the prototype of a hypothetical period of irreality, whose consequence [*apodosi*] is constituted by "I believe that one could reply." Here Machiavelli creates an optical illusion that – differently from his tendency to express himself in a direct way, when not provocative – aims to conceal the substance of his thought. Earlier Machiavelli seems to say that the argument of short-term memory can be used to refute the thesis of the eternity of the world, then (with the hypothetical prototype placed after the consequence [*apodosi*]) he shows the conceptual inconsistency of that argument. Therefore: if one does not see that there exist many causes that determine the loss of historical memory (but there are such causes and they are seen: thus it is an absurd hypothesis), then one could use the argument against those who maintain that the world is eternal, etc.' (Machiavelli 1993: 251). For an overview of the Machiavellian position in the history of the question, cf. Bianchi 1987.

was opposed to both Platonism (specifically the *Timaeus*) and Christianity. The second thesis has the same polemical objectives: it takes aim at both the Platonic theory of memory as *anamnesis* and the Sacred Scriptures as the memory of the history of humanity from its origins (the 5,000 years that Machiavelli mentions correspond precisely to the antiquity of the world to which Genesis refers).

The combination of these two theses leads to a new conception of historical knowledge; it presents itself not as the conceptual double of the historical totality, but as a fragment spared from the destruction of human memory. This fragment of human memory is in no way the expression of the totality: no reason (understood as Sense) presides over its survival. This fragment is only what remains from the encounters among the forces of nature and human society, and the encounters of different societies among themselves. The error of Platonism and Christianity, of which Hegel will accomplish an impressive synthesis, consists precisely in projecting the fragment on to totality, an error that finitises the world and establishes a powerful alliance between memory and truth, an alliance that in turn founds the grand continent of idealism.

Let us now turn to the Machiavellian distribution of the causes of forgetting. Machiavelli begins his exposition of that 'which comes from men', that is, social causes:

For when a new sect – that is, a new religion – emerges, its first concern is to extinguish the old to give itself reputation; and when it occurs that the orderers of a new sect are of a different language, they easily eliminate it. This thing is known from considering the modes that the Christian sect took against the Gentile. It suppressed all its orders and all its ceremonies and eliminated every memory of that ancient theology. It is true that they did not succeed in eliminating entirely the knowledge of the things done by its excellent men. This arose from having maintained the Latin language, which they were forced to do since they had to write this new law with it. For if they had been able to write with a new language, considering the other persecutions they made, we would not have any record of things past. Whoever reads of the modes taken by Saint Gregory and by the other heads of the Christian religion will see with how much obstinacy they persecuted all the ancient memories, burning the work of the poets and the historians, ruining images, and spoiling every other thing that might convey some sign of antiquity. So if they had added a new language to this persecution, in a very brief time everything would be seen to be forgotten. It is therefore to be believed that what the Christian sect wished to do against the Gentile sect, the Gentile sect would have done against that which was prior to it. And because these sects vary two or three times in five or six thousand years, the memory of the things done prior to that time is lost; and if, however, some sign of them remains, it is considered as something fabulous and is not lent faith to – as happened to the history of Diodorus Siculus, which, though it renders an account of forty or fifty thousand years, is nonetheless reputed, as I believe it to be, a mendacious thing.[73]

The theses declared by Machiavelli are of great philosophical importance. They are:

1. The Christian religion is nothing other than one *sect* among others.[74]
2. Religious sects are temporal apparatuses of power[75] that tend by nature to hegemony, and the logic that regulates the relationships between them on the world stage is that of war.
3. The memory of the spiritual culture of an epoch resides entirely within the materiality of the language that expresses it; language does not have the expressive centrality of a subject and, therefore, cannot be subject to absolute control. Consequently, a language can be entirely destroyed, but in the case in which it resists destruction, it escapes the attempts of power to control it. Its materiality is the *de facto* guarantee of its acentricity and its asystematic structure.[76]

[73] *Discourses on Livy* II, 5; Machiavelli 1996: 139. Regarding the 'mendaciousness' of Diodorus Siculus's history, Sasso writes: 'admitting (in principle) the "veracity" of those sparse fragments, he realised that "verifying them" was, however, impossible. In order to verify them it would have in fact been necessary to resort to the "context", or to the reality that, destroyed in the things themselves, was also dissolved in human memory. [. . .] To Greek history [. . .] Machiavelli seems to make a double, although coherent, rebuke: not only of having constructed a "fairy tale", but also, first of all, of not taking into account the methodogical difficulty that the investigation of the remote past was closed in on itself.' According to Sasso, Machiavelli does not want to claim that 'the history of Diodorus Siculus is a fairy tale because he speaks of very old things', but on the contrary, that 'it is not possible to ascertain the truth of the most ancient past insofar as its context is destroyed, and what remains of it, if anything, is only fragments, among which, precisely because they are nothing but fragments, we cannot rigorously decide which are true and which are false' (Sasso 1987: 378–83).

[74] This thesis is clearly at the root of Spinoza's arguments against Albert Burgh.

[75] Cf. the following passage from Spinoza's letter to Burgh: 'the organization of the Roman Church, which you praise so highly, is well-designed politically, and profitable for many' (*Ep.* LXXVI [to Albert Burgh]; CWS II, 477).

[76] Here again we can find an opposition *ante litteram* to Hobbes's conception of language

The combination of these three philosophical propositions outlines a theory of history in which memory, far from constituting the instrument of a more powerful knowledge, is what is at stake in the struggles between different sects: the winner attempts to destroy the memory of the vanquished and impose its own story of the world as the only truth (an attempt that can succeed only if the vanquished is destroyed right to its material roots, language).[77]

We can now consider the passage where Machiavelli presents 'the causes that come from heaven', that is, the natural causes of the destruction of memory:

> As to the causes that come from heaven, they are those that eliminate the human race and reduce the inhabitants of part of the world to a few. This comes about either through plague or through famine or through an inundation of waters. The most important is the last, both because it is more universal and because those who are saved are all mountain men and coarse, who, since they do not have knowledge of antiquity, cannot leave it to posterity. And if among them someone is saved who has knowledge of it, to make a reputation and a name for himself he conceals it and perverts it in his mode so that what he has wished to write alone, and nothing else, remains for his successors.[78]

and truth, which according to Lebrun, far from being an overturning of Platonism, is more of a daring rescue 'by moving the realisation of the "Truth" from knowledge to the "Institution"' (Lebrun 1983: 6). Balibar provides a discussion of Lebrun's interpretation as well as its alternatives regarding the modern conception of truth in Balibar 1992b. He proposes reading the Hobbes–Spinoza opposition through the contrast of institution of the truth–constitution of the truth: 'Spinoza opposes an entirely causal problematic to the juridical problematic in Hobbes' (Balibar 1992b: 20).

[77] It is interesting to note that Spinoza had access, in his own library, to historiographical models entirely opposite to Machiavelli. Saavedra, for example, claims that the imposition of the Latin language, against the multiplicity of languages existing in Spain, was inspired by Roman reason of state as well as divine providence, so that the message of the Gospel could spread: 'it was for reason of state (if not divine inspiration, so that the Gospel could spread more easily) that they made sure that all of the world was Roman, not only in the unity of political power, but also in conformity of languages, by reducing them all to Latin' (Saavedra 1681: 147–8). Saavedra's historical reconstruction is in general dominated by the influence of 'divine providence'.

[78] *Discourses on Livy* II, 5. Machiavelli 1996: 139–40. Here is Machiavelli's justification of the three phenomena of the natural destruction of memory, which is not devoid of a theological-moral aspect that is precisely the object of Spinoza's anti-teleological critique in the appendix to *Ethics* I: 'That these inundations, plagues, and famines come about I do not believe is to be doubted, because all of the histories are full of

Here are the philosophical theses that can be drawn out of this passage:

1. The history of humankind is profoundly rooted in nature, whose power can brutally make entire civilizations disappear. Consequently, the continuity of memorial narrative is nothing other than the continuity of a fragment, of an island that emerges above the flood of oblivion.
2. Memory does not uniformly permeate society: there is a stratification of memory within society that excludes the model of expressive causality and the *pars totalis*.[79]
3. Memory is much more an instrument of power and therefore the perversion of truth for a political goal than it is the adequate consciousness of the past.

Together these three theses constitute a theoretical position that can be read as a refutation of the great systems of idealism *ante litteratum*.

However, an unexpected source for this passage can be identified in Plato's *Timaeus*. There is actually a passage in Plato's cosmological work that Machiavelli's text seems to be modelled on in several respects. In the dialogue, a story is told about the existence of a city in ancient Greece whose inhabitants are very similar to those Socrates speaks of in the *Republic*. Plato underscores that what is in question in this story is not an invented myth but a true discourse. The reason why the memory of this city is lost is that the Greeks are all 'young in spirit', because in the city there is not 'any old opinion of traditional antiquity, no white-haired teacher for the age'. And this is the reason, according to the narration given by the old Egyptian priest to Solon:

> There have been, and there will continue to be, numerous disasters that have destroyed human life in many kinds of ways. The most serious of

them, because this effect of the oblivion of things is seen, and because it seems reasonable that it should be so. For as in simple bodies, when very much superfluous matter has gathered together there, nature many times moves by itself and produces a purge that is the health of that body, so it happens in this mixed body of the human race that when all provinces are filled with inhabitants (so that they can neither live there nor go elsewhere since all places are occupied and filled) and human astuteness and malignity have gone as far as they can go, the world must of necessity be purged by one of these three modes, so that men, through having become few and beaten, may live more advantageously and become better' (ibid.).

[79] Balibar defines this principle as 'the social homoeomery' [*l'homéomérie sociale*]: this consists in thinking that 'within every social (or political, or cultural) whole, the "parts" or "cells" are necessarily similar to the whole itself' (Balibar 1992a: 44).

these involve fire and water, while the lesser ones have numerous other causes. And so also among your people the tale is told that Phaethon, child of the Sun, once harnessed his father's chariot, but was unable to drive it along his father's course. He ended up burning everything on the earth's surface and was destroyed himself when a lightning bolt struck him. This tale is told as a myth, but the truth behind it is that there is a deviation in the heavenly bodies that travel around the earth, which cause huge fires that destroy what is on the earth across vast stretches of time. When this happens all those people who live in the mountains or in places that are high and dry are more likely to perish than the ones who live next to rivers or by the sea. Our Nile, always our savior, is released and at such times too, saves us from this disaster. On the other hand, whenever the gods send floods of water upon the earth to purge it, the herdsmen and shepherds in the mountains preserve their lives, while those who live in cities, in your region, are swept by the rivers into the sea. [. . .] Now of all the events reported to us, no matter where they've occurred – in your parts or in ours – if there are any that are noble or great or distinguished in some other way, they've all been inscribed here in our temples and preserved from antiquity on. In your case, on the other hand, as in that of others, no sooner have you achieved literacy and all the other resources that cities require, than there again, after the usual number of years, comes the heavenly flood. It sweeps upon you like a plague, and leaves only your illiterate and uncultured people behind. You become infants all over again, as it were, completely unfamiliar with anything there was in ancient times, whether here or in your own region. And so, Solon, the account you just gave of your people's lineage is like a nursery tale. First of all, you people remember only one flood, though in fact there had been a great many before. Second, you are unaware of the fact that the finest and best of all the races of humankind once lived in your region. This is the race from whom you yourself, your whole city, all that you and your countrymen have today, are sprung, thanks to the survival of a small portion of their stock. But this has escaped you, because for many generations the survivors passed on without leaving a written record.[80]

The essential point of Plato's narrative figures equally in Machiavelli's text: floods destroy the memory of humanity because the only survivors are illiterate. However, as is frequently the case in the history of philosophy, apparently similar arguments are inscribed in opposed theoretical

---

[80] Plato 1997: 1230–1.

strategies.[81] The flood functions in Plato as an argument in favour of a lost original wisdom (a conception that Nietzsche would define as 'Egypticism'), a thesis of the progressive fall of the ages made paradigmatic by Diodorus Siculus (which will inspire Vico's *course of nations*, inverting the arrow of time), whose history Machiavelli qualifies as a *mendacious thing*. For Machiavelli there is no lost originary wisdom, but only memory that has disappeared forever, or the political mystification of memory.

Machiavelli outlines a theory of history that eliminates the metaphysical dyad of Origin and End while ceaselessly affirming the aleatory necessity of encounters – encounters between virtue and fortune – in the form of multiple material forces: the materiality of the apparatuses of religious power, the materiality of languages, hunger, sicknesses, natural disasters, and the cultural stratification of society. The memory of a civilisation is therefore a fragile fragment of matter in the face of the immense power of nature, which has no teleological respect towards it. It can survive this immense power for some time and imagine itself to be eternal, projecting itself over the totality of time, but its destiny is, despite everything, oblivion.

This theoretical framework enables an explanation of the real meaning of Machiavelli's reference to Roman history, which apparently plays the origin role in a philosophy of history where Christianity would constitute the moment of loss, of crisis, and the future Italy the moment of the rebirth of ancient virtue. Actually, however, the Etruscan people, more ancient than the Romans, could also have had the role of an original reference point. And it is precisely in taking this possible objection as a counter-attack (which is actually the opinion of Coluccio Salutati and Leonardo Bruni) that Machiavelli evokes the Etruscans in the final lines of *Discourses on Livy* II, 4, which ignite the following chapter dedicated to oblivion that we have been examining:

---

[81] Sasso emphasises the difference between these two texts as follows: 'However, it is true that the above-mentioned agreement does not also concern the tone and structure of the two texts. Both in the *Laws*, as well as the *Timaeus*, primitive humanity – of which no particular memory survives – is presented with mythically positive characteristics. It appears alien from the "malice" that Machiavelli, instead, suspects, or even establishes, in the one who, having saved himself from extermination and finding himself with some notion of the destroyed past, transmits it to posterity, but disfigures and alters it' (Sasso 1987: 201). Sasso claims that this difference does not invalidate the agreement between the texts. For my part, I maintain that the rejection of the myth of origin and the alliance between memory and truth involves a strict distance taken against Platonism; given this antithetical theoretical horizon, the agreements between the texts thus play the role of a warning to the astute reader: 'we are refuting Plato'.

And if the imitation of the Romans seems difficult, that of the ancient Tuscans should not seem so, especially to the present Tuscans. For if they could not, for the causes said, make an empire like that of Rome, they could acquire the power in Italy that their mode of proceeding conceded them. This was secure for a great time, with the highest glory of empire and of arms and special praise for customs and religion. This power and glory were eliminated so much that although two thousand years ago the power of the Tuscans was great, at present there is almost no memory of it. This thing has made me think whence arises this oblivion of things.[82]

And at the end of the chapter on the causes of the destruction of memory, Machiavelli adds:

Tuscany was then, as was said above, once powerful, full of religion and of virtue, and had its customs and ancestral language, *all of which were eliminated by Roman power*. So, as was said, the memory of its name alone remains of it.[83]

Thus, Rome is not the *Ursprung* of a philosophy of history that thinks its own memory in terms of destiny [*Schicksal*], but a material fragment of the past that has withstood the ravages of time, one that can play the political role of being a model in the present against the dominant Christian model. The Etruscan model would have been just as valid, but nothing remains of this powerful and virtuous people except the name.[84]

This reading of Machiavelli allows us to interpret Spinoza's texts from a different perspective. What becomes visible for us through Machiavelli's anti-philosophy of history is a theory of history that refuses a conception of temporality understood as a linear, serial succession of events, thought as a decline, progression, or even cyclical return on itself. It is in the passage from the logic of *ordo sive series* (which is at the same time the logic of inmost essence) to the logic of *ordo sive connexio* (which is the logic of the identity of essence and power) that Spinoza transposes Machiavelli's historical-political insights on to an ontological level. This transfer can be summarised in three moves.

---

[82] *Discourses on Livy* II, 4; Machiavelli 1996: 138.
[83] *Discourses on Livy* II, 5; Machiavelli 1996: 139–40. My emphasis.
[84] On Machiavelli's criticism of the 'realist illusion of original facts', see Lefort 1986: 541–6.

1. The affirmation, as Hegel well knew, through the concept of God as *causa sui*, of the effect contained in the originary thing (the *Ursache* as the *ursprüngliche Sache*), or the deconstruction of the concept of origin.
2. The position, as an effect of the system, of the infinite intellect in *Natura naturata*, not therefore as the planning intelligence of the world, but as the infinite process of the knowledge of its facticity.[85]
3. Memory as the inadequate knowledge of the past and an instrument of power, and not as anamnesis of a truth that is always-already present in the soul.

Philosophical modernity (to use a once-fashionable phrase) is built precisely on the repression of these three theses.[86] If we consider, for example, Leibniz's system, whose latent or manifest influence on later philosophy is enormous, it is clear that it is elaborated against the logic of the *ordo sive connexio* and on the point-by-point inversion of Spinoza's theses. It could be objected that in the Leibnizian universe everything hangs together and therefore everything is interconnected, but this is actually nothing but an optical illusion that cannot be sustained by a more attentive look. Indeed, in the Leibnizian universe nothing truly touches, nothing encounters anything, and each monad remains the prisoner of the giant panopticon that is God, who, having established the serial laws of each monad in the moment of creation, produces the appearance of the encounter. The risk of the encounter is neutralised by the harmony of the series, pre-established by the divine intellect, wherein the complete notion of each individual lies:

> God originally created the soul (and any other real unity) in such a way that everything must arise for it from its own depths, through a perfect spontaneity relative to itself, and yet with a perfect conformity to external things. [. . .] This is what makes every substance represent the whole universe exactly and in its own way, from a certain point of view, and makes the perceptions or expressions of external things occur in the soul at a given time, in virtue of its own laws, as if in a world apart, and as if there

---

[85] In his famous Munich lecture on Spinoza, Schelling claims that Spinoza's God is 'that which can *only* be (and not also that which is able not to be), it is for that reason that which *only* is [*das nur Seyende*], i.e., being [*das Seyende*] which is by the exclusion of all non-being – by the exclusion of all potentiality – of all freedom (for freedom is non-being). Accordingly it is being [*das Seyende*] without potentiality, and, in *that* sense, powerless being, because it absolutely does not have the power of another being [*Seyn*] in itself' (Schelling 1994: 65).

[86] On the relationship between Spinoza and Leibniz, cf. Morfino 1994: 179–86.

existed only God and itself. [. . .] There will be a perfect agreement among all these substances, producing the same effect that would be noticed if they communicated through the transmission of species or qualities, as the common philosophers imagine they do.[87]

In this sense, to take up the example that Bayle provides in his article on Rorarius,[88] I never truly hit the dog with a cane, but the two serial laws, me and the dog, synchronised *ab origine*, ensure that in the moment when the movement of my arm that hits the dog is represented, the dog feels pain. There is seemingly no difference here, but a closer look at the theory of pre-established harmony shows that the dog's pain is God's choice *ab aeterno*, while for Spinozist theory it would be nothing but the aleatory effect of a necessary weave.

The theoretical power of Machiavelli and his argument about memory as a source for Spinoza is measured in all its breadth at the moment Spinoza sets out his reading of Scripture. Indeed Spinoza, following Machiavelli in my view, considers the Bible not as a true memory of the origin and history of the world, but as the imaginary[89] record of real history:

> For many things are related in Scripture as real, and were even believed to be real, which were, nevertheless, only representations and imaginary things [*In Scriptura enim multa, ut realia narrantur, et quae etiam realia esse credebantur, quae tamen non nisi repraesentationes, resque imaginariae fuerunt*].[90]

This imaginary memory, this past imagined by rudimentary opinions, is not a simple incorrect knowledge of history. Instead, it takes part in history by playing a political role: memory is the discipline of the body through the

---

[87] Leibniz 1989: 143–4.

[88] 'I understand why a god passes immediately from pleasure to pain when, being very hungry and eating some bread, he is suddenly beaten with a stick. But that his soul would be constructed so that at the instant he is hit, he feels pain and would so even though he were not hit and even though he continued eating bread without trouble and without being stopped – this is what I cannot understand' (Bayle 1991: 238).

[89] Daniela Bostrenghi emphasises the rarity of the term *imaginarius* in Spinoza as opposed to the frequency of terms such as *imago, imaginatio, imaginari* (*imaginarius* is used three times in the *Ethics* and six times in the *TTP*): 'the adjective indicates, therefore, a privation of reality (imaginary = what is not real), which does not, however, undermine the constitutive and structuring function of the same prophetic *imaginatio*' (Bostrenghi 1997: 107).

[90] *TTP* VI, 57; *CWS* II, 165.

obedience inscribed by customs in the daily life of the actions of the people. The memory of ancient times therefore plays a function that is disarticulated by the link with the truth, and instead articulated on the one hand with the spontaneous teleological prejudice of the imagination, and on the other with the inscription in the body of a code of behaviour conforming to social life.

Other elements of Machiavelli's conception of memory appear in Spinoza's work and at different levels of conceptual elaboration. For example, in *TTP* VII, when Spinoza articulates his method of reading Scripture,[91] he declares the methodological rule that separates his reading from the tradition:

> To sum up briefly, I say that the method of interpreting Scripture [*methodus interpretandi Scripturam*] does not differ at all from the method of interpreting nature, but agrees with it completely. For the method of interpreting nature consists above all in putting together a history of nature, from which, as from certain data, we infer the definitions of natural things. In the same way, to interpret Scripture it is necessary to prepare a straightforward [*sincera*] history of Scripture and to infer from it the mind [*mens*] of Scripture's authors, by legitimate inferences, as from certain data and principles.[92]

The interpretation of Scripture must therefore be based on 1) a reconstruction of its history grounded in an exact knowledge of the nature and properties of the Hebrew language [*natura et proprietates linguae*]; 2) an account of the sentences [*sententiae*] of each book, organising them under main headings and noting those which are obscure, ambiguous and contradictory; 3) an account of all of the circumstances concerning the prophetic books through which memory was transmitted: the life, concerns and cultural references of the author, what occasioned its writing, the time it took to write it, the public to which it was addressed, and its language. In addition, the fortune of each book must be taken into consideration, in the triple sense of the original reception, its history and readings, and its acceptance among the sacred books.[93]

It is thus clear, as Spinoza himself openly affirms, that the question that must be posed to Scripture is not about its truth, but its meaning ('We

---

[91] On Spinoza's method of reading, cf. Strauss 1965, which accurately retraces the sources. Cf. also Zac 1965; Tosel 1984: 105–26.

[92] *TTP* VII, 6–7; CWS II, 171.

[93] *TTP* VII, 23; CWS II, 175.

are concerned only with the meaning of the utterances, not with their truth').[94] The meaning of this text offers itself to us as the complex weave of multiple durations, irreducible to the linear model of *logos*.[95] This sense is first of all linked to the materiality of a language whose structure, because of its singular constitution, is a source of ambiguity.[96] It is usually linked to the singular customs and structure of each author, as well as the circum-stances of its writing, namely the modalities of the author's encounter with their time. Finally, it is indissociable from successive encounters with other singular structures and apparatuses of power to which written books are submitted.

According to Spinoza, the reconstruction of this meaning must be based on the material memory of the language, which both scholars and the people preserve, because the meaning of words hinges on networks of relations that can neither be decided upon or dominated by single individuals. No one can arbitrarily change the meaning of a word in order to mystify, because the meanings of words reside in a weave of institutional relations in both the scholarly practice of writing that goes into the texts of the tradition and in the everyday communicative action of the masses. One must (instead) be wary of interpretative traditions such as those of the Pharisees[97] or the Roman Church, who have political interests in modifying the meaning of the argument of Scripture:

---

[94] *TTP* VII, 16; CWS II, 173.

[95] According to Blumenberg, Spinoza does not only maintain the factual non-unity of the Bible, but also 'its principle of impossibility as such': 'No revelation could communicate to man what was completely unknown, and nothing can take place elsewhere than in the heads of the members of the linguistic and epochal community, in their conditions. What was said with angelic language, for humans would simply mean nothing. A god who wanted to reveal himself would have to conceal what he is. Consequently he would not have anything to communicate, and that book would remain empty' (Blumenberg 1984: 102).

[96] 'In addition [. . .] there is the very nature and constitution of the language. So many ambiguities arise from this that it is impossible to devise a method which will teach you how to find out with certainty the true meaning of all the utterances of Scripture. For besides the causes of ambiguity common to all languages there are certain others in this language from which a great many ambiguities are born' (*TTP* VII, 47; CWS II, 180).

[97] In reconstructing Spinoza's conception of the Hebrew tradition, Chamla emphasises the apparent entirely negative judgement towards the Pharisees, but at the same time an even greater theoretical incompatibility with the adversary position of the Sadducees, who propose a backwards look to a sort of literal intangibility of the truth. Cf. Chamla 1996: 152–4.

We've shown, then, the way to interpret Scripture, and at the same time demonstrated that this is the only way to find its true meaning [*verus sensus*] with great certainty. Of course, if anyone has a certain tradition about this, *or* a true explanation received from the Prophets themselves (as the Pharisees claim), I concede that he is more certain of the meaning of Scripture. Similarly, if anyone has a High Priest who cannot err concerning the interpretation of Scripture (as the Roman Catholics boast). Nevertheless, since we cannot be certain, either of this tradition or of the authority of the High Priest, we also cannot found anything certain on these things. For the most ancient Sects of the Christians denied [the authority of the Pope], and the most ancient Sects of the Jews denied [the Pharisaic tradition]. Moreover – not to mention other objections now – if we pay attention to the chronology [*ad seriem annorum*] the Pharisees received from their Rabbis, by which they extend this tradition all the way back to Moses, we shall find that it is false. [. . .]

So a tradition like that must be very suspect to us [*Quare talis traditio nobis admodum debet esse suspecta*]. It's true that in our Method we are compelled to suppose that *one tradition of the Jews is uncorrupted*: the meaning of the words of the Hebrew language [*significatio verborum linguae Hebraicae*] which we have accepted from them. But though we don't doubt that tradition at all, we still doubt that tradition [about the meaning of passages in Scripture]. For it could never be to anyone's advantage to change the meaning of a word [*verborum significatio*]; but it could often be to someone's advantage to change the meaning of an utterance [*sensus orationis*]. It's extremely difficult to change the meaning of a word. Anyone who tried to do this would be forced, as a part of the process, to explain all the authors who wrote in that language and used that word in its accepted meaning. Either he would have to do this according to the temperament and mind of each author [*ingenium vel mens*], or else he would have to distort them very carefully.

Moreover, both the common people and the learned preserve language; but only the learned preserve books and the meanings of utterances. So we can easily conceive that the learned could have changed or corrupted the meaning of an utterance in some very rare book which they had in their 'power', but not that they could have changed the meaning of words. Moreover, if someone wants to change the meaning of some word to which he has become accustomed, it will be difficult for him to observe the new meaning afterward both in speaking and in writing. These and other reasons easily persuade us that it could not occur to anyone to corrupt a language, but that it could often occur to someone to corrupt the thought of a writer by changing his utterances or by misinterpreting them.[98]

The knowledge of the meaning of Scripture therefore passes through the knowledge of the Hebrew language (for which the material continuity of the use of the language is necessary, and not the spiritual continuity of the truth), because it is impermeable to the attempt to modify the meaning of words for political goals, and instead radically refuses the authority of those interpretative traditions that can have a political interest in changing the meaning of the argument, such as those of the Pharisees or Roman Catholics. This analysis corresponds to an essential approach in Machiavelli's argument about memory. On the one hand, it corresponds to the material memory of language that belongs to the people ('both the common people and the learned preserve language'), and escapes every attempt of the semantic police, where instead the Hobbesian utopia resides. On the other hand, it corresponds to the alteration and perversion of memory for political goals, which must in any case take account of this materiality.

The method Spinoza proposes for interpreting Scripture requires, in order to clarify the meaning of each book, a perfect knowledge of the Hebrew language and the history of what happened with each book of Scripture [*historia casuum omnium liborum Scripturae*]. In terms of the difficulty of restoring these histories, Spinoza introduces another Machiavellian theme: the destruction of memory by natural and political events. First of all, time has eroded the very memory of the language:

> To begin with, a great difficulty in this method arises from the fact that it requires a complete knowledge [*integra cognitio*] of the Hebrew language. But where is this now to be sought? Those who spoke and wrote in Hebrew in ancient times left nothing to posterity regarding its foundations and teaching. Or at least we have absolutely nothing from them: no Dictionary, no Grammar, no Rhetoric. Moreover, the Hebrew nation has lost all its marks of distinction and honor – this is no wonder, after it has suffered so many disasters and persecutions [*clades & persecutiones*] – and has retained only some few fragments of its language and of a few books. For almost all the names of the fruits, birds, fish, and many other things have perished in the injuries of time [*temporum injuria*]. Again, the meaning of many nouns and verbs which occur in the Bible is either completely unknown or is disputed.

[98] *TTP* VII, 38–42; CWS II, 178–80. Translation modified.

We lack, not only all these things, but also and especially, a phrase-
ology of this language. For time, the devourer, has obliterated from the
memory of men almost all the idioms and manners of speaking peculiar to
the Hebrew nation [omnes fere tempus edax ex hominum memoria abolevit].[99]

The meaning of the argument [orationis sensus] thus cannot be reconstructed
from the use of the language [ex linguae usu], and remains lost forever. The
causes of this loss, whose theorisation implies the rupture with a fundamental
dogma of every philosophy of history (the belief in the continuity of meaning, of logos), are political and natural at the same time. On the one hand,
there is the disintegration of political unity (Babylonian wickedness and
the diaspora), the defeats, the persecutions, and on the other, the injuries of
time, natural calamities. These two types of causality are summarised in that
extraordinary conclusive synthesis that, bringing new life to the Greek myth
of Chronos, makes visible the destructive power of time with an image that
has crossed through Western literature from Ovid to Shakespeare: tempus
edax, 'time, the devourer'.[100]

Language, therefore, is linked to the daily life of the people and is a means
of transmission that cannot be subjected to political control. Yet it is continually eroded by the devouring power of time, which manifests as material
destruction in the form of defeats, persecutions and natural calamities for
the community that conserves language. Spinoza inscribes the concept of
tradition itself into very precise material limits. It eludes the linear logic
of series and is instead subordinated to the complex logic of connexio, the
fabric, the weave that is a continual loss and transformation of meaning,[101]
whose origin is nothing more than a material genesis, an encounter whose

---

[99] TTP VII, 44–5; CWS II, 180. Translation modified.

[100] In his translation, Droetto surprisingly renders this with the neutral 'passage of time'
[andar del tempo], whereas Fergnani puts it much better as 'time's voracity' [voracità del
tempo]. See Spinoza 1972: 407.

[101] Here is an important passage from chapter eight on the theme: 'Though such a history
is very necessary, the Ancients still neglected it. Or if they wrote any of it (or handed
it down [in an oral tradition]), that has perished by the assault of time [temporum
injuria]. So a large part of the foundations and principles of this knowledge has fallen
into oblivion. This loss is one we might still have endured, if those who subsequently
transmitted the texts had stayed within the proper limits, and in good faith transmitted to their successors the few things they had received or found, without concocting
new things out of their own brains. The result has been that the history of Scripture
has been left, not only incomplete, but also quite faulty. The foundations of the
knowledge of the Scriptures are not just too slight to have allowed the whole [history
of Scripture] to be built on them; they are defective' (TTP VIII, 1–2; CWS II, 192).

aleatory necessity frees it from every value-laden meaning: Nietzsche would say an *Entstehung* (emergence) and not an *Ursprung* (origin).

The second difficulty arises from the interpretation of Scripture, namely the ignorance of the circumstances in which the texts were written and who the authors of the text are, which again emphasises the problem of material genesis.

> There is yet another difficulty in this method: it requires a history of the circumstances of all the books of Scripture. For the most part we do not know this history. Either we are completely ignorant of the authors (or, if you prefer, Writers) of many of the books, or else we have doubts about them. [. . .] Moreover, for the books whose writers we do know, we also do not know on what occasion or at what time the books were written [*qua occasione, neque quo tempore*]. In addition, we do not know into whose hands all the books fell, nor in which copies so many different readings [*variae lectiones*] were found, nor, finally, whether there were not many other readings in other copies.
>
> If we read a book which contains incredible or incomprehensible things, or is written in very obscure terms, we don't know its author, or when or on what occasion it was written, it will be pointless for us to become more certain of its true meaning. If we're ignorant of all these things, we can't know anything about what the author intended, or could have intended. On the other hand, when we know these things properly, we determine our thoughts in such a way that we're not predisposed by any prejudice. So we don't attribute to the author – or to the one on whose behalf the author wrote – more or less than is just. And we don't think about any other things other than those the author could have had in mind, or which the time and occasion required.[102]

Scripture is thus not the true memory of the past, or tradition as the transmission of a continuous meaning from God to the successive generations of the Hebrew people (a tradition that is identified with the totality itself of history). Instead, Scripture is the imaginary memory of a fragment whose meaning is lost forever, along with the record of the conjuncture that gave rise to it. It is not an accident that Spinoza repeatedly uses the term *occasio*.[103]

---

[102] *TTP* VII, 58–60; CWS II, 183.

[103] The index of the *TTP* alerts us to sixteen occurrences of this term in the text (CWS II, 694). Only in chapter seven does Spinoza use it five times, and always in a pair with the term *tempus* (using it at *TTP* III, 101, 101, 102, 103, 109, 110; CWS II, 175, 175, 176, 183, 183).

This negation of an originary meaning, the divine *logos* that would be transmitted intact to successive generations (the God of Abraham, Isaac, Jacob, etc.), is also the negation, on a political level, of a mythical first cause that presents itself with the pen strokes of a legislator inspired by God who establishes the eternal order of a society.[104] This negation, through the analysis of the singular history of the Hebrew people, gets rid of the idea of a legislator God. Indeed, this history emphasises the imaginary status of a God who transmits laws to the people. After their exodus, no longer subject to the laws of another nation, the Hebrews, again in possession of their own natural right, had the possibility of establishing new laws and occupying new lands. In these conditions, they opted to stipulate a pact with God:

> When they'd been placed in this natural condition, they decided to transfer their right only to God, not to any mortal. That was Moses' advice and they had the utmost trust in him. Without further delay they all promised equally, in one voice [*omnes aeque uno clamore promiserunt*], to obey all God's commands absolutely, and not to recognize any other law except what he would establish as law by Prophetic revelation.[105]

The Hebrew state thus had the form of a theocracy in which God was the only monarch. However, Spinoza immediately adds that 'truly all these things consisted more in opinion than in fact' [*Verum enimvero haec omnia opinione magis, quam re constabant*].[106] The divine transmission of the law to the people is therefore just as imaginary as the idea of a legislator *in one stroke*, of which moreover the pact of the people with God in one voice [*uno*

---

[104] The parallel between God and a unique legislator, used in positive terms to legitimate the proper foundation of science on entirely new bases, is found in Descartes: 'Peoples who have grown gradually from a half-savage to a civilized state, and have made their laws only in so far as they were forced to by the inconvenience of crimes and quarrels, could not be so well governed as those who from the beginning of their society have observed the basic laws laid down by some wise law-giver. Similarly, it is quite certain that the constitution of the true religion, whose articles have been made by God alone, must be incomparably better ordered than all the others' (*AT* IX, 12; Descartes 1985: 116–17). God, the legislator and the method play the same role, albeit on different theoretical levels: they provide the guarantee of existence on the ontological, political and epistemological levels, respectively. It is not an accident that Spinoza rejects every transcendent guarantee, in order to study pure facticity and its dynamics on both the ontological and political levels, as well as the cognitive.

[105] *TTP* XVII, 27; *CWS* II, 301.

[106] *TTP* XVII, 32; *CWS* II, 302.

clamore] is the mirror image. The citizens who turn to God all together in order to interpret commands cannot but take note of the impossibility of such an operation: because the *interpres*, the prophet, is the one who mediates between God and the people, this would be possible only in the event that a sort of reciprocal mediation of everyone in relation to everyone could happen. But this is excluded by the nature of prophetic knowledge. A homogeneous collective interpretation is not possible because of the differences in the imaginative structure of each individual prophet, which Spinoza described in *TTP* II.

However, Spinoza does not limit himself to demonstrating the impossibility of a legislator God. He also negates the possibility of a legislator man, of a Moses who has the privilege to speak to God face to face. Just as Machiavelli had done for Rome, in analysing the Hebrew state, Spinoza shows that its constitution after Moses escapes the classic typology:

> Moses [. . .] left the state to be administered by his successors in such a way that he couldn't be called either popular, or aristocratic, or monarchic, but theocratic. For one person had the right of interpreting the laws and of communicating God's replies, and another had the right and power to administer the state according to the laws already explained and the replies already communicated.[107]

This constitution of the state does not correspond to the initial project of Moses, but is rather the consequence of the people's adoration for the golden calf, which brought Moses to exclude the firstborn from the sacred ministry in order to confine it to the Levite tribe.

The biblical passage shows how the new constitution, far from being the fruit of rational planning, had its origin in unprecedented violence which established a new relation of force within society.

> 26 Then Moses stood in the gate of the camp, and said, 'Who is on the Lord's side? Come to me!' And all the sons of Levi gathered around him. 27 He said to them, 'Thus says the Lord, the God of Israel, "Put your sword on your side, each of you! Go back and forth from gate to gate throughout the camp, and each of you kill your brother, your friend, and your neighbour."' 28 The sons of Levi did as Moses commanded, and about three thousand people fell on that day. 29 Moses said, 'Today you have ordained yourselves for the service of the Lord, each one at the cost

---

[107] *TTP* XVII, 41; CWS II, 304–5.

of a son or a brother, and so have brought a blessing on yourselves this day.'[108]

This exclusion of the people from the sacred ministry would generate a state of permanent sedition, which will lead to the dissolution of a state that has been rendered fragile and incapable of resisting the blows of fortune.[109] Spinoza here deconstructs the myth of the legislator's omnipotence, demonstrating that legislative action is inscribed in the relations of force of a conjuncture – in the materiality of an occasion that renders it possible and determines it. As Machiavelli already before him, Spinoza, approaching the singular object of his study, abandons the idea of a first cause from which a linear time flows in order to analyse it in its singular *connexio*, in the interweaving that constitutes its political form not *in one stroke*, but 'by chance, and in more times, and according to the accidents', that is, through the combination of partial measures determined by circumstances.

---

[108] Exodus 32:26–9. This is the version of Exodus present in Spinoza's library (Testamenti Veteris Biblia 1618: 100). Translator's note: Spinoza's Latin edition reads as follows: '26 Subsistens Mosche in porta castrorum edixit, quisquis *est* Jehovae, ad me *aggregator*: sic aggregati sunt ad eum omnis filii Levi. 27 Dixitque illis, sic ait Jehova Deus Jisrelis, apponite quisque gladium suum femori suo: transite et redite per castra de porta in portam, & occidite quisque fratrem suum, & quisque amicum suum, & quisque propinquum suum. 28 Quod fecerunt filii Levi secundum edictum Moschis; & ceciderint de populo illo, eo ipso die, ad tria millia virorum. 29 Dicebat enim Mosche, consecrate ministerium vestrum hodie Jehovae, quum quis filio suo, aut fratri sup aderat: &iditurus est vobis hodie benedictionem.' Cf. the Spanish translation, also included in the archival list at the Hague: 'Y parose Moseh en puerta del real y dixo, quien por.A.comigo: y apañarose à todos hijos de Levi. Y dixo à ellos, assi dixo.A. dio de Ysrael, poned cada uno su espada sobre su anca, passad y torros, y varon à su cercano. E hizieron hijos de Levi como palabra de Moseh, y cayó del pueblo en el dia esse como tres mil varones. Y dixo Moseh, henchistes vuestras manos oy à.A., que cada uno en su hijo, y en su hermano: y para dar sobre vos oy benedicion' (Biblia 1646: 65).
[109] *TTP* XVII, 103–12; *CWS* II, 319–20.

Conclusion

Works on the sources of philosophy generally have the limit of being one-sided. Given its objective of emphasising the importance of one way of thinking in the formation of another, in most cases such research ends up either demonstrating a sort of repetition of a hidden source behind the argument that has merely been adapted to new times, or it puts in motion an *Aufhebung* of which the 'original' source is a necessary moment. Spinoza, whose thought allows for the widest possible interpretative spectrum (from neoplatonism to materialism), is extremely opportune for this type of analysis. Indeed, as Macherey has highlighted, Spinoza is 'located at the crossroads of several cultures'.[1] The material fabric from which he produced his work derives, to cite only the best-known sources, from the Jewish tradition, the Arabic enlightenment, neoplatonism, the Italian Renaissance, scholasticism, Spanish baroque culture, and, undoubtedly, Bacon, Hobbes and Descartes. The temptation to select the red thread – the fundamental source of which Spinozist philosophy would be nothing but an original repetition – from within the complex weave of these traditions is strong: here then is where we would find that Spinoza, beneath his simple Latin, actually thinks in Spanish, Portuguese, Hebrew and/or Scholastic Latin. I believe instead that Spinoza's thought is irreducible to any of its sources, and, moreover, cannot be thought as the result of a successful combination between elements of Descartes, Hobbes, Plotinus, Maimonides, etc.

As such, I will be wary of saying that Spinoza thought in Italian, or better yet, in Florentine, in the *sparse and powerful* style of the cursed secretary. Further, such an operation, which would consist in searching for a simple and transitive origin in the material weave that composes Spinoza's texts, would do nothing to restore a clearer image of Spinoza's philosophy. To

---

[1] Macherey 1992: 29.

think a Machiavellian Spinoza would mean searching through Spinoza's work for the Machiavelli-enigma rather than illustrating the conclusive meaning of Spinoza's philosophy.[2]

However, refusing to conclude by stitching up with the help of the conceptual instruments of classical metaphysics – such as cause, essence, telos and origin – does not entail sceptically abandoning the task of conceptualising the Spinoza–Machiavelli relation. Such a refusal instead precisely furnishes a methodological warning against every type of simplifying temptation.

The Spinoza–Machiavelli encounter must be thought without the help of teleological models. It must be thought as a plural encounter: an encounter of Spinoza the reader with the materiality of the Florentine language in one of the five 'Testina' editions of Machiavelli's complete works, and with the materiality of Silvestro Tegli's Latin translation of *The Prince* in one of the two editions, 1560 or 1580; an encounter with the image of Machiavelli established in Latin by the work of Bacon and Clapmar, in Spanish by Gracian, Quevedo, Perez and Saavedra, in Italian by Leti, in Dutch by the van Hove brothers and Glazemaker's translation of Descartes' letters; and yet more encounters whose traces have perhaps been devoured by time. We should emphasise again the risk of reducing Spinoza's reading to the list of his archives in The Hague, as well as the risk of imagining Spinoza engaged in a kind of monographic research on the image of Machiavelli as it emerges from the work in his library. And yet what we can detect in this plurality of possible encounters, besides the traditional image of Machiavelli as the devil incarnate, the living antithesis of Christianity (an image that Spinoza will explicitly oppose in the *TP*), is the display of certain impulses for thinking several fundamental philosophical problems that stem precisely from a confrontation with Machiavelli. From this point of view, what seems especially important is Bacon's inversion of Machiavelli's argument about oblivion, where in opposition to the Florentine secretary he reaffirms the historical centrality of religion founded on the rock (while others are built on sand), as well as the letters between Descartes and Elisabeth, where the problem of the relation between force and law is posed aporetically (a structural aporia similar to the one between the cogito and clarity that Spinoza will encounter at another level of Cartesian philosophy).

This plural encounter has left material traces in Spinoza's production at different levels: 1) an explicit level, with the two citations in the *TP*; 2) an implicit level, with the strategic repetition of key Machiavellian arguments

---

[2] 'The question of Machiavelli will probably remain one that never closes or exits from the archives' (Croce 1952: 176).

in his two great political works; and 3) an ontological level, in the *Ethics*, as the modification of an extensive conceptual structure in relation to the *TdIE*. The path I have traced within the materiality of Spinoza's texts has shown, beyond ideal genealogies of a materialist current, the powerful effects that the encounter with Machiavelli produced in the theoretical structure of the mature Spinoza.

1) We have seen, at a first level, that the citations in the *TP* are by no means happenstance, but on the contrary are indispensable to the argumentative strategy of the chapters in which they are inserted. The first citation immediately emphasises the fact that Spinoza does not classify Machiavelli, whom he defines as *sapiens* and *prudentissimus*, among the politicians, who are instead, with a concession to common opinion, defined as cunning [*callidi*], and above all whose practice he characterises as guided more by fear than reason. Moreover, if we consider the entire part of the *TP* on political ontology, namely the first five chapters, we find that Spinoza's references to Machiavelli constitute its alpha and omega: Machiavelli is evoked in the first paragraph of the first chapter, at the moment Spinoza answers the question 'what is political philosophy?', at the moment he traces a line of demarcation between the theological-political imagination of man and the effectual truth of the weave of passions that compose human society. And then Machiavelli is evoked again in the final paragraph of chapter five, where the question of the purpose of political theory is posed, whose answer, formulated by Spinoza through an interpretation of the *acutissimus florentinus*, is freedom. Machiavelli is thus summoned not as one political thinker among others, but as a universal individuality – on the same level as Euclid – as the founder of modern politics. The sole difference between them lies in the fact that political theory is itself traversed by the political struggle it describes, and for this reason it appears to lack the universality of geometry. The praise Spinoza addresses to Machiavelli consecrates an exemplary theoretical path: it is the praise of a theory that is at the same time an instrument of liberation from religious prejudice. Proposing an interpretation of *The Prince* that underlines its paradoxical character, Spinoza refuses, however, to inscribe this paradox into the dilemma between monarchy and republicanism. Machiavelli's thought is a thought of the necessity of contingency, which rejects the Platonic logic of the best kind of regime. Spinoza's aim is to illuminate the interventions in the conjuncture, which are nothing but the structure of habits, customs and laws of the multitude, or the historical form taken by the relations of ideas and passions that traverse the multitude.

The second citation, found at the beginning of *TP* X, is actually a summary of *Discourses on Livy* III, 1 which Machiavelli dedicates to the necessity of the return to principles. What is essential here is that the principle, the origin, is not thought in the terms of originary peace, as in the Platonic *topos*, but as a relation of forces, an encounter of passions. In other words, to use Hegelian terminology, origin is not thought as *Ursache* but rather as *Wechselwirkung*, and this allows Spinoza to describe, beyond every essentialism and teleology, the model of political praxis as an intervention in the conjuncture, by means of the disjunction borrowed from Machiavelli's style: *aut virtus aut fortuna*.

2) At a second level, we have also seen the silent repetition of Machiavellian arguments in both the *TTP* and the *TP*. Contrary to Adolph Menzel's claim at the outset of the twentieth century, Machiavelli is quite present in the *TTP*. First, in defining the terms 'God's guidance', 'God's external aid', 'God's internal aid', 'God's election' and 'fortune', Spinoza's concepts are extremely close to Machiavelli's pair of virtue and fortune, which Spinoza leverages to deconstruct the myth of election. Second, recalling only the most important points, when Spinoza describes the importance of the political function of religion for the constitution of the state, what is revealed, as Balibar was the first to show, is a strict parallelism between Spinoza's account of Moses establishing power and Machiavelli's account of Numa – a parallelism confirmed even in minute textual details. And finally, third, we have seen the insertion of Machiavelli's paradigm regarding the observance of faith from *The Prince* XVIII into the theoretical framework of natural law theory. This paradigm is at least present at the terminological level, and extends Machiavelli's metaphor of the centaur, half-man, half-beast, to all of society, thereby eliminating the radical discontinuity between the Hobbesian state of nature and civil society.

The *TP*, where Spinoza's preoccupation with the theological dimension has disappeared, is precisely characterised by the centrality of removing the discontinuity between the natural state and civil society. It is made within a reflection that now seems liberated from the natural law horizon that had inspired it. Indeed, natural individual right and the pact disappear, while the collective power of the multitude, as a fundamental element in the constitution of the state, appears on the theoretical scene (and regarding this point, Spinoza's use of the plural for the term *contractus* in its sole occurrence in the *TP* clearly indicates the change in terrain that has taken place). The references to *The Prince* XVIII, which we found in *TP* II, 12 as well as *TP* IV, 5–6, where Spinoza describes the dissolution of the state as the consequence of popular hatred and indignation, are just as important in this conceptual movement. This sums up a theme that Machiavelli insists on several times throughout *The Prince* and *Discourses on Livy*, as well as in some extraordinary pages of the *Florentine Histories*.

As we have emphasised, therefore, the continuity of the reading and strategic use of Machiavelli in both works lies precisely in Spinoza's double-inversion of the Hobbesian theoretical-political problematic. First, Spinoza overturns Hobbes's natural law theory with the affirmation of the impossibility of establishing a juridical foreclosure of the state of nature by means of a social pact. Second, Spinoza overturns legal positivism by refusing the sovereign's ability to determine the *salus populi*. Spinoza's introduction of the theme of popular hatred and indignation in the *TP* signals that he definitively renounced thinking the constitution or dissolution of a society by means of an abstract and utilitarian model of calculating rationality for a conception of society as the complex weave of passions.

As such, I think that what Spinoza finds in Machiavelli's theory of politics and history is the path towards a model of reason that is different than the Hobbesian model of calculating reason, which extends the mathematical paradigm to the totality of the real.[3] In confronting historical-political questions, Spinoza abandons a system of thought founded on a serial logic and a form of transitive causality in order to affirm a rationality founded on the complex logic of a mesh of passions. Such complexity lies at the origin of the apparent simplicity of individuals and their rational calculations. It is for this reason, as Matheron has shown, that Hobbesian theory seems to take the form of a utopia for Spinoza. Machiavelli's influence on Spinoza therefore touches a deep metaphysical root. Indeed, this new conception of reason does not simply repeat Machiavelli, but is the effect of the encounter between Machiavelli's politics and Spinoza's metaphysics, an effect that produces in Spinoza a change in both the metaphysical and political fields.

3) It is thus at the level of the extensive metaphysical structures of Spinoza's ontology that the effects of Machiavelli's politics must be measured. To this end I have formulated the hypothesis, on the basis of a passage in the appendix to *Ethics* I indicated by Balibar, that the causes allowing humans to lay waste to the *dark forest* of teleological prejudice cannot be limited to mathematical knowledge: Machiavelli's theory of politics and history must be added to the second kind of knowledge of the common notions of the social body. This hypothesis leads, in addition, to a clarification of the third kind of knowledge. The example Spinoza provides in *Ethics* II, 40

---

[3] Hobbes writes: 'For reason, in this sense, is nothing but *reckoning* (that is, adding and subtracting) of the consequence of general names agreed upon for the *marking* and *signifying* of our thoughts' (Hobbes 1994: 22–3).

remains obscure precisely because of the fact that mathematical essences, as the very properties common to things, cannot have a singular essence. The third kind of knowledge should thus be understood as the knowledge of the singular history of a people. Machiavelli provides an example of this with the Romans in the *Discourses on Livy*, and Spinoza outlines his own by taking up Hebrew history in chapters seventeen and eighteen of the *TTP*. In both cases, it is on the basis of re-elaborating an imaginary narrative (Titus Livy for Machiavelli, and the Bible for Spinoza) through the common notions of the social body that the adequate knowledge of a singular essence of a people is produced.

However, the application of *ratio* to the historical-political field entails a thorough modification of its structures. If indeed the second kind of knowledge means *scire per causas*, then the adjustment to the concept of cause that follows from the encounter with Machiavellian thought must be analysed. In the sketch of the ontology that we traced in the *TdIE*, Spinoza divides beings into two series – fixed and eternal things, and things subject to change. The knowledge of things subject to change assumes a bracketing of their order of existence, which offers nothing but an exterior knowledge and does not permit access to their *inmost essence*. What must instead be focused on is the series of fixed and eternal things and the laws inscribed within them, which make up the true code of the series of changeable things. No science of the contingent, of the series of changeable things, is therefore possible, but only a science of the necessary, of fixed and eternal things. As such, there could not be a science of relations and circumstances, which concerns the series of changeable things, and therefore there could be no science of history and politics. However, what is decisive in this ontological sketch is the concept of series that Spinoza used to define the causal order and concatenation of the inner essence of things. In the *TdIE*, the causal order is a serial order that confers a logical-mathematical undertone to Spinoza's ontology at that time.

My hypothesis is that the encounter with Machiavelli, likely contemporaneous with the drafting of the *TTP* (this period at least constitutes the endpoint of his reading of Machiavelli), had the consequence of Spinoza's redefinition of the concept of cause. Indeed, the term *series* disappears from the *Ethics*, and the term *connexio* appears in its place. *Connexio* defines the order of *Natura naturata* as the immanent effect of the causal power that constitutes the order of *Natura naturans* (while in the *TdIE*, God is said to be *causa prima*, but never *causa immanens*). The concept of the individual loses the anthropomorphic simplicity and unity that conferred its inmost essence in the *TdIE* (namely, what remained beyond exterior relations and existential circumstances), yielding to the complexity of a proportional relation in which essence and power do not differ, and power is the capacity to enter into relation with the external. Cause therefore loses the anthropomorphic simplicity of a juridical relation in order to take on the structural plurality of complex relations with the outside. All of these elements were excluded as inessential from the adequate knowledge of things in the *TdIE*. It is perhaps barely exaggerating to say that the essence–existence relation is inverted from the *TdIE*: the essence of things now resides in the accomplished fact of the existential relations and circumstances that have produced their existence. In other words, the essence of a thing is not conceivable until after its power of acting reveals its true interiority. We could here read the influence of Machiavelli's concept of virtue understood as action rather than its Christian meaning of withdrawal from the world.[4] This redefinition of cause as order by connection (as Balibar proposes to translate the formula *ordo et connexio*) owes a lot to the Machiavellian notion of the occasion, which expresses precisely the primacy of the relation between things over their inmost essence, and the primacy of the aleatory over every theology or teleology of cause.

The logic of *ordo et connexio* leads Spinoza to think the temporality of history beyond all linear representations produced by the memory's way of functioning through concatenation, and independently from every first cause, which in politics takes the form of an omnipotent legislator. The space of history and politics is constituted by the complex *connexio* of different levels of being whose knowledge *sub specie aeternitatis* precisely supposes abandoning the absolutisation and simplification of time that memory puts into place. And it is precisely in the deconstruction of the ancient alliance between memory and truth that Spinoza again meets the Machiavelli of the chapter in the *Discourses on Livy* dedicated to oblivion. Far from corresponding to the sincere history of the past (the anamnesis of an eternity always-

---

[4] It seems that Spinoza was well aware of the Machiavellian critique of Christianity as what would have made 'the world effeminate' (*Discourses on Livy* II, 2; Machiavelli 1996: 131); he reproduces it in his own reading when he claims regarding the Hebrews that 'the foundations of their religion [made] their hearts unmanly' [*fundamenta suae religionis eorum animos effœminarent*] (*TTP* III, 55; CWS II, 124). Strauss has constructed a genealogy for this line of thought: 'The passions for "worldly honor" or "worldly glory" which animate political life and which manifest themselves in terrible and vigorous deeds, and not merely in endurance of sufferings, are the nexus out of which Machiavelli and Giordano Bruno draw their rejection of the Christian ideal, which allegedly fosters quietism' (Strauss 1965: 48). According to Strauss, the Machiavelli–Bruno line makes up one of the three sources of the critique of religion in the seventeenth century, with the others being Epicurus and Averroes.

already there), memory is nothing but the inadequate knowledge of the past, indissolubly linked to the materiality of the language that expresses it, and also an instrument of mystification in service to power. The affirmation of the contingency of memory and the contingency of tradition,[5] the demystification of memory as imaginary knowledge of a surviving fragment, and the excess of the power of nature surreptitiously erected as the centre of the universe and time: Spinoza's philosophy has been considered the only philosophy capable of thinking the Copernican revolution in all its radicality; perhaps we could say the same thing about the Machiavellian revolution.[6]

Reading Spinoza in light of Machiavelli thus carries us to an interpretation of his thought that escapes both from the philosophy of history and from every form of nihilism. Spinoza strives to understand history and politics through the logic of *ordo sive connexio*, which is not the simple and linear order that memory inscribes into habit,[7] but a complex order, the effect of encounters of differential necessity.[8] Different levels of being interfere with one another beyond any pre-established harmony (these levels are not permeated by a *Zeitgeist* precisely because there can be no absolute contemporaneity, no *absolute Zugleich*), producing the effects of causality, understood not as the absence of necessity, but as the encounter of differential necessity. History is not subject to the law of a linear temporality; it is the effect of the emergence of a level of being that owes its existence to the duration of the encounter of multiple necessities. The question of meaning, evoked by Leibniz's fundamental question 'why is there something rather than nothing?', is therefore, from this perspective, abolished: there is no other meaning except the complex weave of necessities, the differential articulation of durations and rhythms. The foundation is not beyond the

---

[5] In the corollary of *Ethics* II, 31; CWS I, 472, Spinoza establishes an equation between contingency [*contingentia*] and the possibility of corruption [*possibilitas corruptionis*].

[6] Carlo Sini, in a remark following an old judgement of Feuerbach, defines Spinoza's thought as 'Copernican *par excellence*' (Sini 1992: 91).

[7] In reference to the scholium I recalled above, Laurent Bove writes: 'It is thus beyond the imaginary couple formed by the images of (repetitive) Order and the contingency relative to it (as the rupture of order) that the reader of the *Ethics* must think the eternal and infinite necessity of nature' (Bove 1996: 148).

[8] Bove's parallel between Spinoza and Epicurus is here very interesting: 'the Epicurean affirmation of chance then becomes the affirmation of the existence of the infinite in its differential necessities. This positive conception of chance, which does not contradict the affirmation of a universal causality, one can suppose Spinoza to have read in Lucretius' (Bove 1996: 149). In this sense, it is perhaps useful to recall the importance of Lucretius for the formation of Machiavelli's thought; he transcribed *De rerum natura*, probably in order to possess a copy (Bertelli 1961; Bertelli 1964).

series, as in Leibniz, but in the *connexio*, as immanent cause, which is, however, not reflected in the *conatus*, precisely because it is not an image that
can be reflected, but rather the weave itself thought as conjunction and not
always-already as conjuncture.

Bibliography

Albiac, G. (1987), *La sinagoga vacia: un estudio de las fuentes marranas del espinosismo*, Madrid: Libros Hiperión.

Albiac, G. (1988), '"Recuperar lo pasado": L'axe épicurisme/machiavélisme dans l'histoire apologétique d'Abraham Pereyra', *Archives de Philosophie* 51, 2: 39–53.

Althusser, L. (1990), 'Is It Simple to be a Marxist in Philosophy?', trans. G. Lock, in G. Elliott (ed.), *Philosophy and the Spontaneous Philosophy of the Scientists & Other Essays*, London: Verso, pp. 203–40.

Althusser, L. (1997), 'The Only Materialist Tradition: Spinoza', trans. T. Stolze, in W. Montag and T. Stolze (eds), *The New Spinoza*, Minneapolis: University of Minnesota Press, pp. 3–20.

Althusser, L. (1999), *Machiavelli and Us*, trans. G. Elliot, London: Verso.

Althusser, L. (2006), *Philosophy of the Encounter: Later Writings, 1978–87*, trans. G. M. Goshgarian, ed. F. Matheron and O. Corpet, London: Verso.

Althusser, L., E. Balibar, R. Establet, P. Macherey and J. Rancière (2015), *Reading Capital: The Complete Edition*, trans. B. Brewster and D. Fernbach, London: Verso.

Altini, C. (1998), 'Spinoza lettore di Machiavelli', *Bolletino della società di studi fiorentini* 3: 31–8.

Andújar, A. H. (1989), *La teoria del Estado de Spinoza*, Seville: Universidad de Sevilla.

Aquinas, T. (2006), *Summa Theologiae: Questions on God*, ed. B. Davies and B. Leftow, Cambridge: Cambridge University Press.

Archives de Philosophie (1994), 57, 3.

Aristotle (1984a), *Complete Works, Volume I*, ed. J. Barnes, Princeton: Princeton University Press.

Aristotle (1984b), *Complete Works, Volume II*, ed. J. Barnes, Princeton: Princeton University Press.

Armogather, J. R., and J. L. Marion (1976), *Index des* Regulae ad directionem ingenii *de René Descartes*, Rome: Edizioni dell'Ateneo.

Bachelard, G. (2000), *The Dialectic of Duration*, trans. Mary McAllester Jones, Manchester: Clinamen Press.

Bacon, F. (1641), *Semones Fideles, Ethici, Politici, Œconomici sive Interiora rerum. Accedit Faber fortunae &c.*, Lug. Batavorum, Apud Franciscum Hackium.

Bacon, F. (1861), *The Advancement of Learning*, ed. William Aldis Wright, Oxford: Clarendon Press.

Bacon, F. (1985), *The Essays*, ed. John Pitcher, London: Penguin Books.

Bacon, F. (1999), *Selected Philosophical Works*, ed. Rose-Mary Sargent, Indianapolis: Hackett Publishing.

Bacon, F. (2000), *The New Organon*, ed. L. Jardine and M. Silverthorne, Cambridge: Cambridge University Press.

Balibar, E. (1990), 'Individualité, causalité, substance. Réflexions sur l'ontologie de Spinoza', in E. Curley and P. F. Moreau (eds), *Spinoza: Issues and Directions (Proceedings of the Chicago Spinoza Conference, 1986)*, Leiden: Brill. pp. 58–76.

Balibar, E. (1992a), 'Foucault and Marx: The Question of Nominalism', in T. J. Armstrong (ed.), *Michel Foucault: Philosopher*, New York: Routledge, pp. 38–56.

Balibar, E. (1992b), 'L'institution de la vérité: Hobbes et Spinoza', in D. Bostrenghi (ed.), *Hobbes e Spinoza: Scienza e politica*, Naples: Bibliopolis, pp. 3–22.

Balibar, E. (1997a), *Spinoza: From Individuality to Transindividuality*, Delft: Eburon.

Balibar, E. (1997b), '*Jus Pactum Lex*: On the Constitution of the Subject in the *Theologico-Political Treatise*', in W. Montag and T. Stolze (eds), *The New Spinoza*, Minneapolis: University of Minnesota Press, pp. 171–206.

Balibar, E. (1998), *Spinoza and Politics*, trans. P. Snowdon, London: Verso.

Barbaras, F. (1996), 'Spinoza et Democrite', *Studia Spinozana* 12: 12–27.

Baumgarten, A. (2013), *Metaphysics*, trans. and ed. C. D. Fugae and J. Hymers, London: Bloomsbury.

Bayle, P. (1991), *Historical and Critical Dictionary: Selections*, trans. R. H. Popkin, Indianapolis: Hackett Publishing.

Benjamin, W. (1968), 'Theses on the Philosophy of History', in W. Benjamin, *Illuminations*, trans. H. Zohn, New York: Schocken Books, pp. 253–64.

Bennett, J. (1996), 'Spinoza's Metaphysics', in D. Garrett (ed.), *The Cambridge Companion to Spinoza*, Cambridge: Cambridge University Press, pp. 61–88.

Berns, T. (2000), *Violence de la loi à la Renaissance. L'originaire du politique chez Machiavel et Montaigne*, Paris: Kimé.

Bertelli, S. (1961), 'Noterelle machiavelliane: un codice di Lucrezio e di Terenzio', *Rivista storica italiana* 73: 544–53.

Bertelli, S. (1964), 'Noterelle machiavelliane. Ancora su Lucrezio e Machiavelli', *Rivista storica italiana* 76: 774–90.

Bertman, M., H. De Dijn and M. Walther (eds) (1987), 'Hobbes and Spinoza', *Studia Spinoziana* 3: 21–347.

Bertrand, M. (1983), *Spinoza et l'imaginaire*, Paris: Presses universitaires de France.

Bianchi, L. (1987), *L'inizio dei tempi Antichità e novità del mondo da Bonaventura a Newton*, Florence: Olschki.

Biblia (1646), *Biblia en lengua espanola*, Amsterdam: Impressesadorie de Gillis Joost.

Blumenberg, H. (1984), *La leggibilità del mondo*, trans. B. Argenton, Bologna: Il Mulino.

Bobbio, N. (1963), *Locke e il diritto naturale*, Turin: Giappichelli.

Bobbio, N. (1965), *Da Hobbes a Marx*, Naples: Morano.

Bock, G. (1990), 'Civil Discord in Machiavelli's *Istorie Fiorentine*', in G. Bock, Q. Skinner and M. Viroli (eds), *Machiavelli and Republicanism*, Cambridge: Cambridge University Press, pp. 181–202.

Boethius (1990), *The Consolation of Philosophy*, trans. P. G. Walsh, Oxford: Clarendon Press.

Bonicalzi, F. (1997), 'La causalité dans la science cartésienne', in O. Depré and D. Lories (eds), *Lire Descartes Aujourd'hui*, Louvain: Editions Peeters.

Bonnant, G. (1965), 'Les impressions genevoises au XCII siècle de l'édition des œuvres de Machiavel', *Annali della scuola speciale per archivisti e bibliotecari dell'Università di Roma* 5.

Bordoli, R. (1994), *Memoria e abitudine. Descartes, La Forge, Spinoza*, Milan: Geurini.

Borges, J. L. (1972), 'Spinoza', trans. R. Howard and C. Rennert, in J. L. Borges, *Selected Poems 1923–1967*, ed. N. T. di Giovanni, London: Allen Lane, The Penguin Press, pp. 212–13.

Bostrenghi, D. (1992a), 'Aspetti della imaginatio negli scritti di Spinoza', *Bollettino dell'Associazione Italiana degli Amici di Spinoza* III: 35–44.

Bostrenghi, D. (1992b), *Hobbes e Spinoza: Scienza e politica*, Naples: Bibliopolis.

Bostrenghi, D. (1997), *Forme e virtù della immaginazione in Spinoza*, Naples: Bibliopolis.

Bouveresse, R. (1992), *Spinoza et Leibniz. L'idée d'animisme universel*, Paris: Vrin.

Bove, L. (1996), *La strátegie du conatus: Affirmation et résistance chez Spinoza*, Paris: Vrin.

Bove, L. (1999), 'La réalisme ontologique de la durée chez Spinoza lecteur de Machiavel', in L. Bove (ed.), *La recta ratio: Criticiste et Spinoziste? Hommage en l'honneur de Bernard Rousset*, Paris: Presses de l'Université de la Sorbonne, pp. 47–64.

Bovero, M. (1992), 'Hobbes e Spinoza', in D. Bostrenghi, (ed.), *Hobbes e Spinoza: Scienza e politica*, Naples: Bibliopolis, pp. 673–9.

Breton, S. (1982–83), 'Hegel ou Spinoza. Réflexions sur l'enjeu d'une alternative', *Cahiers Spinoza* 4: 61–87.

Burot, L. (1992), 'Le vocabulaire du contrat, du pacte, et de l'alliance: quelques enjeux lexicaux', in Y. C. Zarka (ed.), *Hobbes et son vocabulaire*, Paris: Vrin, pp. 187–205.

Cahné, P. -A. (1977), *Index des Discours de la méthode de René Descartes*, Rome: Edizioni dell'Ateneo.

Campanella, T. (1967), *Metaphysicorum dogmatum / Metafisica, Vol. II*, trans. and ed. G. De Napoli, Bologna: Zanichelli.

Canone, E. , and G. Totaro (1991), 'Il *Tractatus de Intellectus emendatione* di Spinoza: Index locorum', *Lexicon Philosophicum* 5: 21–2.

Canziani, G. (1980), *Filosofia e scienza nella morale di Descartes*, Florence: La Nuova Italia.

Caporali, R. (2000), *La fabbrica dell' "Imperium": Saggio su Spinoza*, Naples: Liguori Editore.

Cassirer, E. (2007), *The Myth of the State*, trans. M. Lukay, Hamburg: Felix Meiner.

Chamla, M. (1996), *Spinoza e il concetto della tradizione ebraica*, Milan: Franco Angeli.

Clapmar, A. (1641), *De arcanis rerumpublicarum*, Amsterdam: Ludovicum Elzevirum.

Corsano, A. (1948), *U. Grozio. L'umanista, il teologo, il giurista*, Bari: Laterza.

Cortellazzo, M., and P. Zolli (1985), *Dizionario etimologico della lingua italiana 3/I–N*, Bologna: Zanichelli.

Costa, P. (1999), *Storia della cittadinanza in Europa, Vol. 1*, Rome–Bari: Laterza.

Cristofolini, P. (1985), 'Esse *sui juris* e scienza politica', *Studia Spinozana* 1: 53–71.

Cristofolini, P. (1987), *La scienza intuitiva di Spinoza*, Naples: Morano.

Cristofolini, P. (1988), 'Imagination joie et socialité selon Spinoza', in R. Bouveresse (ed.), *Spinoza: Science et religion*, Paris: Vrin, pp. 47–33.

Cristofolini, P. (1993), *Spinoza per tutti*, Milan: Feltrinelli.

Cristofolini, P. (1995), *Scienza Nuova: Introduzione alla lettura*, Rome: La Nuova Italia Scientifica.

Cristofolini, P. (1996), 'Note di un traduttore', *Bollettino Spinoziano* 7: 5–12.

Cristofolini, P. (1997), 'Le parole-chiave del *Trattatto politico* e le traduzione moderni', in P. Totaro (ed.), *Spinoziana: Ricerche di terminologia filosofica e critica testuale*, Florence: Olschki, pp. 23–38.

Cristofolini, P. (1999), 'La paix comme vertu de l'homme libre', unedited conference paper given in Amsterdam, October.

Cristofolini, P. (2001), *Vico pagano e barbaro*, Pisa: ETS.

Cristofolini, P. (2003), 'Spinoza e l'acutissimo fiorentino', in V. Morfino and F. Del Lucchese (eds), *Sulla scienza intuitiva in Spinoza: Ontologia, politica, estetica*, Milan: Ghibli.

Croce, B. (1952), *Indagni su Hegel e schiarimenti filosofici*, Bari: Laterza.

D'Andrea, D. (1997), *Prometeo e Ulisse. Natura umana e ordine politico in Thomas Hobbes*, Florence: La Nuova Italia.

De Bujanda, J. M., R. d'Avignon and E. Stenek (eds), *Index des livres interdits, VIII: Index de Rome 1557, 1559, 1564. Les premiers index romains et l'index du Concile de Trente*, Centre d'études sur la Renaissance, Geneva: Editions de l'Université de Scherbrooke.

De Deugd, C. (1966), *The Significance of Spinoza's First Kind of Knowledge*, Assen: Van Gorcum.

De la Court, J., and P. de la Court (1937), *La Balance politique, Livre premier*, trans. M. Francès, Paris: Librarie Félix Alcan.

De la Court, P. (1662), *Politike Discoursen*, Leyden, By Pieter Hackius: In 't Jaar.

De Michelis Pintacuda, F. (1967), *Le origini storiche culturali del pensiero di Ugo Grozio*, Florence: La Nuova Italia.

De Witt, J. [P. van Hove] (1669), *Aanwysing der heilsame politike gronden en Maximen van de Republieke van Holland en West-Vriesland*, Leiden–Rotterdam: Hakkens.

Del Lucchese, F. (1999–2000), 'Le statut philosophique du conflit chez Machiavel et Spinoza', Mémoire de D. E.A.

Del Lucchese, F. (2001), '"Disputare" e "combattere": Modi del conflitto nel pensiero politico di Niccolò Machiavelli', *Filosofia politica* XV, 1: 71–95.

Del Lucchese, F. (2009), *Conflict, Power, and Multitude in Machiavelli and Spinoza: Tumult and Indignation*, London: Continuum.

Del Lucchese, F., F. Frosini and V. Morfino (eds) (2015), *The Radical Machiavelli: Politics, Philosophy, and Language*, Leiden: Brill.

Delbos, V. (1990), *La problème moral dans la philosophie de Spinoza et dans l'histoire du spinozisme*, Paris: Presses universitaires de France.

Deleuze, D. (1988), *Spinoza: Practical Philosophy*, trans. Robert Hurley, San Francisco: City Lights.

Deleuze, D. (1992), *Expressionism in Philosophy: Spinoza*, trans. Martin Joughin, New York: Zone Books.

Des Cartes, R. (1641), *Brieven*, trans. J. H. Glazemaker, Amsterdam: Tymon Houthaak.

Descartes, R. (1985), *The Philosophical Writings of Descartes, Volume I*, trans. John Cottingham, Cambridge: Cambridge University Press.

Descartes, R. (1991), *The Philosophical Writings of Descartes, Volume III*, trans. John Cottingham, Cambridge: Cambridge University Press.

Di Vona, P. (1960), *Studi sull'ontologia di Spinoza*, Florence: La Nuova Italia.

Di Vona, P. (1969), *Studi sull'ontologia di Spinoza Parte II*, Florence: La Nuova Italia.

Di Vona, P. (1977), 'La definizione dell'essenza in Spinoza', *Revue Internationale de Philosophie* 31, 119–20: 39–52.

Di Vona, P. (1990), *Aspetti di Hobbes e Spinoza*, Naples: Loffredo.

Di Vona, P. (1995), *La conoscenza* Sub specie aeternitatis *nell'opera di Spinoza*, Naples: Loffredo.

Diodato, R. (1990a), *Sub specie AEternitatis: Luoghi dell'ontologia spinoziana*, Milan: CUSL.

Diodato, R. (1990b), *Superficialità della bellezza*, Milan: Melograno.

Diodato, R. (1994), *Immagine dell'assente: Vermeer, Spinoza*, Milan: Melograno.

Diodato, R. (1997), *Vermeer, Góngora, Spinoza: L'estetica come scienza intuitiva*, Milan: Bruno Mondadori.

Dionisotti, C. (1980), *Machiavellerie: storia e fortuna di Machiavelli*, Turin: Einaudi.

Dotti, U. (1979), *Niccolò Machiavelli: La fenomenologia del potere*, Milan: Feltrinelli.

Duchesnau, F. (1978), 'Modèle cartésien et modèle spinoziste dans l'être vivant', *Cahiers Spinoza* 2: 241–85.

Dujovne, L. (1945), *Spinoza. Su vida, su época, su obra, su influencia, Vol. IV (La influencia de Baruj Spinoza)*, Buenos Aires: Imprenta López.

Duprat, G. (1980), 'Expérience et science politiques. Machiavel, Hobbes', *Cahiers Vilfredo Pareto* 49: 101–30.

Elisabeth of Bohemia and R. Descartes (2007), *The Correspondence Between*

Princess Elisabeth of Bohemia and René Descartes, trans. and ed. L. Shapiro, Chicago: University of Chicago Press.

Esposito, R. (1984), *Ordine e conflitto: Machiavelli e la letteratura politica del Rinascimento italiano*, Naples: Liguori.

Esposito, R. (1996), 'Introduzione: Termini della politica', in R. Esposito (ed.), *Oltre la politica: Antologia del peinsiero 'impolitico'*, Milan: Bruno Mondadori, pp. 2–3.

Faraklas, G. (1997), *Machiavel: Le pouvoir du prince*, Paris: Presses universitaires de France.

Filippi, I. (1985), *Materia e scienza in Spinoza*, Palermo: Libreria Dario Flaccovio Editore.

Forni, E. (1990), 'Verso la filosofia della storia: Una possibile interpretazione della Provvidenza nel Trattato teologico-politico', *Annali di Storia dell'Esegesi* 7, 1: 29–43.

Francès, M. (1951), 'Les réminiscences spinozistes dans le *Contrat social* de Rousseau', *Revue Philosophique de la France et de l'Etranger* 76, 1: 61–84.

Gallicet Calvetti, C. (1972), *Spinoza lettore del Machiavelli*, Milan: Vita e Pensiero.

Gamba, B. (1839), *Serie dei testi di lingua e di altre opere importanti nella italiana letteratura scritte dal secolo XIV al XIX*, Venice: Gondoliere.

Garin, E. (1993), *Machiavelli tra politica e storia*, Turin: Einaudi.

Gebhardt, C. (1923), 'Spinoza gegen Clapmarius', *Chronicon Spinozanum* 3: 344–7.

Gentili, A. (1964), *De Legationibus Libri Tres*, trans. G. J. Laing, New York: Oceana Publications.

Gerber, A. (1906), 'The Mutual Relations of the Five Prints of the Testina and the Terminus Post Quem of the Original', *Modern Language Notes* 21, 6: 171–5.

Gerber, A. (1962), *Niccolò Machiavelli: Die Handscriften, Ausgaben und Ubersetzungen seiner Werke im 16. und 17. Jahrhundert*, Turin: Bottega d'Erasmo.

Gerbier, L. (1999), 'Histoire, médecine et politique: Les figures du temps dans le *Prince* et les *Discours* de Machiavel', PhD thesis, Université de Tours.

Giancotti, E. (ed.) (1970), *Lexicon Spinozanum*, 2 vols, La Haye: Martinus Nijoff.

Giancotti, E. (1995), *Studi su Hobbes e Spinoza*, Naples: Bibliopolis.

Gilead, A. (1985), 'The Order and the Connection of Things', *Kant Studien* 76: 72–7.

Glare, P. G. W. (ed.) (1982), *Oxford Latin Dictionary*, Oxford: Clarendon Press.

Gouhier, H. (1973) *Descartes: Essais sur le* Disours de la méthode, *la métaphysique et la morale*, Paris: Vrin.

Gracian, B. (1653), *El Criticón*, En Huesca: por Juan Nogues.

Gramsci, A. (1966), *Note sul Machiavelli*, Turin: Einaudi.

Grotius, H. (2005), *The Rights of War and Peace, Book 1*, trans. and ed. R. Tuck, Indianapolis: Liberty Fund.

Guena, M. (1998), 'La tradizione repubblicana e i suoi interpreti: Famiglie teoriche e discontinuità concettuali', *Filosofia politica* 12, 1: 101–32.

Gueroult, M. (1968), *Spinoza Dieu ('Ethique', 1)*, Paris: Aubier.

Gueroult, M. (1974), *Spinoza II – l'ame*, Paris: Aubier.

Guerret, M., A. Robinet and P. Tombeur (1977), *Spinoza: Ethica – Concordances, Index, Listes de fréquences, Tables comparatives*, Louvain-la-Neuve: UCL.

Guzzo, A. (1924), *Il pensiero di Spinoza*, Florence: La Nuova Italia.

Habermas, J. (1973), *Theory and Practice*, trans. J. Viertel, Boston: Beacon Press.

Hammacher, K. (1977), 'The Cosmic Creed and Spinoza's Third Mode of Knowledge', in S. Hessing (ed.), *Speculum Spinozanum 1677–1977*, London: Routledge & Kegan Paul, pp. 183–96.

Harrington, J. (1977), The Commonwealth of Oceana, in The Political Works of James Harrington, Volume 1, ed. J. G. A. Pocock, Cambridge: Cambridge University Press, pp. 155–360.

Hegel, G. W. F. (1976), *Science of Logic*, trans. A. V. Miller, New York: Humanities Press.

Hegel, G. W. F. (1991), *The Encyclopedia Logic, Part I of the Encylopaedia of Philosophical Sciences with the Zusätze*, trans. T. F. Geraets, W. A. Suchting and H. S. Harris, Indianapolis: Hackett Publishing.

Hegel, G. W. F. (1997), *Phenomenology of Spirit*, trans. A. V. Miller, Oxford: Oxford University Press.

Hegel, G. W. F. (2008), *Outlines of a Philosophy of Right*, trans. T. M. Knox, rev. S. Houlgate, Oxford: Oxford University Press.

Herder, J. G. (1967–68), *Gott, Einige Gespräche*, in J. G. Herder, *Sämliche Werke*, Vol. 3, ed. C. Redlich, New York: Georg Olms.

Hess, M. (1961), *Philosophische und sozialistische Schriften: 1837–1850*, Berlin: Akademie Verlag.

Hobbes, T. (1839), *The English Works of Thomas Hobbes of Malmesbury, Volume I*, ed. W. Molesworth, London: John Bohn.

Hobbes, T. (1994), *Leviathan, with Selected Variants from the Latin Edition of 1668*, trans. and ed. E. Curley, Indianapolis: Hackett Publishing.

Hobbes, T. (1995), *Three Discourses: A Critical Modern Edition of Newly Identified Work of the Young Hobbes*, ed. N. Reynolds and A. Saxonhouse, Chicago: University of Chicago Press.

Hobbes, T. (1998), *On the Citizen*, trans. and ed. R. Tuck and M. Silverthorne, Cambridge: Cambridge University Press.

Horkheimer, M. (1993), 'Beginnings of the Bourgeois Philosophy of History', in M. Horkheimer, *Between Philosophy and Social Science: Early Writings*, trans. and ed. G. F. Hunter, M. S. Kramer and J. Torpey, Cambridge, MA: MIT Press, pp. 313–88.

Hubbeling, H. G. (1967), *Spinoza's Methodology*, Assen: Van Gorcum.

Jacobi, F. H. (1994), *The Main Philosophical Writings and the Novel Allwill*, trans. D. di Giovanni, Montreal: McGill-Queen's University Press.

Jacobi, F. H. (2000), *Über die Lehre des Spinoza in Briefen an den Herrn Moses Mendelssohn*, Hamburg: Felix Meiner.

Jankélévitch, V. (1980), *Le Je-ne-sais-quoi et le Presque-Rien, Vol. I: La Manière et l'Occasion*, Paris: Seuil.

Joachim, H. H. (1940), *Spinoza's Tractatus de intellectus emendatione*, Oxford: Clarendon Press.

Jonas, H. (1979), 'Spinoza and the Theory of Organism', in M. Grene (ed.), *Spinoza: A Collection of Critical Essays*, Notre Dame: University of Notre Dame Press, pp. 259–78.

Kaegi, W. (1960), 'Machiavelli a Basilea', in D. Cantimore (ed.), *Meditazioni storiche*, Bari: Laterza, pp. 155–215.

Kant, I. (1998), *Critique of Pure Reason*, trans. and ed. P. Guyer and A. W. Wood, Cambridge: Cambridge University Press.

Kneale, M. (1979), 'Eternity and Sempiternity', in M. Grene (ed.), *Spinoza: A Collection of Critical Essays*, Notre Dame: University of Notre Dame Press, pp. 227–40.

La Peyrère, I. (1655), *Systema theologicum ex Prae-Adamitarum hypothesi pars prima*, Amsterdam: Elzevir.

Land, J. P. N. (1889), 'De bibliotheek van Spinoza', *De Nederlandsche Spectator* 15 (13 April 1889): 117–19.

Languet, H. (1994), *Vindicae contra tyrannos, or, concerning the legitimate power of a prince over the people, and of the people over a prince / Stephanus Junius Brutus, the Celt*, trans. and ed. G. Garnett, Cambridge: Cambridge University Press.

Larivaille, P. (1982), *La pensée politique de Machiavel. Les Discours sur la première décade de Tite-Live*, Nancy: Presses universitaires de Nancy.

Laux, N. (1994), *Imagination et religion chez Spinoza: La 'potentia' dans l'histoire*, Paris: Vrin.

Lazzeri, C. (1990), 'Les racines de la volonté de puissance: Le "passage" de Machiavel à Hobbes', in Y. C. Zarka and J. Bernhardt (eds), *Thomas Hobbes: Philosophie première, théorie de la science et politique*, Paris: Presses universitaires de France, pp. 225–46.

Lazzeri, C. (1998), *Droit, pouvoir et liberté. Spinoza critique de Hobbes*, Paris: Presses universitaires de France.

Lebrun, G. (1983), 'Hobbes et l'institution de la vérité', *Manuscritto* 6, 2: 105–31.

Lefort, C. (1986), *Le travail de l'oeuvre*, Paris: Gallimard.

Leibniz, G. W. (1989), *Philosophical Essays*, trans. R. Ariew and D. Garber, Indianapolis: Hackett Publishing.

Lessing, G. E. (1991), *La religione dell'umanità*, trans. and ed. N. Merker, Rome–Bari: Laterza.

Lessing, G. E. (2005), *Philosophical and Theological Writings*, trans. and ed. H. B. Nisbet, Cambridge: Cambridge University Press.

Leti, G. (1671), *Le visioni politche*, Germania.

Lucas, H. (1988), 'Margen y centro: Dos formas de critica (Hegel/Derrida) a la filosofía del estado de Spinoza y Hegel', *Taula* 9: 47–73.

Lucretius (1992), *De Rerum Natura*, trans. W. H. D. Rouse, Cambridge, MA: Harvard University Press.

Lukács, G. (1966), *The Young Hegel: Studies in the Relations between Dialectics and Economics*, trans. R. Livingston, Cambridge, MA: MIT Press.

Macherey, P. (1992), *Avec Spinoza: Etudes sur la doctrine et l'histoire du spinozisme*, Paris: Presses universitaires de France.

Macherey, P. (1994), *Introduction à l'Ethique du Spinoza. La cinquième partie, les voies de la libération*, Paris: Presses universitaires de France.

Macherey, P. (1997), *Introduction à l'Ethique de Spinoza: La seconde partie, la réalité mentale*, Paris: Presses universitaires de France.

Macherey, P. (1998), *Introduction à l'Ethique de Spinoza: La première partie, la nature des choses*, Paris: Presses universitaires de France.

Macherey, P. (2011), *Hegel or Spinoza*, trans. S. M. Ruddick, Minneapolis: University of Minnesota Press.

Machiavelli, N. (1560), *De Principe Libellus*, Basel: Pietro Perna.

Machiavelli, N. (1580), *De Principe Libellus*, Basel: Pietro Perna.

Machiavelli, N. (1958), *Machiavelli: The Chief Works and Others, Volume II*, trans. A. H. Gilbert, Durham, NC: Duke University Press.

Machiavelli, N. (1971), *Tutte le opere*, ed. M. Martelli, Florence: Sansoni.

Machiavelli, N. (1985), *The Prince*, trans. H. C. Mansfield, Princeton: Princeton University Press.

Machiavelli, N. (1988), *Florentine Histories*, trans. L. F. Banfield and H. C. Mansfield, Princeton: Princeton University Press.

Machiavelli, N. (1993), *Opere politiche, Vol. II*, ed. G. M. Anselmi, Turin: Boringhieri.

Machiavelli, N. (1996), *Discourses on Livy*, trans. H. C. Mansfield and N. Tarcov, Princeton: Princeton University Press.

Machiavelli, N. (1997), *Opere, Vol. I*, ed. C. Vivanti, Turin: Einaudi-Gallimard.

Maggiore, G. (1927), 'Due Anniversarie (Machiavelli e Spinoza)', *Critica fascista* 5.

Marion, J. L. et al. (1996), Index des Meditationes de prima philosophia de R. Descartes, Paris: Annales littéraires de l'Université de Franche-Comté.

Marvall, J. -A. (1955), *La philosophie politique espagnole au XVII siècle dans ses rapports avec l'esprit de la Contre-Réforme*, Paris: Vrin.

Matheron, F. (1969), *Individu et communauté chez Spinoza*, Paris: Les Éditions de Minuit.

Matheron, F. (1971), *Le Christ et le salut des ignorants chez Spinoza*, Paris: Aubier.

Matheron, F. (1978), 'Spinoza et la décomposition de la politique thomiste: Machiavélisme et utopie', *Archivio di filosofia (Lo spinozismo ieri e oggi)* 47, 1: 29–60.

Matheron, F. (1986), 'Spinoza and Euclidean Arithmetic: The Example of the Fourth Proportional', in M. Grene and D. Nails (eds), *Spinoza and the Sciences*, Dordrecht: Kluwer Academic Publishers, pp. 125–50.

Matheron, F. (1988), 'Les modes de connaissance du *Traité de la Réforme de l'Entendement* et les genres de connaissane de l'*Ethique*', in R. Bouveresse (ed.), *Spinoza: Science et religion*, Paris: Vrin, pp. 97–108.

Matheron, F. (1990), 'Le problème de l'évolution de Spinoza du *Traité théologico-politique* au *Traité politique*', in E. Curley and P. F. Moreau (eds), *Spinoza: Issues and Directions (Proceedings of the Chicago Spinoza Conference, 1986)*, Leiden: Brill, pp. 258–70.

Matheron, F. (1994), 'L'indignation et le "conatus" de l'Etat spinoziste', in M. Revault D'Allons and H. Rizk (eds), *Spinoza: Puissance et ontologie*, Paris: Kimé, pp. 153–65.

Meinecke, F. (1976), *Die Idee der Staatsräson in der neueren Geschichte*, Munich/Vienna: Oldenbourg.

Meinsma, K. O. (1983), *Spinoza et son cercle: Etude critique historique sur les hétérodoxes hollandais*, Paris: Vrin.

Melchionda, M. (1979), *Gli 'Essayes' di Francis Bacon. Studio introduttivo e commento*, Florence: Olschki, pp. 3–56.

Mendelssohn, M. (1983), *Jerusalem: Or, On Religious Power and Judaism*, trans. Allan Arkush, Lebanon, NH: University Press of New England.

Menzel, A. (1902), 'Machiavelli und Spinoza', *Grünhuts Zeitschrift für das Privat und Öffentliches Recht der Gegenwart* 29: 567.

Meschini, F. (1996), *Indice dei Principia Philosophiae di René Descartes, Indici lemmatizzati, frequenze, distribuzione di lemmi*, Florence: Olschki.

Mignini, F. (1979), 'Per la datazione e l'interpretazione del *Tractatus de intellectus emendatione*', *La Cultura* 17: 87–160.

Mignini, F. (1981), *Ars imaginandi: Apparenza e rappresentazione in Spinoza*, Naples: Edizioni Scientifiche Italiane.

Mignini, F. (1983), *Introduzione a Spinoza*, Rome–Bari: Laterza.

Mignini, F. (1985), 'Nuovi contributi per la datazione e l'interpretazione del *Tractatus de intellectus emendatione*', in E. Giancotti (ed.), *Spinoza nel 350 anniversario della nascita*, Naples: Bibliopolis, pp. 515–25.

Mignini, F. (1987), 'Données et problèmes de la chronologie spinozienne entre 1656 et 1665', *Revue des Sciences Philosophiques et Théologiques* 71: 9–21.

Mignini, F. (1988), 'Per una nuova edizione del *Tractatus de intellectus emendatione*', *Studia Spinozana* 4: 15–35.

Mignini, F. (1997), 'Annotazioni sul lessico del *Tractatus de Intellectus Emendatione*', in P. Totaro (ed.), *Spinoziana: Ricerche di terminologia filosofica e critica testuale*, Florence: Olschki, pp. 107–23.

Moreau, J. (1971), *Spinoza et le spinozisme*, Paris: Presses universitaires de France.

Moreau, P. F. (1975), *Spinoza*, Paris: Seuil.

Moreau, P. F. (1985), 'Politiques du langage', *Revue Philosophique de la France et de l'Etranger* 110, 2: 189–94.

Moreau, P. F. (1989), *Méthode et métaphysique*, Paris: Presses universitaires de France.

Moreau, P. F. (1990), 'Fortune et théorie de l'histoire', in E. Curley and P. F. Moreau (eds), *Spinoza: Issues and Directions (Proceedings of the Chicago Spinoza Conference, 1986)*, Leiden: Brill, pp. 298–305.

Moreau, P. F. (1994), *Spinoza: L'expérience et l'éternité*, Paris: Presses universitaires de France.

Morfino, V. (ed.) (1994), *Spinoza contra Leibniz*, Milan: Unicopli.

Morfino, V. (1997), *Substantia sive Organismus*, Milan: Geurini.

Morfino, V. (ed.) (1998), *La Spinoza-Renaissance nella Germania di fine Settecento*, Milan: Unicopli.

Morfino, V. (2000), *Sulla violenza: Una lettura di Hegel*, Pavia–Como: Ibis.

Morfino, V. (2014), *Plural Temporality: Transindividuality and the Aleatory Between Spinoza and Althusser*, Leiden: Brill.

Mugnai, M. (1976), *Astrazione e realtà*, Milan: Feltrinelli.

Mugnier-Pollet, L. (1976), *La philosophie politique de Spinoza*, Paris: Presses universitaires de France.

Mulier, E. H. (1990), 'A Controversial Republican: Dutch Views of Machiavelli in the Seventeenth and Eighteenth Centuries', in G. Bock, Q. Skinner and M. Viroli (eds), *Machiavelli and Republicanism*, Cambridge: Cambridge University Press, pp. 247–64.

Namer, E. (1961), *Machiavel*, Paris: Presses universitaires de France.

Negri, A. (1991), *The Savage Anomaly: The Power of Spinoza's Metaphysics and Politics*, trans. M. Hardt, Minneapolis: University of Minnesota Press.

Nourisson, J. F. (1892), 'La bibliothèque de Spinoza', *Revue des deux mondes* 152: 811–33.

Orsini, N. (1936), *Bacone e Machiavelli*, Genoa: Emiliano degli Orfini.

Pacchi, A. (1998), 'Hobbes e la filologia biblica al servizio dello Stato', in A. Lupoli (ed.), *Scritti hobbesiani (1978–1990)*, Milan: Franco Angeli, pp. 185–201.

Padovani, U. A. (1937), *Cartesio e Machiavelli: Osservazioni sui rapport tra politica e morale*, Milan: Vita e Pensiero.

Parel, A. J. (1992), *The Machiavellian Cosmos*, New Haven, CT: Yale University Press.

Peña Echevarría, J. (1989), *La filosofía política de Espinoza*, Valladolid: Universidad de Valladolid.

Peña Garcia, V. (1974), *El materialismo de Spinoza*, Madrid: Revista de Occidente.

Perez, A. (1644), *Las Obras y Relaciones*, Geneva: Juan de Tornes.

Perini, L. (1967), 'Ancora sul libraio-tipografico Pietro Perna e su alcune figure di eritici italiani in rapporto con lui negli anni 1549–1555', *Nuova rivista storica* 51: 363–85.

Perini, L. (1990), 'Amœnitas typographicae', in S. Rota Ghibaudi and F. Barcia (eds), *Studi politici in onore di Luigi Firpo, Vol. I: Richerche sui secoli XIV–XVI*, Milan: Franco Angeli, pp. 905–71.

Plato (1997), *Complete Works*, ed. J. Cooper, Indianapolis: Hackett Publishing.

Popkin, R. H. (1979), *The History of Scepticism from Erasmus to Spinoza*, Berkeley: University of California Press.

Popper, K. (1982), *The Open Universe: An Argument for Indeterminism*, London: Hutchinson.

Pozzi, P. (1994), 'La biblioteca di Spinoza', in J. M. Lucas and J. Colerus (eds), *Le vite di Spinoza*, Macerata: Quodlibet, pp. 149–74.

Praz, M. (1962), 'Machiavelli e gl'inglesi dell'epoca elisabettiana', in M. Praz, *Machiavelli in Inghilterra*, Florence: Sansono, pp. 97–151.

Procacci, G. (1995), *Machiavelli nella cultura europa*, Rome–Bari: Laterza.

Proietti, O. (1995), *Osservazioni, note e congetture sul testo latino e nederlandese del* TP, Macherata: Università degli Studi di Macerata.

Proietti, O. (1997), 'La tradizione testuale del *Tractatus politicus*: "Examinatio" per un'edizione critica', in P. Totaro (ed.), *Spinoziana: Ricerche di terminologia filosofia e critica testuale*, Florence: Olschki, pp. 125–53.

Proietti, O. (2001), 'Per una cronologia degli scritti postumi di Spinoza: Terenzio e il *Petronius* di M. Hadrianides (Amsterdam, 1969)', *Quaderni di storia* 27: 105–54.

Quevedo, F. (1660), *Obras*, Brussels: Dela Emprenta de Francisco Foppens.

Quevedo, F. (1661), *Obras, Secunda Parte*, Brussels: Dela Emprenta de Francisco Foppens.

Quevedo, F. (1980), *L'heure de tous et la fortuna raisonnable / La hora de todos y la fortuna con seso*, trans. and ed. J. Bourg, P. Dupont and P. Geneste, Paris: Aubier.

Raab, F. (1965), *The English Face of Machiavelli: A Changing Interpretation*, London: Routledge & Kegan Paul.

Ravà, A. (1930), 'Un contributo agli studi spinoziani: Spinoza e Machiavelli', in *Studi filosofici-giuridici dedicati a G. Del Vecchio, tomo II*, Modena: Società tipigrafica modenese, pp. 299–313.

Ravà, A. (1958), *Studi su Spinoza e Fichte*, Milan: Giuffrè.

Regnault, F. (2012), 'The Thought of the Prince', trans. C. Kerslake, rev. S. Corcoran, in K. Peden and P. Hallward (eds), *Concept and Form: Key Texts from the* Cahiers pour l'Analyse, *Vol. I*, London: Verso, pp. 229–57.

Rensi, G. (1993), *Spinoza*, ed. A. Montano, Milan: Guerini.

Rivaud, A. (1906), *Les notions d'essence et d'existence dans la philosophie de Spinoza*, Paris: Alcan.

Robinet, A. (1978), *Le langage à l'âge classique*, Paris: Klincksieck.

Robinson, L. (1928), *Kommentar zu Spinozas* Ethik, *Erster Band*, Leipzig: Meiner.

Rossi, P. (1999), *Naufragi senza spettatore: L'idea di progresso*, Bologna: Il Mulino.

Saavedra, D. (1681), *Corona Gothica Castellana, y Austriaca*, En Amberes: En Casa de Juan Bautista Verdussen.

Sasso, G. (1987), *Machiavelli e gli antichi, Vol. I*, Milan–Naples: Riccardo Ricciardi Editore.

Sasso, G. (1993), *Niccolò Machiavelli*, 2 vols, Bologna: Il Mulino.

Schelling, F. W. J. (1994), *On the History of Modern Philosophy*, trans. A. Bowie, Cambridge: Cambridge University Press.

Schmitt, C. (1986), *Scritti su Thomas Hobbes*, trans. C. Galli, Milan: Giuffrè.

Schopenhauer, A. (2012), 'On the Fourfold Root of the Principle of Sufficient Reason', in A. Schopenhauer, *On the Fourfold Root of the Principle of Sufficient Reason, On Vision and Colours, On Will in Nature*, trans. and ed. D. E. Cartwright, E. E. Erdmann and C. Janaway, Cambridge: Cambridge University Press.

Semerari, G. (1970), 'La teoria spinoziana della imaginazioni', in F. Adorno, A. Antonaci and N. Badaloni (eds), *Studi in onore di Antonio Corsano*, Manduria: Lacaita, pp. 747–64.

Senellart, M. (1989), *Machiavélisme et raison d'Etat*, Paris: Presses universitaires de France.

Senellart, M. (1995), *Les arts de gouverner. Du regimen médiéval au concept de gouvernement*, Paris: Seuil.

Servas van Rooijen, A. J. (ed.) (1888), *Inventaire des livres formant la bibliothèque de Bénédict Spinoza La Haye*, Paris: Tengeler-Monnerat.

Sini, C. (1992), *La verità pubblica e Spinoza*, Milan: CUEM.

Solari, G. (1927), 'La dottrina del contratto in Spinoza', *Rivista di filosofia* 17: 317–53.

Solari, G. (1974), *La filosofia politica, Vol. I*, Bari: Laterza.

Spinoza, B. (1925), *Opera*, 5 vols, trans. and ed. C. Gebhardt, Heidelberg: Carl Winters Universitätsbuchhandlung.

Spinoza, B. (1954), *Œuvres complètes*, trans. and ed. R. Callois, M. Francès and R. Misrahi, Paris: Gallimard.

Spinoza, B. (1962), *Emendazione dell'intelletto, Principi di filosofia cartesiana, Pensieri metafisici*, trans. and ed. E. De Angelis, Turin: Boringhieri.

Spinoza, B. (1972), *Trattato teologico-politico*, trans. A. Droetto, ed. E. Giancotti, Turin: Einaudi.

Spinoza, B. (1984), *Traité sur la réforme de l'entendement*, Paris: Vrin.

Spinoza, B. (1985), *The Collected Works of Spinoza, Volume I*, trans. and ed. E. Curley, Princeton: Princeton University Press.

Spinoza, B. (1992), *Traité de la réforme de l'entendement*, trans. and ed. B. Rousset, Paris: Vrin.

Spinoza, B. (1999), *Trattato politico*, trans. and ed. P. Cristofolini, Pisa: Edizioni ETS.

Spinoza, B. (2004), *Tradado Teológico-Político*, trans. D. Pires Aurélio, Lisbon: Casa Da Moeda.

Spinoza, B. (2016), *The Collected Works of Spinoza, Volume II*, trans. and ed. E. Curley, Princeton: Princeton University Press.

Sportelli, S. (1995), *Potenza e desiderio nella filosofia di Spinoza*, Naples: Edizioni Scientifiche Italiana.

Strauss, L. (1948), 'How to Study Spinoza's *Theologico-Political Treatise*', *Proceedings of the American Academy for Jewish Research* 17: 69–113.

Strauss, L. (1965), *Spinoza's Critique of Religion*, New York: Schocken Books.

Strauss, L. (1987), 'Niccolò Machiavelli', in L. Strauss and J. Cropsey (eds), *History of Political Philosophy, Third Edition*, Chicago: University of Chicago Press, pp. 296–317.

Suarez, F. (1965), *Disputationes Metaphysicae*, Hildesheim: Georg Olms.

Testamenti Veteris Biblia (1618), Hanoviae: Typis Wechelianis.

Timm, H. (1964), *Gott und die Freiheit: Studien zur Religionsphilosophie der Goethezeit Band 1: Die Sponozarenaissance*, Frankfurt am Main: Klostermann.

Tosel, A. (1984), *Spinoza, ou, Le crépuscule de la servitude: Essai sur le Traité théologico-politique*, Paris: Aubier.

Turlot, F. (1988), 'La question de l'essence chez Spinoza', in R. Bouveresse (ed.), *Spinoza: Science et religion*, Paris: Vrin, pp. 11–18.

Van Hove, J. (1662), *Politieke Weegschaal*, Amsterdam: Dirk Dirksz.

Vernant, J. P. (2006), 'Mythic Aspects of Memory', in J. P. Vernant, *Myth and Thought among the Greeks*, New York: Zone Books, pp. 115–38.

Vico, G. (1948), *The New Science*, trans. T. G. Bergin and H. Fisch, Ithaca, NY: Cornell University Press.

Vico, G. (1977), *Principi di scienza nuova d'intorno alla comune natura delle nazioni*, ed. M. Veneziani, Florence: Olschki.

Villa, E. (1919), 'Di un giudizio dello Spinoza su Machiavelli', *Athenaeum* 7, 4: 190–6.

Visentin, S. (1998), 'Assolutismo e libertà: L'orizzonte republicano nel pensiero politico olandese del XVii secolo', *Filosofia politica* 12, 1: 67–85.

Vulliaud, P. (1934), *Spinoza d'après les livres de sa bibliothèque*, Paris: Bibliothèque Chacornac.

Walther, M. (1985), 'Die Transformation des Naturrechts in der Rechtsphilosophie Spinozas', *Studia Spinozana* 1: 73–104.

Walther, M. (1990), 'Institution, Imagination und Freiheit bei Spinoza: Eine kritische Theorie politischer Institutionen', in G. Göhler, K. Lenk, H. Münkler and M. Walther (eds), *Politische Institutionen in gesellschaftlichen Umbruch*, Opladen: Westdeutscher.

Wolff, C. (1984), *Opuscula Metaphysica*, ed. J. Ecole, Hildesheim: Georg Olms.

Wolfson, H. (1932), *The Philosophy of Spinoza: Unfolding the Latent Process of his Reasoning*, Cambridge, MA: Harvard University Press.

Wuellner, B. (1956), *Dictionary of Scholastic Philosophy*, Milwaukee, WI: Bruce Publishing.

Yovel, Y. (1989), *Spinoza and Other Heretics: The Marrano of Reason*, Princeton: Princeton University Press.

Zac, S. (1965), *Spinoza et l'interprétation de l'Ecriture*, Paris: Presses universitaires de France.

Zac, S. (1989), *Spinoza en Allemagne: Mendelssohn, Lessing, et Jacobi*, Paris: Méridiens Klincksieck.

Zourabichvili, F. (1994), 'L'identité individuelle chez Spinoza', in M. Revault D'Allons and H. Rizk (eds), *Spinoza: Puissance et ontologie*, Paris: Kimé, pp. 85–110.

Index

EU Authorised Representative:

Easy Access System Europe Mustamäe tee 50, 10621 Tallinn, Estonia

gpsr.requests@easproject.com

Printed and bound by CPI Group (UK) Ltd, Croydon, CR0 4YY

12/08/2025

01934810-0006